Profits,
Power, and
Prohibition

SUNY Series in New Social Studies on Alcohol and Drugs
Harry G. Levine and Craig Reinarman, editors

Profits, Power, and Prohibition

Alcohol Reform and the Industrializing of America, 1800–1930

JOHN J. RUMBARGER

STATE UNIVERSITY OF NEW YORK PRESS

Published by
State University of New York Press, Albany

Printed in the United States of America

For information, address State University of New York Press, State University Plaza, Albany, N.Y., 12246

Library of Congress Cataloging-in-Publication Data

Rumbarger, John J., 1938–
Profits, power, and prohibition : Alcohol reform and the industrializing of America, 1880–1930 / John J. Rumbarger.
p. cm.—(SUNY series in new social studies on alcohol and drugs)
Includes index.
ISBN 0–88706–782–4. ISBN 0–88706–783–2 (pbk.)
1. Prohibition—United States—History. 2. Temperance—United States—History. 3. United States—Industries—History. I. Title. II. Series.
HV5089.R84 1988
363.4'1'0973—dc19 88–1884
CIP

For Janet and Emily Elizabeth

Contents

Part II
The Middle Years:
The Tradition Fails, 1865–1890

Preface

For more than fifteen years John Rumbarger's manuscript *Profits, Power, and Prohibition* has held a reputation as something of an underground classic to students of nineteenth and early twentieth century American temperance history. In 1976, for example, I encountered a graduate student at the Massachusetts Historical Society who, like me, was researching the temperance movement. Discussing our mutual interests, my fellow researcher mentioned two items that he found especially valuable: an article by Herbert Gutman and Rumbarger's dissertation.

Linking these two names was oddly appropriate. In the late 1960s Rumbarger and Gutman became friends and through that friendship Rumbarger first absorbed the works of the British historians, Christopher Hill, Eric Hobsbawm and above all Edward Thompson. These writers perspectives meshed well with those which Rumbarger had encountered as a student of Gabriel Kolko and Thomas C. Cochran. Gutman's work, like Thompson's, stressed the importance of working-class struggles and culture, and in the 1970s began to reshape scholarly thinking about American society.

Rumbarger, on the other hand, concerned himself with similar questions about America's dominant classes and in particular with their utopian dream that the temperance reform could help bring about a perfectly harmonious capitalist social order.[1] In *Profits, Power, and Prohibition* Rumbarger argues that wealthy and powerful Americans played critical roles in helping to establish, support and lead the temperance and prohibition movements, and that they did so out of their larger efforts to transform America into an industrial capitalist social order. Fifteen years ago this view of temperance was still so heretical as to appear unthinkable—at least to some early readers of the manuscript.

The dominant view of temperance at that time had been developed first by Richard Hofstadter and then expanded by Joseph Gusfield. This view focused on temperance as an issue of "status politics" which, as Gusfield has recently explained, they had explicitly developed "as a concept in opposition to 'class politics.'" In *The Age of Reform* Hofstadter had ignored the role of wealthy businessmen in reform movements. He argued that prohibitionists, like other reformers, were motivated by concerns about their own social status—about whether their way of life dominated America. Prohibition, Hofstadter maintained, was the product of the "country mind" upset about the city's way of life and of nativist concerns about the behavior of immigrants. Prohibitionism "was carried about America," he said, "by the rural-evangelical virus." Hofstadter even went so far as to suggest that prohibitionism was not part of the Progressive movement.[2]

Several historians have pointed out that Hofstadter was wrong about much of this. From the early nineteenth century on, temperance and prohibition leadership and ideology was urban, professional, and progress-oriented—"progressivist." As *Profits, Power, and Prohibition* reveals, the temperance and prohibitionist "virus" actually came from Boston, New York, Philadelphia and other metropolitan centers, and that it was spread by prominent members of the eastern business establishment—men who were decidedly urban and cosmopolitan in outlook.[3]

In *Symbolic Crusade* Joseph Gusfield skillfully developed Hofstadter's notion of status politics and, unlike almost anyone else since prohibition, he sought to really understand what made temperance supporters so distressed about drinking. In order to do that Gusfield employed two analytic strategies. First, he focused on alcohol as a symbolic issue; this was, I think, a crucial insight and a major contribution to understanding temperance and alcohol in America. Second, and less happily, he focused exclusively on "noneconomic issues" and on temperance as "disinterested reform."

> It is within an analytic context of concern with noneconomic issues that we have studied the Temperance movement. . . . Typical of moral reform movements, Temperance has usually been the attempt of the moral people, in this case the abstainers, to correct the behavior of the immoral people, in this case the drinkers. This issue has appeared as a moral one, divorced from any direct economic interests in abstinence or indulgence. This quality of "disinterested reform" is the analytical focus of our study."

Temperance was far more self-interested than Gusfield recognized. For middle-class men and women it was an attempt, partly realistic and partly deluded, to protect themselves, their families and their communities. Middle-class temperance advocates always defined their crusade in terms of everyone's material, physical, and spiritual self-interest.[4]

According to *Profits, Power, and Prohibition*, Gusfield's most significant problem was that he ignored the participation and leadership of wealthy employers. Indeed, Rumbarger's book can be read, in part, as an extended, illustrated answer to Hofstadter, Gusfield and others as to why it is so important to include capitalists in the telling of American history, especially of American reform movements.

One of the great strengths of *Profits, Power, and Prohibiton* is that Rumbarger never takes his eye off the wealthy capitalists who played major roles in the making and ongoing development of the temperance campaign in America. Indeed, so overwhelming is the evidence that Rumbarger presents, and so persuasive and penetrating is his general argument, that this book should change forever the scholarly debate about temperance and prohibition. As a result, eventually it will be widely acknowledged that large employers believed that the questions of drinking, temperance, and prohibition were of vital economic importance, that rich businessmen helped organize the first temperance organizations, and that wealthy capitalists provided crucial financing and leadership for temperance organizations throughout the nineteenth century and in the first two and a half decades of the twentieth.

Rumbarger shows that for over one hundred years employers participated in the temperance crusade because of their concern with the behavior and lifestyles of their workers. Capitalists insisted that churches and other morally uplifting institutions were much better places than the taverns, barrooms or saloons for their workers to spend their time. Employers believed that workers who did not drink were usually more efficient, orderly, disciplined, easier to manage and control, and less likely to make trouble on the job than workers who did drink.

In the last ten or fifteen years a number of other historians have noted and studied the roles played by wealthy businessmen in temperance. In *Sobering Up*, the first monograph on the early temperance movement since John Allen Krout's 1925 classic, Ian Tyrell has clearly established that antebellum temperance was neither the invention of a declining elite nor of rural backwater Americans; rather temperance was at the cutting edge of industrial and capitalist cultural reform. In *A Shopkeeper's Millennium* Paul Johnson has made a series of similar observations about both temperance and evangelical Christianity in the 1830s. Roy Rosenzweig, in *Eight Hours for What We Will*, has described working-class resistance to the upper-class and employer orientation of nineteenth and early twentieth century temperance. In *Retreat from Reform* Jack Blocker, like Rumbarger, has shown how the emergence of the Anti-Saloon League constituted a retreat from the more populist politics of the Prohibition Party.[5]

Rumbarger's analysis preceded this revisionist work and here he has absorbed the more recent studies into his analysis. But *Profits, Power, and Prohibition* has a much greater sweep than these studies. Rumbarger begins in the early nineteenth century and ends in the 1920s, after passage of the Eighteenth Amendment. Repeatedly in his account he returns to the concerns of a substantial portion of the wealthy temperance men whom he terms "conservatives." Throughout the history of the movement the conservatives sought to balance their desire to spread the temperance ethic to workers with their equally strong wish to minimize friction and antagonism among social classes, especially between capitalists and workers. The conservatives' strategies and actions within the movement constitute one of the major hitherto hidden stories of temperance which Rumbarger has brought to light. The conservative temperance response of the twentieth century Rumbarger terms "antisaloonism" because of its focus on eliminating the urban working-class pub. Antisaloonism united Progressives who supported the Anti-Saloon League as well as many who initially opposed prohibition legislation (notably members of the Committee of Fifty). Finally, in his Epilogue, Rumbarger discusses how conservative capitalists who had supported prohibition revised their ideas in the new conditions of the 1920s and then led the campaign for repeal. The important point here is not so much that they switched sides, but that so many rich men remained so involved in alcohol politics and continued to shape the development of alcohol policy to serve their interests as they understood them.[6]

Rumbarger clearly views temperance ideology as based on fantasy and delusion about both the capacities of American capitalism and the effects of drink and abstinence. However, for understandable reasons, he resists evaluating many of the specific employer and temperance claims he discusses about the pernicious effects of drink and the beneficial effects of abstinence on workers. To this day the issue remains highly charged and difficult to sort out. For many years, most historians, sociologists, and journalists routinely regarded temperance movement ideas as exaggerated and wrong. It seemed self-evident to so many writers that alcohol was not the demonic substance and unmitigated evil which temperance advocates and prohibitionists believed it to be. Recently, however, popular and scholarly writings have tended, more than ever before, to view temperance ideology as a sensible and reasonable response to alcohol use and abuse.[7]

I'd like to briefly outline my ways of understanding this whole question, for I believe they are consistent with Rumbarger's analysis. It is important to note that *per capita* alcohol consumption was higher in the eighteenth century than for most of the nineteenth, and that it has remained at a relatively lower level up to the present.[8] Alcohol was certainly abused in the nineteenth century, as it was prior to then, and as it still is today. However, on the basis of my own research, and that of other historians and social scientists, I want to suggest that:

1) As Rumbarger observes, temperance and prohibitionist antialcohol arguments and claims were often extravagant and wrong. As to the extent of social problems caused by drink—such as poverty, crime, and orphaned children—temperance ideology *was* exaggerated and obsessive. Similarly, liquor and the saloon were not nearly as harmful to business efficiency and productivity as businessmen and temperance advocates often claimed. Temperance advocates routinely made alcohol a scapegoat for problems caused by larger political and economic forces—a fact well supported by *Profits, Power, and Prohibition.*

2) Though often wrong and exaggerated, in America temperance ideas functioned as a very effective procapitalist ideology. Temperance conceptions and claims shifted attention away from the structural sources of social problems and blamed individuals and the substance alcohol for poverty, unemployment, slums, and other social and urban problems. The scapegoating character of temperance ideology helped undermine middle-class support for working-class labor struggles. (One often-used argument was that if workers didn't drink they wouldn't need higher wages, and so long as they drank higher wages wouldn't make any difference). As Rumbarger makes clear, temperance spread a proemployer, procapitalist world view and explanation of social problems.

3) Temperance was part of a bourgeois cultural offensive that attacked not simply drinking but rather an entire working-class life-style symbolized, in temperance ideology, by drinking. In this sense, the temperance crusade very rationally and effectively served employer interests. The campaign against drink and for abstinence was a campaign on behalf of the so-called industrial virtues of "industry, *sobriety* and thrift." *Sobriety,* as interpreted by temperance advocates and other moral reformers, meant much more than simply "not drunk," and *abstinence* meant more than "not drinking." Abstinence and sobriety defined a character type, a personality, and a whole set of values and behaviors that upper-class and middle-class reformers sought to promulgate and develop in themselves and in others. This "temperate" character type or life style was disciplined, orderly, hard-working, frugal, responsible, morally correct, and self-controlled; it thoroughly fused the Protestant ethic and the ethos of capitalism. Despite the gross distortions and inaccuracies of so many temperance movement claims about drink, the temperance and prohibition campaigns, as Rumbarger shows, did help implant this "temperate" culture and its life-style and values deeper into American society.

4) Temperance and employer claims about the life-style changes associated with abstinence from drink were often true—*especially when abstinence resulted from religious conversion or participation in a temperance organization.* That was because abstinence or "sobriety" was never understood as a behavior by itself, but as part of an entire life style. Then, as now, it was assumed that the real sign of "sobriety" or "abstinence" was that it was accompanied by other even more important behaviors, especially "industry" and "thrift."

In short, in America, alcohol and the saloon served as symbolic enemies in the larger capitalist-sponsored enterprise of social, cultural and psychological transformation. The temperance reform was a central part of that enterprise and—as Rumbarger demonstrates—wealthy employers, among the campaign's earliest and most steadfast supporters, shaped much of its ideology and politics to suit their needs.

Profits, Power, and Prohibition is being published after the Reagan presidency—the most pro-upper-class and pro-big business administration since that of Calvin Coolidge, if not of the entire twentieth century. In the name of productivity, efficiency and economic growth, the Reagan administration redistributed income and wealth to the wealthiest portion of the population and reduced government supervision of big business. This book's focus on the role of wealthy businessmen in shaping American thought and politics is an idea whose time has truly come, again.[9]

Harry G. Levine
Queens College
City University
of New York

Acknowledgments

I am indebted to many people who assisted me in various and numerous ways, ranging from friendly concern to rigorous criticism, as I worked on this study. None, however, bears responsibility for its configuration or conclusions. Specifically, I am grateful to Gabriel and Joyce Kolko for their enduring support, criticism, and encouragement through some difficult times. In addition, I owe Thomas C. Cochran a particular debt of gratitude for sustaining my research and writing.

John L. Shover permitted me to address his graduate seminar while my work was progressing, and I gained much valuable criticism from him and his students. J. Joseph Huthmacher read and supported an earlier version of the manuscript, while subjecting it to his own inimitable wit. Throughout, Herbert Gutman was an abiding friend and acerbic critic. Other such friends include Albro Martin and Edward Pessen. I owe special thanks to Robert Irwin, former director of the University of Pennsylvania Press, who provided both the opportunity and guidance to make needed editorial revisions.

Others who read parts of the manuscript or otherwise assisted me include Jim Dougherty of the National Endowment for the Humanities, R. K. Webb, former editor of the *American Historical Review*, and participants in the professional research seminar of the National Archives and Records Administration.

Scholars are well aware of the professionalism and dedication of the Archives staff. Congress, however, should be better apprised of its excellence. So, to Gerald Haines, Leonard Rapport, Elsie Freeman, Jill Brett, Meyer Fishbein, Mike McReynolds, Trudy Peterson, Dave Van Tassel, Jim Hastings, Bill Valentine, Frank Burke, John Taylor, Bob Wolfe, Mary Walton Livingston, Sam Walker, Milt Gustafson, Harold Pinkett, Dave Eggenberger, Virginia Purdy, and many others, permit me now to say, "thank you."

No study of this sort can be accomplished without the professional involvement of research and manuscript curators and librarians. To so many of them I owe thanks for the guidance they provided me. The collections of private and public records to which they afforded me access are listed elsewhere in this book; it is appropriate, however, that I record here my gratitude to the several staffs of Yale University, Columbia University, New York Public Library, University of Chicago, Library of Congress, Rockefeller Archives, Ohio Historical Society, Michigan Historical Collections, Presbyterian Historical Society, Forest History Society, and National Archives and Records Administration, who made it possible for me to utilize their invaluable materials while preparing this book.

Finally, I owe special thanks to Harry Levine of Queens College and Rosalie Robertson of SUNY Press. Without them, quite simply, there is no book. To my wife, Janet, whose endurance of it never waned, I can only add that what I need to say to her continues to lie beyond my capacity for words and deeds.

Introduction

The history of America's temperance reform presents kaleidoscopic patterns of a people stressed and distressed by the common drinking practices of their society. For more than a century, hosts of social, fraternal, religious, and political organizations struggled to cope with the drink evil as they understood it, first, by mounting campaigns of moral suasion and, eventually, by organizing for political action.

The conventional image of this "Cold Water Army" is not flattering: evangelical zeal—never a prized commodity within the liberal establishment—is viewed as the core of a movement that traversed the grounds of zealotry, fanaticism, and, finally, obsession. Such dark hues pervading our social landscape have been attributed to middle-class anxieties generated largely by its own morbid concerns to have its success acknowledged. It transpires, in other words, that while the American nation was establishing itself as an industrial colossus and world power, and as a model of liberal, pragmatic democracy, it nurtured narrowly sectarian forces deeply suspicious of the forces transforming America, while, at the same time, comprising a substantial portion of them. It is almost as if two different nations were being built by two different peoples.

Most explanations of this anomaly are securely moored to Richard Hofstadter's view that temperance and prohibitionism were or became "a historical detour, a meaningless nuisance, an extraneous imposition on the main course of history." People wishing to understand "the development of great economic issues [or] the main trends of class politics," Hofstadter maintained, would find nothing of value in the temperance movement. Hofstadter's judgment rests upon his perception of the movement as composed of fanatical and marginal social types, uprooted by and reacting against the main currents of American history. His artfully wrong-headed synthesis of the movement as a "rural evangelical virus" remains today the basis of much popular and scholarly understanding of the anti-liquor movement.[1]

While the ideological suppositions of these views are Hofstadter's, their theoretical elaboration and refinement became the work of Joseph Gusfield.[2] As did Hofstadter, Gusfield divorced the temperance and prohibition movement from the dynamics of political economy. Gusfield argued that an American politics of consensus had elevated permanently status preoccupations to the front rank of national political concerns, and that politics now involved a hurly-burly of groups seeking validation of their social status. He maintained that the middle classes regarded the diversity of life styles that characterized industrial America as presenting social and cultural threats to their own "social respect and honor."

For Gusfield and Hofstadter, the drive for national prohibition had become an act of "symbolic politics" that employed the state as a coercive mechanism, not to obtain or maintain material advantage, but rather to acquire social respect from one's countrymen. For "the sober abstaining citizen seek[ing] from public acts [to] reaffirm the dominance and prestige of his style of life," constitutional prohibition represented symbolically the superiority of his cultural values over those of his social peers.[3] Gusfield reaffirmed Hofstadter's assertion that prohibition had nothing to do with orthodox political economy, but he disagreed that it represented a "pointless interruption of the American political system." On the contrary, Gusfield argued that a "politics of status goals" had become an enduring American political characteristic.[4] Despite this departure from Hofstadter's canon, Gusfield's argument remains crucially dependent upon Hofstadter's strictures concerning temperance and political economy.

Gusfield viewed temperance as a "disinterested" reform, one that had no direct bearing upon such matters as social class and economic position. Temperance, he maintained, could best be understood as a "non-economic [issue] divorced from any direct economic interests in abstinence or indulgence."[5] Despite his disclaimers, Gusfield worked with a concrete model of America's political economy—one that enabled him to believe that certain historical phenomena can be examined apart from the world of getting and keeping. Thus, somewhat like philosophical phenomenologists, Gusfield "bracketed" a phenomenon in order to reveal its essence. But historical reality has a way of refusing to remain bracketed.

Given the evident extent of America's commitment to capitalism, it is not difficult to see how Gusfield and other observers of temperance reform have regarded it as they have. In their model, as increasing abundance permits more and more groups to enter the orbit of politics, conflict operates on culture, for it has nowhere else to find expression. Politics becomes the means for both gaining formal recognition of one's economic achievement and social honor for one's cultural proclivities or life style. In short, consensus politics gives us "pluralist" America—in a paradoxically mass society.

In this account, the antiliquor movement is depicted as, at best, tangential to issues of political economy. Neither economic substance nor political power are involved. The actors in this drama appear as obscure, resentful of the world confronting them, and seeking to take refuge in their status by abandoning "genuine" reform and securing for themselves and families symbolic honor that is supposed to be accomplished by the suppression of alien drinking.[6]

The burden of this book is to challenge as directly as possible Hofstadter's and Gusfield's notion that temperance reform was merely a status concern of the middle classes; that this reform was tangential to our nation's political economy; and that the morbid hues it cast over our social landscape were unrelated to our fascination with modern capitalism. I hope to show that men of power and substance defined, directed, and controlled the movement for drink reform. Moreover, I hope to make clear that wealthy capitalists regarded temperance reform as integral and necessary to establishing a capitalist, industrial social order.

What and whom do I mean by men of power and substance? Rather than attempt to define abstractly such a phenomenon, I wish to offer examples of them drawn from my own family, and thus remain concerete and empirical in my argument.[7]

On January 16, 1889, *The DuBois* [Pennsylvania] *Express* recorded the death of the city's founder, John Jacob Rumbarger, beneath the lugubrious headline, "Life's Fitful Fever O'er." Rumbarger's anonymous eulogist described him, who had brought to a wilderness in 1865 both a railroad and the lumbering industry, as one who deliberately shunned "efforts to reach the Dead Sea fruit of riches or political preferment." Rather, Rumbarger was "a man of mark" because of his vision of a social order dedicated to general prosperity. For the obituary writer, the fact that John Rumbarger died, relatively speaking, a wealthy man, was of lesser importance than his visionary exploitation of his capital. Rumbarger had liberally endowed his town's first two churches, the Methodist Episcopal (his own) and the Roman Catholic (his tenants') with land and money; he was equally generous in support of the local school.

In the course of his life of lumbering and farming in western Pennsylvania, Rumbarger adopted the Methodist Episcopal church for the business contacts it afforded him, and became an abstainer from "ardent spirits," although he never actively participated in the post–Civil War prohibition movement. This, in itself, is not surprising: the Prohibition party hardly had been organized, and only then largely on paper, when Rumbarger passed his sixtieth birthday in 1871. But, as a man intimately knowledgeable of lumbering and railroading, he would not "countenance" strong drink among his workers.[8]

John Jacob Rumbarger's sons and grandsons not only carried on his pioneering entrepreneurship and abstemious convictions, they played important roles in the development of the country's lumber industry.[9] Their company furnished timber for the Union Pacific Railroad and for the Civil War Union's defenses in the midwest. It was the first in the United States to quarter saw interior finishing oak (for the Providence, Rhode Island, city hall). Its products were exhibited at Philadelphia's Centennial Exposition, and won an August St. Gaudens prize medal at the World's Columbian Exposition.[10] In the early 1880s the firm pushed its operations into West Virginia, using narrow gauge railroads and Shay locomotives to bring out the state's hardwoods and, thereby, earn for J. L. Rumbarger the title "the cherry[wood] king" of eastern lumbering.[11]

These latter two generations of "sawmill barons" remained faithful to their temperance inheritance, forswearing the use of ardent spirits, while nurturing their Republican politics to a point that allowed J. L. Rumbarger to declare Theodore Roosevelt "the greatest statesman that ever lived."[12] While they were undoubtedly entrepreneurial capitalists, they were equally alert to the need to modernize their company's business organization, and were among the first in their industry to achieve a vertical integration that gave them control of raw materials, manufacturing plants, distribution, and sales.[13]

In summary, these three generations of businessmen were innovative capitalists whose temperance and religious convictions were integral to their enterprises. The world they confronted encouraged their optimism, expansionism, and a view of history that led them to Rooseveltian progressivism. They did not seek, in the words of Geoffrey Blodgett, to protect their families from "endemic social disorder in nineteenth century America . . . to recapture a remembered vision of social stability so that virtue might thrive again." Nor were they fleeing fusion "with authentically radical currents of social protest."[14] Rather, theirs was a pursuit of a social order that took successful business enterprise as both its goal and its means. When national prohibition arrived, both J. L. and his son John Rumbarger quietly expressed their satisfaction that none of their sons nor employees would ever again have to confront the evil of drinking.[15]

It was such men as these who filled the interstices of the temperance movement. Their business interests ordered their lives, controlled their activities, and informed their convictions. As such, the business interests of three generations of these men may be considered to constitute a utopian vision of society. Consider, for example, those endorsements of national constitutional prohibition presented to the Senate judiciary committee in 1914. Millionaire textile manufacturer and real estate developer William F. Cochran of Baltimore urged prohibition because, "until this question of the liquor matter is solved we cannot expect to solve our industrial problems," which, he maintained, would also require "efficient" unionization of the labor force. Cochran's larger concerns were reiterated by Mrs. Howard M. Hoge, president of the Virginia Women's Christian Temperance Union, who informed the committee that her organization spoke for "insurance companies and railroad people . . . and men representing almost every branch of mercantile business." According to Hoge and her Massachusetts counterpart, prohibition would "result in the preservation of our industries and our ascendancy in the great world affairs of today."[16] Such people were not retreating into the past; their testimony affirmed what three generations of "temperance men"—men of capital—were seeking to build.

This epochal undertaking, however, required a working class that appeared always to elude the grasp of America's capitalist developers. Hence, T. T. Waterman's complaint to his congressman, George O'Shaunessy, in December 1917, immediately before the Senate's vote on constitutional prohibition, that his teaming and hauling business was "almost unable to get men, while many of the saloons are filled with what should be able bodied men, but . . . who will only work a few hours a day so that they may get more liquor."[17] What Waterman and my grandfather could not obtain by their own resources, constitutional prohibition sought to obtain for them and their social class: a labor force submissive to the exigencies of business enterprise. Such a prospect lay beyond their means if not their needs, but they had the power to define those needs and see them acted upon at the highest level of American government.

Herein lies the historical significance of the temperance and prohibition movements: men of power and substance—"men of mark"—articulated and refined a utopian vision of society at the heart of which lay an abstemious and cooperative workforce perpetually manufacturing wealth for others. Such temperance men were among the first to view America's workers as a "national capital asset" to be husbanded by reform and government.[18]

Temperance ideology was based both on obsessions concerning the effects of drinking and middle-class fantasies about capitalism's capacity to establish a rational social order. Both obsessions and fantasies were maintained in the face of considerable evidence to the contrary.[19] If, for example, one were to take seriously all that was written and preached about the evils of drink in America, one could only conclude that the nation's sprawling empire, which spanned a continent in less than a century, had been the labor of three generations of riotous drunks and debilitated paupers. An appetite for strong drink, however, was among the least of problems besetting American workers, chief of which were to obtain steady work and make ends meet. Nevertheless, the drink problem obsessed their employers because their temperance ideology explained success and failure in the marketplace by reference to drinking and abstinence. Thus, temperance ideology accounted for myriad labor problems—shortages, irregularity, productivity, and wages among them. It did not, however, account for the role entrepreneurial capitalism played in determining who would succeed and who would fail. Still less did temperance ideology fathom the reality that in a regime of business success and failure, failure itself is a necessary component of success. Here lay the origins of fantasy and obsession: confronting a world they could not see as illusory, temperance reformers viewed business success and failure in terms of labor's productivity. Having established in their own minds a causal nexus between drinking and abstinence on the one hand and productivity on the other, temperance capitalists sought to introduce the coercive power of the state to implement drink reform. This decision, in turn, presented them with a host of problems concerning where to direct this power and, above all, how to negotiate the shoals of popular electoral politics.

These problems divided the capitalist leadership of the reform movement. Those whom I term conservatives were sensitive to any politics that might arouse working-class hostility to drink reform. They opposed the 1838 Massachusetts Fifteen Gallon Law as a tax upon the poor and not the rich. But these same conservatives in the 1850s seized the banner of Maine Law prohibition, which penalized manufacturers as well as retailers, to carry forward their objective. However, when eventually drink reform was caught up in the vortex of Abolitionist politics, the movement's conservative capitalists resisted all efforts to bring temperance—Maine Law prohibition—into the broader stream of bourgeois reform. Following the Civil War, these conservative capitalists regrouped around the National Temperance Society and Publication House and unsuccessfully opposed middle-class efforts to form a national and popular Prohibition party.

Confronted by the new party's challenge, America's men of power broadened their prohibitionist analysis of the "labor problem" as a way to demonstrate both the futility of third-party reform and the need for a drinkless social order. In so doing, they recognized, as temperance reform's middle-class and third-party supporters did not, the limits on capital's power to achieve the national dream of wealth for all. Consequently, they developed a hybrid variant of temperance ideology, which I have termed "antisaloonism." It was principally the work of corporate, eastern metropolitan capitalists seeking a secure political basis for continued economic development, and incorporated both opponents of prohibition and the dominant antidrinking organization of the era, the Anti-Saloon League of America.

Within the temperance movement, the alternative to and opponent of antisaloonism in the last decade of the nineteenth century was third-party prohibitionism and its broad-gauge program of reform. The Prohibition party challenged the conventional wisdom of the day about American capitalism and, most important, sought to recall the middle class to its republican heritage; the party pointed out that the state is not a neutral instrument, but rather the consequence of political power. In sanctioning the liquor traffic, the Prohibitionists argued, the state had become an agent of "class interests," pauperizing workers and neglecting development of the domestic market in search of foreign markets. The Prohibition party epitomized middle-class discontent with the course of nineteenth-century industrialization.

The party's disruptions of local and state politics eventually compelled conservative temperance men to reassess their antiliquor strategy. They were, for the most part, located in the country's eastern and urban areas. These men were usually described as "men of large interests" or closely associated with them, and they had been instrumental in establishing a national network of state and local temperance societies that by the 1880s appeared to be slipping from their grasp.

These conservative capitalists reevaluated "the liquor problem" and developed a paternalistic ideology of antisaloonism. In seeking to undermine the third-party politics of the Prohibition party and establish what one antisaloonist called "prohibition in fact," antisaloonist critics focused upon the industrial life style of America's polyglot workers rather than upon people directly and politically involved in the liquor traffic itself. Antisaloonists, in other words, sought both to curtail drinking and to quell third-party agitation for suppression of the liquor traffic.

Antiliquor conservatives directed attention to the urban saloon as the root of industrial America's liquor problem. At the same time, they pointed to "powerful economic forces," by which they meant large industrial corporations, that would mitigate the saloon evil by their dominance over the labor market. Antisaloon reformers believed that such propitious circumstances did not require popular political agitation. Rather, they thought that expedient cooperation with established economic and civil powers would gradually impose progressively tighter restrictions on what they regarded as the working classes' principal social institution.[21]

The antiprohibitionism of the antisaloon movement did succeed in rallying middle-class antiliquor reformers to the vigilante-like politics of nonpartisanship, but it failed dismally to establish "prohibition in fact." No succession of legislative triumphs at the local and state levels ever succeeded in lowering substantially per capita increases in drinking (which, in any case, never threatened the foundations of the nation's evident, if mercurial, prosperity). By 1913 antiprohibitionist antisaloonism as a national strategy to crush the working-class saloon had become bankrupt. No amount of local antiliquor/antisaloon legislation could rationalize the labor supply, whose maldistribution and transient nature had become structural features of national economic life. Nor could it effect the nation's rootless underclass of workers. But antisaloonism had achieved one notable and enduring victory: it had healed politically the split within the ranks of property and had helped to end its debate about the nature and purpose of industrial society. In so doing it brought sufficient numbers of America's propertied classes into vague agreement that successful industrialization required national prohibition for the protection of capital's "national asset": the laboring classes.

Antisaloon capitalists turned to constitutional prohibition to achieve their goals of a saloonless working class and political stability. The Eighteenth Amendment did not result from middle-class status anxieties; nor was it brought about by rural animus toward urban immigrants and industrialization. Rather, prohibition triumphed because enough urban capitalists believed such a ban was, in existing circumstances, a necessary precondition of the social reform required to ensure successful and permanent transformation of American society into an industrial order characterized by political stability and labor's social quiescence.

I hope this book leaves its readers with the realization that self-conscious property interests have played decisive roles in our nation's reform history while advancing their own material interests. These roles included that of the disinterested social reformer. Capitalists, perhaps better than others, grasped the precariousness of their position in a market economy subject to the vagaries of political democracy. They grasped as well the possibilities of employing other agencies as instruments to bulwark rather than change basic social arrangements. If there is anything distinctive about America's capitalist antiliquor movement, it is the relative facility with which it was guided through the shoals and eddies of much larger social transformations. In large part this guidance derived from a well ordered hierarchy of values that itself sustained several generations of empire builders and enabled them to identify and use levers of social and economic power with consistent and firm purpose.

A proper understanding of our history, therefore, demands inquiry not only into the visions, dreams, hopes, values, aspirations, and nightmares of the propertyless, but also into those of the powerful as well. Temperance reform well exhibits the need for such inquiries if we are to achieve an objective understanding of our past. If this book points in such a direction, it will have served its purpose.

Part I

The Early Years: The Movement Defines Itself, 1800–1870

1

The Social and Ideological Origins of Drink Reform, 1800–1836

The roots of the temperance movement can be found in those social forces working to develop the expansionist tendencies of the American economy. Neither an abstract Puritan heritage nor paternalist conservatism can explain satisfactorily the dynamics that produced the movement to extirpate liquor drinking from America's culture.[1] The earliest temperance societies, like that organized in Litchfield, Connecticut, in 1787, resulted from the efforts of wealthy farmers to curtail drinking among their laborers during harvest time.[2] Such efforts were sporadic and limited by the fact that alcoholic beverages were a major commodity of agricultural production and commerce. Tactical boycotts were also crippled by the exigencies of the harvest and scarcity of labor. When the temperance movement became a significant factor in Jacksonian America, resistance to it would come from many agricultural regions.[3]

Nevertheless, these early societies defined the movement's strategic objective: the increase of productivity by the elimination of daily work breaks for alcoholic refreshment and its unpredictable consequences. These societies also illustrated a mutual desire on the part of property holders to obtain a uniform standard of labor, regardless of considerations that worked to set them in opposition to each other. These employers assumed that it was their prerogative to determine the social conditions that would lower the costs of production. In a market economy such considerations constituted sufficient reason to eliminate customary drinking, and the more so when labor scarcity deprived employers of a traditional instrument of capital accumulation, low wages.

Early concern about popular drinking was forcefully articulated by Benjamin Rush, whose writing on the subject became an ideological touchstone for the temperance movement.[4] Rush first expressed his anxiety over "intemperate" drinking in a political tract he appended to his essay, "Hints Towards the Natural History of Pennsylvania," in February 1774. Firmly opposed to the continuation of British rule in the colonies, Rush also believed popular drinking constituted an obstacle to the development of American liberty and commerce. If future greatness depended upon eliminating both the British and the drinking of distilled beverages, Rush proved unwilling to permit the state a role in the latter. He believed such action would be "a remedy as unequal to the design as it is destructive to liberty and commerce." His objective could best be obtained by employing "the force of severe manners" to curtail the social habits of drinking.[5]

Rush's rejection of mercantilist instruments of regulation led him to rely upon voluntary associations of property owners to accomplish the reform he sought. His solution, which aimed at avoiding the dilemma created by attacking one form of commerce and property with the state, inspired a considerable portion of the temperance movement. Yet, it also proved to be a source of enduring division within the movement.

The war with Great Britain suspended Rush's antiliquor concern until June 1782 when he attacked the custom of supplying farm laborers with daily rations of liquor. Rush's polemic, "Against Spiritous Liquors," focused its argument on his contention that "'the custom cost farmers dearly in money and lost time.'" In 1784, by which time he was himself, investing heavily in land, Rush published his classic attack on customary drinking, *An Enquiry into the Effects of Spiritous Liquors Upon the Human Body, and their Influence Upon the Happiness of Human Society.*

Rush's *Enquiry* was the direct result of his close observation of Pennsylvania's rural population, which, he believed, needed to be taught to act "'in such a manner as not to defraud [its] creditors or neglect . . . family . . . [and] to amass wealth.'" The quality of Pennsylvania's population in 1784 was highly uneven by Rush's standard. The major ethnic groups were the Scots-Irish and Germans; the former were Calvinists and the latter predominately pietist and quietist offshoots of Lutheranism and Anabaptism. Of the two, Rush preferred the communalistic Germans whose social habits he believed were more likely to increase land values and rents. On the other hand, the individualistic and rootless Scots-Irish epitomized for Rush all the social evils of the intemperate use of alcoholic beverages. The physician-land speculator noted in his diary of 1784 that in the Scots-Irish region surrounding Carlisle, Pennsylvania, "'the quantity of rye destroyed and of whisky drunk in these places is immense . . . and its effects upon their industry, health, and morals are terrible.'"

Rush was grappling with the complex problems of absentee ownership, in which the maximization of profits from ground rents, land improvement, and marketable commodities were all inextricably tied up with the social habits of the indigenous and, sometimes, as in the case of the Scots-Irish, uncooperative population. He promoted education as a way to develop "severe manners" of industry and temperance, advancing the idea that an industrious rural population was a major capital asset. He utilized the Philadelphia Society for Promoting Agriculture and Rural Affairs to spread his propaganda and became active in the formation of local antiliquor societies. By 1789 the *Pennsylvania Packet* was reprinting his *Enquiry* annually before every harvest season.[6]

Typical of the fruits of Rush's pioneering efforts was the temperance society formed by property owners in the Moreau-Northumberland region of Saratoga County, New York. At the beginning of the nineteenth century these agriculturally rich townships supported a diversified local economy of farming, lumbering, milling, and some rudimentary manufacturing.[7] The political and social life of the area was dominated by a squirearchy, but, as elsewhere, it was difficult for them to engage in business enterprise without supplying workers with their customary alcoholic beverages.[8] What distinguished Moreau-Northumberland's temperance pioneers was professional training among those who galvanized the squirearchy into action against liquor drinking.

Billy Clark had studied medicine; Esek Cowan had read law; Lebbius Armstrong was trained for the ministry. All three invested their surplus professional income in land and agricultural production. Clark, for example, owned several farms and had a large investment in a local paper mill. Cowan was a prosperous farm owner with a reputation for innovative husbandry. More important, however, for the purposes of temperance reform, was the common world view—quite like Rush's—the three shared. In one degree or another Moreau's temperance reformers believed society could improve with individual discipline and practical innovation, and that the criterion of improvement was business profits. William Hay, who subsequently headed the society, recalled that Clark was "convinced of the necessity of self-culture, and consequently acquired what are pertinently termed *business habits*." Hay admiringly described Clark as "pecuniarily successful as a physician and a businessman," and also wrote approvingly of Esek Cowan's various employments as a jurist, farmer, and classical scholar. For this kind of man "recreation was only change of employment," and employment was directed towards profit.[9]

The men who founded the Moreau-Northumberland antiliquor movement, and those who sustained it viewed society as "usually" undergoing a process of "progress or decline," but always as a phenomenon that "divides itself into three grades—the highest being above, and the lowest being below moral restraint." The implied rebuke to the principal social classes, capital and labor, was continued in the assertion that the "middle class" was the engine of social progress: "from that medium class," William Hay wrote, "most improvements, inventions, discoveries have proceeded." They contended that the object of government should be to enlarge their number while "reform must increase it."[10]

These ideological conceptions nurtured temperance reform. But the reformers' stance towards other social classes was flexible: traditional rank or position was not an obstacle for association with like-minded men, provided the requisite social virtues of practical knowledge and disciplined effort could be demonstrated. Despite this apparent democratic appeal, the political ideology of a temperance "middle" class did not look to a reordering of society. Forged as it was in the crucible of business enterprise, it sought ultimately to redirect the energies and activities of capital and labor, but not to alter their social relationship. In the social context of Jeffersonian America, however, temperance ideology was radical in both theory and practice since it claimed to seek another reallocation of wealth and property according to utilitarian norms even as it sought an increase in social productivity. The assumption of the permanency of social stratification, to be dominated by a rationally selected elite, was but poorly masked by notions of individual worth taken to be demonstrated by the social virtues of innovation and discovery wedded to a discipline, including temperance, congenial to business. Because of this critical defect, temperance reformation, insofar as it envisioned a distinct "middle" class, was necessarily procapitalist.

The idea of a middle class proved especially valuable to the socialization process required by young America, which in the period 1820–50 could not compel people to alter their customary behavior sufficiently to modify the social order's value system. Indeed, the idea that personal characteristics and behavior were a form of capital may be seen as the *sine qua non* of American economic development in these years. Thus, all manner of ideologies, both secular and religious, that encouraged the development of internal modes of self-discipline as forms of "moral capital" were encouraged by the early advocates of liquor reform.[11]

During the decades of the 1820s and 1830s temperance reform wherever it appeared became a political effort to create a social order universally congenial to entrepreneurial capitalism. It was during these years that the perceptions of men like Benjamin Rush and Billy Clark took root in business activity outside of agriculture, and attracted attention from such established institutions as the Protestant churches. But while local societies of employers who mutually agreed "that hereafter we will carry on our business without the use of distilled spirits as an article of refreshment, either for ourselves or those whom we may employ" remained on the reform scene, they proved insufficient to the task of extending temperance sentiment.[12] To meet this need and to deal with the realities facing various enterprises, their politicization was required.

In Jeffersonian and Jacksonian America, maritime commerce ranked with agriculture in its importance to the economy. Here, too, liquor was customarily provided for laborers. A popular song of the day conveys some idea of the realities confronting and attitudes of merchant seamen in this respect and of the magnitude of the task confronting reformers:

> Now the storm is raging and we are far from shore.
> The good old ship is tossing about
> And the rigging is all tore.
> . . . .
> Now the storm is over and we are safe and well
> We will go into a public house
> And we'll sit and drink our fill.
> We will drink strong ale and porter
> And we'll make the rafters roar
> And when our money is all spent
> We'll go to sea once more.
>
> "The Holy Ground" ca. 1840

In shipbuilding, workers enjoyed ceremonial provisions of strong drink in addition to their daily rations. At the completion of each major stage of construction they joined with shipowners and masters to toast their work's progress. Thus when the keel was put down, the ribs erected, the decking laid, and the masts raised and stepped there would be general celebrations fueled by large amounts of whiskey.[13]

The earliest efforts at reform in these employment areas followed the boycott tactics that were being developed by agricultural temperance societies. In Medford, Massachusetts, for example, a local shipbuilder, Thacher Magoun, refused to permit rum or distilled spirits to be used in his shipyard. Magoun's 1817 no-rum edict was immediately interpreted by his laborers as "practically an increase in the working time, the employer thus saving the cost of time as well as the cost of the rum."[14] Other Medford shipbuilders followed Magoun's lead, even to the point of raising wages.[15] These boycotts could only be partially effective, however, because of the apprentice system and the grog shop, which furnished money and the means to smuggle the contraband refreshment into the yards.[16]

By 1819, temperance advocates outside of agricultural societies had developed an analysis of the liquor problem that would eventually permit them to go beyond the limits of the boycott, and thus politicize the temperance movement. Thomas Hertell's *An Expose of the Causes of Intemperate Drinking and the Means by which It May Be Obviated* considered the entire social order to be the obstacle to temperance reform.[17] Hertell implied that reform could only succeed if society in general were reformed with respect to drinking.

Hertell, who served for more than a dozen years on the bench of New York City's maritime court, asserted that his antiliquor convictions proceeded from the fact that "intemperate drinking is inimical to agricultural and mechanical, as well as moral improvement." He maintained that neither distillers nor the grog shop lay at the root of the problem; both were symptoms and consequences. The real cause of society's intemperate drinking was to be found in the "intemperate use of ardent liquor [which] originates in the fashions, habits, customs, and examples of what are called the upper or wealthy classes of the community." Because of the universal employment of such drinks by society's elites in both public and private, Hertell concluded that "inebriating drinks" had gained sanction as the "median universally adopted by society for manifesting friendship and good will, one to another."[18]

Hertell believed that society's lower orders habitually emulated the upper, and so he argued that self-reformation by the wealthy must come before a general reform. Moreover, Hertell insisted that without a general temperance reform, nascent manufacturing enterprizes could not hope to succeed for "there is scarcely to be found among the laboring class, any who do not drink, and drink too much." Drinking customs were depriving manufacturers of quality manpower. "What single measure," he asked rhetorically, "would do more to further [manufacturing and agricultural development] than the destruction of the custom of giving ardent spirits to working people of every description."[19]

Hertell's analysis of the liquor problem pulled together several strands in the developing temperance movement, and extended the focus of the reformers' concerns beyond agriculture and commerce to manufacturing. The reform impulse had derived from the pragmatic observation that customary drinking diminished productivity. Initially, reformers focused on the ordinary drinks—"ardent spirits"—of the working class as the principal source of abuse, and they continued to rely on the boycott as the means of curtailing and eliminating drinking.

On the other hand, Hertell insisted on the need of society's elites (including the churches) to exercise rigid self-restraint. Only when this class acted to end its sanction of drinking would "useful industry . . . become fashionable," and would "the already over-run and overrated learned professions" be abandoned for the "honorable calling" of the mechanical trades.[20] Hertell looked to the formation of an antiliquor class consciousness that would act not only to protect its traditional base in agriculture and commerce, but also extend its concerns to American manufacturing. Of primary significance, however, is the fact that this attention to the responsibility of America's elite for the general well-being of society gave the temperance reform its peculiarly moralistic character, its ambivalence about the use of the state, and its connection with the Protestant churches.

During the years leading to the politicization of the temperance movement, American society underwent severe stress. Between 1800 and 1820, war and depression, accompanied by the introduction of the factory system, released latent hostilities that frequently expressed themselves in inchoate public drunkenness and disrespect towards religious and secular authority—or so it seemed to men like Lyman Beecher, the Congregationalist clergyman-reformer.[21] Yet Beecher's consideration of social policy did not produce any effort to define the liquor problem in ways fundamentally different from those discussed. Indeed, during these years the established churches wedded themselves firmly to the emerging temperance movement in ways that sought to reinforce the movement's fundamental purposes. In 1812, for example, Beecher brought an ad hoc report before the General Association of Congregational and Presbyterian clergy wherein he asserted that intemperance was the mutual problem of the "Civil and Religious order," and recommended that employers cease providing liquor to their employees. Beecher also warned his colleagues that their efforts must remain within the boundaries of the "sanction of public sentiment," and thus echoed Benjamin Rush's plea for a regime of severe manners.[22]

Ultimately the concerns of activist clergymen like Beecher were identical to those of men like Thomas Hertell and Mathew Carey, the Philadelphia publisher who helped establish the Philadelphia Society for the Promotion of National Industry. In 1820 Carey brought out Beecher's sermon, "The Means of National Prosperity," which encouraged the expansion of manufacturing, presupposing an abstemious social order, and outlined a role for the nation's churches in fostering this development.

According to Beecher, social honor had to be awarded to mechanical and manual laborers. "That nation cannot be prosperous and free," he argued, echoing Carey's well known neo-Hamiltonian doctrines, "whose labouring population are consigned to relative ignominy."[23] The only impediments to social honor that Beecher would acknowledge were "ignorance, indolence, and immorality."[24] Otherwise: "Let the road to honor and influence be open alike to all classes of society . . . and the consequence will be, contented families, and national wealth—We shall have no mobs of discontented labourers to annoy us—an no standing armies to protect and enslave us."[25]

Like Hertell, Beecher saw in the habits of American society's dominant social class obstacles to the millennium of an autarchic and dry economy. Rooting out these abuses required a disciplined elite effort "of setting our own houses in order, of checking by our example, the innovation of expensive and gaudy fashions, of maintaining simplicity of living, and resisting that expensive luxury, which is creeping in under the cover of festivity and the hospitalities of friendship [i.e., social drinking], and of rearing up our families in habits of useful industry."[26]

In this general socioeconomic context, Beecher outlined a distinctive social role for Christian churches: "Finally—the institutions of the Christian religion are an important means of national prosperity," because accumulated wealth "in the hands of an irreligious nation, is the sword for suicide in the hands of a madman."[27] A complementary function of the church would be to reconcile those who could not share in the expected increase, but from whose toil it would come, and to demonstrate "that there is no collision of interest, or of foundation for envy, between the several classes of men, whose exertions are required to promote the general welfare."[28] In Beecher's view, the flaunting of wealth in the face of structural inequality was irrational; but the man who reacted to it by seeking "to alienate from each other the different classes of society, is more execrable in his deeds than the asassin or the incindiary."[29] The social radical was the true enemy of the church, which, by implication, would stand for the inequitable production and distribution of national wealth by helping to discipline all classes with regard to their proper social function.[30] With regard to his own class Beecher meant self-discipline in the form of restraint and encouragement for manufacturing. For the lower orders, restraint would be imposed from above for the sake of increased and diversified production.

The larger vision of temperance reform articulated by Thomas Hertell and Lyman Beecher took firm root within the establishments of the Northeast during and immediately following the Napoleonic wars. Mercantile capital, the center of much early temperance concern, fueled the expansion of the nation's young manufacturing enterprises and brought to them the problems of absentee owners seeking to insure their investments in an unsure world. Made aware during these years of their own role in perpetuating the "drinking usages" of society, American capitalists organized to secure a dry working class. By 1834, Walter Channing, a pioneering member of the Massachusetts Society for the Suppression of Intemperance, recalled with some exaggerated pride that it was only when "men of great consideration . . . solemnly impressed with the ruinous progress of intemperance . . . came out as one man to make an open declaration of their convictions" that temperance reform began to progress.[31]

The American Temperance Society (ATS), founded in January 1826 by Marcus Morton, a colleague of Channing, became the vehicle for the unified expression of class interest and coordinated action that Channing was to praise. Morton, who was "ahead of his time" in matters pertaining to labor reform, organized an umbrella society because of the deepening conviction that existing temperance societies were weak and ineffective. "Their object was," the ATS complained, "to regulate the use of ardent spirits, not to abolish it."[32]

ATS envisioned a decentralized temperance apparatus, hierarchically organized from the local through the national level so that the smallest antiliquor organizations could "regulate their own movements and efforts according to their own views of necessity and expediency, and . . . their own wants and ability."[33] The work of the ATS itself was to provide each and all with a common analysis of the liquor problem that corresponded to the class-conscious need for property owners to abstain totally from the use of distilled liquor, and to aid in the formation of state and local societies that adhered to this view of the problem.[34] To oversee this work, Morton's group decided that a full-time paid secretary would be necessary and solicited contributions from "men of known and expansive benevolence, who are blessed with property," and who shared the view "that a system of general and powerful cooperation may be formed, and that a change may in a short time be effected, which will save an incalculable amount of property, and vast multitudes of valuable lives."[35]

The man chosen to carry out the ATS reform was Justin Edwards of Andover Theological Seminary. In part Edwards's own previous skepticism about the efficacy of total abstinence from the use of distilled liquor became a major asset to the new organization. Prior to joining ATS as its secretary, Edwards had "thought [total abstinence] was going much too far . . . that the temperate use of ardent spirit was, for men who labor, in hot weather, necessary."[36] What persuaded Edwards that the pledge of total abstinence by property owners was indeed efficacious was not theological conviction but an experiment conducted at one of the farms of a member of Morton's group in 1825. The result, Edwards testified, was that laborers "performed more labor with greater ease."

Equally and perhaps more important, in the eyes of ATS, total abstinence from hard liquor produced an apparent change in the attitude of laborers. According to Edwards the regime of enforced abstinence made the men "more respectful and uniform in their deportment . . . more contented with their living; more desirous of being present at morning and evening family devotion . . . more attentive at public worship on the Sabbath."[37] Clearly this class-based reform effort saw a vital link between the docility of workers and their productivity on the one hand, and depriving them of liquor on the other.

The ATS, through the work of Edwards and secretaries of state societies affiliated with it, made repeated attempts to use the churches to advance the goal of abolition. Recognizing that distilleries were, for the most part, owned and operated by members of their own social class, ATS and its affiliates viewed the churches as the most appropriate vehicles available to them for the persuasion and coercion of their own. These efforts had profound and disruptive effects upon the churches and the movement itself, but what should not be lost sight of in the dogmatic hairsplitting over the extent to which abstinence was to be demanded is the intent of the reformers. "Ardent spirits" was the ordinary alcoholic beverage of workers. It had been the indifferent success of societies like the Massachusetts Society for the Suppression of Intemperance in seeking "to discontinue the too free use of ardent spirit" that had led to demands for total abolition. The ATS pledge committed affiliated societies to exclude all who "traffic" in ardent spirits and to "discountenance the use of them throughout the Community."[38] It was thus that the churches became putative instruments of the reformers.

In their endeavor to persuade the churches to condemn both moderate drinking and the liquor traffic, ATS concentrated its efforts on the governing bodies of the various Protestant denominations. Such attempts met with indifferent success. The General Conference of the Methodist Episcopal Church, for example, condemned "the pestilential example of temperate drinking," but only inquired rhetorically if churches which tolerated manufacturers and sellers of whisky could be innocent of wrongdoing. The conference did not condemn the latter or move to excommunicate offending individuals. Thus, ATS had to rely upon the vague hopes of "some leading men" of the conference that by 1836 the church would be rid of the traffickers in drink.[39]

The ATS also sought to bring pressure on the churches to expel liquor dealers through the efforts of such men as Wilbur Fisk, president of Wesleyan University, who castigated total abstinence church members for not insisting upon such expulsions and charged the churches with similar complicity.[40] The ATS executive committee joined in this criticism: "From all parts of the country . . . the greatest difficulties in the way of Temperance Reformation . . . are those members of the church, who still sell ardent spirit."[41]

Such pressures divided the established churches even though they produced condemnations of varying strength from national and state ecclesiastical organizations. The larger ones usually confined their expressions of opinion to vague generalities and left it to specific congregations to act.[42] The Protestant clergy was also encouraged to advance the utilitarian purposes of the reformers. Thus, a Connecticut clergyman maintained that the cause would be well served "if farmers and mechanics would agree not to drink spirits themselves, and not provide them for their workmen."[43]

By 1834 it was clear that the established churches had not made any deep inroads against either moderate drinking or the liquor traffic. In addition, their involvement in reform entailed a necessary hindrance to it since wine was of central importance to the Christian ritual as well as the ordinary drink of the wealthy. When, in the mid-1830s, ATS pushed for total abstinence from all alcoholic beverages and demanded state action against the liquor traffic, the difficulties posed by the churches appeared to outweigh their assets. As one clerical reformer acknowledged to the 1834 New York State Temperance Convention: "I have therefore been pained to see so many inclined to connect their religion with temperance. . . . And I know many individuals, who keep themselves aloof from the temperance society on this account, who would undoubtedly join the ranks, if the cause of temperance could be kept separate from everything else."[44]

While the American Temperance Society concentrated its efforts on arousing the consciousness of property holders through the churches, state societies continued to recruit such people to the cause of temperance by stressing the utilitarian benefits of reform. In July 1833, the *Temperance Recorder*, the official organ of the New York State Temperance Society, reported that the consolidation of the Erie Canal's several towing firms into the Albany and Buffalo Towing Company had enabled the teamsters' employers to gain "control and government" over them, with the result that their intemperate drinking habits had been effectively checked.[45] The same issue praised the society's forwarding of a circular letter to American consuls in Europe, warning émigrés that those who drank would find it difficult to obtain employment, and urging them to affiliate with a temperance society as an aid to finding work. The New York Society, which was dominated by mercantile and landed capitalists like Edward C. Delavan of Albany and Stephen Van Rensselaer of Saratoga, urged "the proprietors of our large, as well as our small manufacturing establishments . . . to take their subject into immediate consideration," since it was clear that intemperance was more dangerous to business prosperity than even foreign competition. The New Yorkers advised that temperance societies be organized within the factories themselves, and that proprietors and owners become the officers: "Unless proprietors or agents take the lead, nothing need be expected; but by their taking the course recommended . . . all under their control will be brought speedily into this 'ark of safety.'"[46]

But the efforts of the New York Society and ATS to use the churches to arouse a class-conscious temperance sentiment in favor of overseas economic expansion ran afoul of the churches' difficulties and weakened the desired condemnation and divided the reformers. Many reformers recognized that the association of temperance with specific political and economic issues detracted from its class appeal.[47] If the temperance movement were to gain the class support that its adherents believed was crucial, temperance morality would have to be divorced from specific secular and religious issues, and its moral appeal would have to come from an agency not associated with the churches.

In May 1833 ATS directors convened a national convention in Philadelphia to consider these questions and to chart the future course of reform.[48] The four hundred delegates from twenty-four states represented the country's mercantile, manufacturing, and landed capital. Indicative of the range and scope of this class of men are Gerrit Smith and Stephen Van Rensselaer. Together with John Jacob Astor, Smith's father had acquired over one million acres of land in upstate New York, some 700,000 acres of which he passed on to his son in 1819. Van Rensselaer's holdings were equally vast. Both men were outstanding proponents of internal improvements and expanded trade with the West. Smith violently opposed a governmental role in expanding these markets, but Van Rensselaer was a strong advocate of such aid.[49]

Other representatives of mercantile wealth included Edward C. Delavan, Roberts Vaux and his son, Richard, of Philadelphia, Samuel Ward of New York whose family's wealth had been invested in the banking firm of Prime, Ward, and King, Samuel Mifflin of Philadelphia, and John Tappan of Boston. Typical of emerging manufacturing representatives were Amasa Walker of Boston, Jonas Chickering, whose piano manufacturing concern of Stewart and Chickering developed the single casting iron frame for making grand pianos, and Matthew Newkirk, whose cotton goods business provided the funds for his railroad investments. Many of them, Delavan, Newkirk, and Smith, for example, had multiple investments in land, transportation, and manufacturing.[50]

Also attending the first national temperance convention were luminaries from the first ranks of law, politics, religion, and science, many bearing some of the oldest family names in America. Reuben Hyde Walworth, chancellor of New York State, was named the convention's president. Joseph H. Lumpkin (whose brother Wilson was a Georgia planter and governor of the state), who would himself become a member of Georgia's Supreme Court, was named convention vice president. Timothy Pitkin, the author of the first major statistical account of American commerce, was a delegate from Connecticut. John McLean, who was to become president of the College of New Jersey, was a delegate. So also was Samuel L. Southard, Democractic senator from New Jersey. Amos Twitchell, a pioneer heart surgeon, represented New Hampshire. Jonas K. Converse of Burlington, Vermont, was a delegate, as were Philadelphia philanthropists John Sargent and Joseph B. Ingersoll; businessmen-publicists such as Mathew Carey, William Goodell, Thomas Bradford, Jr., and Sylvester Graham were typical delegates.

Other men of similar stature, like chemist Benjamin Silliman of Yale, or perhaps less well known, such as George Chambers, largest landowner in Franklin County, Pennsylvania and a reformer in education and agriculture, filled out the complement of delegates to the Philadelphia meeting. Their differences in economic interest, political affiliation, and religious persuasion were transcended by a fundamental class problem: the liquor question.

The convention's standing committee presented to the convention a number of innocuous resolutions, including two calling for "the abolition of the practice of furnishing merchant vessels with ardent spirit or employing men who drink it," and extolling the general desirability of forming "temperance societies in all mechanical and manufacturing establishments." It also attempted to deal with the disaffection of agricultural producers, who argued that their surplus grain could only be marketed as distilled alcohol, by calling upon "the friends of human improvements" to investigate the problem and report their findings through the press.[51] The committee also recommended that prospective immigrants be told about the new abstinence requirements.

But the two major questions before the committee were the relationship of reform to other aspects of political economy and the supposed immorality of the drinking usages of society. The convention had no difficulty with the first of these issues, unanimously resolving that the "SOLE OBJECT" of the ATS and its affiliates was "the promotion of TEMPERANCE."[52]

The question of the immorality of trafficking in liquor was another matter. Not merely was a sizable investment of capital resources involved; traffic was itself business enterprise. In the theoretically neutral world of commerce the question of the nature and desirability of any activity should be resolved in the marketplace. But the paramount political need of the reformers to secularize temperance morality, that is, to obtain a declaration of the immorality of the liquor traffic from a nondenominational authority, pushed such abstract considerations into the background. On the last day of the convention, after much debate, the delegates declared unanimously that "the traffic in ardent spirit as a drink, and the use of it as such, are morally wrong, and ought to be abandoned throughout the world."[53]

Thus a paramount issue of class morality was resolved. Confronted with a question and situation that its own analysis of the liquor problem had created, America's propertied class united behind a declaration that would prove to be a pandora's box. But for the moment the two declarations—the one separating temperance reform from issues of political economy and ecclesiastical concerns and the other reestablishing the secular nature of its moral impulse—paved the way for organizing a national reform effort, superintended by representatives of leading capital interests. Towards this end the convention authorized the formation of a national temperance union. The United States Temperance Union would soon emerge as the legitimate successor of the ATS. Under the guidance of the ATS's old leadership, the USTU would push the reform movement into the political arena, demanding the state revoke its sanctions of the liquor traffic. To further this end Stephen Van Rensselaer financed the publication and distribution of 100,000 copies of the convention's proceedings.[54]

The convention's underlying conviction concerning the immorality of the liquor traffic derived from an implicit assumption that the drinking usages of society supported a socioeconomic order that was no longer viable. Gerrit Smith expressed this conviction when he asked the sixth annual meeting of the ATS to support a resolution condemning the manufacture and sale of whiskey as "violation of the great principles of political economy [which] impose a great burden on the industry and wealth of the country." Explaining his position, Smith declared that the liquor traffic did not produce a genuine value-added commodity, particularly in America where "population is sparce and the demand for labor for useful objects great and incessant." The ATS concurred and passed the resolution. The morality of property, harried by the realities of scarcity, had to be adapted to new needs and circumstances.[55]

Condemnation of the traffic in ardent spirit as immoral by such a nonsectarian body opened the way for employing the instrumentality of the state against drinking. Even before the ATS convened its 1833 convention, it had realized the potential efficacy of this strategy. If the churches could not drive out the rum sellers, their condemnations could be used to move the state. The first public signal of the ATS's intent to move in this direction appeared in 1833. In that year George Cheever reported that the ATS had cited intemperance as the principal cause of all social evil, and stressed its baneful effects on manufacturing. But the main burden of its report shifted from the need for voluntary abstinence by the responsible orders of society to the need to abolish the laws that sustained commerce in alcoholic beverages. The temperance reform "has accomplished comparatively nothing," Cheever maintained, and was unlikely to "as long as legislation sanctions [the liquor traffic]."[56]

A similar critique appeared in the *North American Review*. Temperance reformation had thus far employed "insignificant" measures to date, the *Review's* anonymous critic charged. "It was proposed, by the mere dint of reason, on the part of benevolent individuals unaided by the power of the state . . . to enter the field against one of the strongest of the physical appetites, as indulged to a great degree by that class of the community, least accessible, in all respects, to the force of reason and argument." Temperance work, therefore, must be carried on by every available means including the use of savings institutions, which would protect the poor, and other "auxillaries" such as the churches. Public opinion was the key to successful political action "in this land of free institutions," and the temperance societies were the natural agents for affecting it.[57] While the *Review* did not call for direct political action, its praise of the efforts of the New York Temperance Society and ATS clearly implied such a course.

The question of the legal status of the liquor traffic was first debated at a November 1833 convention of New York temperance societies affiliated with the ATS.[58] The resolutions committee presented a declaration that since the liquor traffic was not only unnecessary but socially injurious, "the laws which sanction that traffic, by licensing men to pursue it, are . . . *morally wrong*, and ought to be so modified, that . . . they should, as far as practicable and expedient, defend the community from its evils."[59] After protracted debate, the resolution was turned over to a select committee for reexamination.

The issue confronting the convention, the same one that had confronted the Philadelphia group, sought a general declaration of the immorality of the "traffic." Yet how could any sort of "traffic" be declared illegal without subverting the notion of commerce itself? Looming in the background was the related issue of the authority of the state and its laws. Could the state propagate or support an immoral law? Could it sustain illicit business enterprise? How could business enterprise or any aspect of it be either illicit or immoral; if it were, what could be said of the authorities of the church and state which sanctioned it?

Faced with these dilemmas, but convinced of the necessity to insist upon its own claims, the gathering from among New York's ruling class compromised. The select committee reported that "no moral reformation can be fully accomplished, and paramountly sustained, when the laws of the country stand in opposition to it; and that so long, therefore, as the laws of the state defend and justify the traffic in ardent spirit, the cause of temperance among us cannot be crowned in triumph."[60] This injunction notwithstanding, the committee reported that some of New York's liquor laws were, on the whole, in keeping with the imperatives of reform; moreover, the abolition of license laws—tantamount to condoning a laissez-faire liquor traffic—"would be of dangerous tendency."

Those aspects of the law with which the committee found favor revealed once again the class nature of temperance reform. New York's law placed no restrictions on the production of distilled liquor, and the committee ignored this fact. Similarly, the committee found no objection to laws permitting the unrestricted sale of whiskey in amounts of five gallons or more. The committee found the law's restraints upon retail sales of smaller amounts, which could be consumed on the premises, to be adequate to prevent abuse. The law's limitation of sale to bona fide tavern keepers for consumption on their premises was also satisfactory because, as the committee explained, all retail sales of any kind were licensed by local authorities. In other words, the production, sale, and distribution of distilled spirits in amounts beyond the range of laborers' physical and pecuniary capacities were safely hedged by the statutes of New York. Hence, the committee recommended "that the efforts of its friends should be mainly directed to the enlightening and reforming of public opinion [and] the temperance pledge [is] the most simple, and at the same time the most effectual instrument which had yet been devised for accomplishing these ends." The committee concluded by arguing that the reform of the state's excise laws would follow the arousing of the sentiment of those who pledged to abstain from the use of whiskey and that "it behooves the friends of temperance to see that the *legal* reform keeps pace with the *moral*.[61]

In the end, this effort to rely solely upon the resources of property would fail because, as Gerrit Smith had already pointed out, America was a society where the demand for labor could not be met. Would-be employers would find the pledge inadequate and the law insufficient. But from the vantage point of 1834, the antiliquor movement had achieved astounding success. It had aroused the consciousness of virtually the entire propertied class, regardless of particular economic or political interest, to the importance of extirpating the use of distilled alcohol as a precondition of capitalist development.[62] It had created a secular temperance morality that avoided the rigidities of various theologies while, at the same time, it had been able to enlist the churches in raising the consciousness of the "employing class." And it had developed its archetypal propaganda institution, the American Temperance Society, which was controlled by entrepreneurs of all sorts, and state and local temperance societies, which were to organize local property interests for the cause. Finally, the reform was being urged in the direction of a political attack on the liquor traffic itself.

When the United States Temperance Union and its affiliates met at Saratoga Springs in 1836, there appeared to remain but two mutually compatible tasks for the reform: first, spread the new gospel that "it has been proved a thousand times, that more labor can be accomplished in a month, or a year, under the influence of simple nourishing food and unstimulating drink than through the aid of alcohol";[63] second, organize and launch a political assault on the liquor traffic itself. To further these ends, the USTU named Reverend John Marsh and Edward C. Delavan to its principal offices. Both were fitting choices for the work. Marsh was related by marriage to the Tappan mercantile family of Boston and New York; his cousin Samuel would head the New York and Erie railroad.[64] Delavan, on the other hand, was an active entrepreneur whose fortune had been made, ironically, as an importer of wine, and who came to the temperance reform after Nathaniel Prime, Lynde Catlin, and he had lost three hundred thousand dollars invested in the manufacture of steam engines and other heavy iron work because, they claimed, of "the unfortunate drinking habits [of the workers], which for best of motives, we ourselves encouraged."[65]

2

The Politics of Moral Reform: Social Class and Nonpartisanship in the Temperance Movement, 1836–1860

The Movement Turns Toward Legislation, 1835–1850

As the organizers of the United States Temperance Union (USTU) set about to spread their gospel of reform and convert the unbelievers in their midst, they did not foresee the thicket of obstacles that would ensnare them. Even had such impediments been recognized, they were largely unavoidable given the assumptions and objectives of the reformers. Moreover, in addition to difficulties of their own making, temperance reformers faced problems arising elsewhere in the political order. Eventually temperance ideology became the "breaking up plow of the Democracy," but the reform itself was lost in the chaos of a social order rushing towards civil war.

The USTU condemned drinking on the basis of a secular and utilitarian analysis of its consequences. Representing this analysis as a new morality, the reformers hoped to obtain voluntary sanctions and restraints from property holders everywhere to curtail the traffic in drink. By the mid-1830s the reformers had come to realize that the immediate interests of the producers and distributors of alcoholic beverages would not give way easily to larger class needs. Yet, by turning to the state for remedies, temperance reformers opened the way for internal division among themselves and for conflict with socially marginal groups whose political support such a move required. Such groups could claim the right to participate in the reform and in the definition of the social order that was to follow. The realization of both possibilities seriously divided the movement.[1]

Concerned about the assumed impact of drinking upon the productivity and related conduct of labor, the USTU and its affiliates proselytized workers as well as their employers. The reformers lavished particular attention on manufacturing enterprise, which, by the 1830s, was attracting substantial mercantile capital. In 1832 for example, Massachusetts affiliates of the USTU praised the mechanics of Boston, stating that there was "no class among us [to which] the body politic [is more] indebted for the good principles, and the good habits, which are the conservative power of our free institutions." The Massachusetts reformers urged "a union of the friends of temperance in the cause of total abstinence from intoxicating stimulants" between themselves and the mechanics.[2] Such blandishments were passed along to workers with indifferent success. Employers established numerous "temperance shops" only to find themselves caught up in labor demands for reducing the work day and/or increasing wages as the price for compliance.[3]

In February 1834, the USTU signaled its urgent concern for the need to use the state to bring workers into the temperance ark by awarding its prize for a temperance essay to a work whose major premise held that "*Labor, diligence in useful employment,* is the source of wealth to both individuals and nations."[4] According to Mark Doolittle, the USTU's prize-winning author, the labor force constituted "the capital of the nation" for which the government had direct responsibility. Consequently the government could not sanction social policies that "induce idleness, [and] dissipation." Nor could it permit labor to be invested in producing commodities dangerous to its own welfare, for this would weaken a major area of capital investment. In other words, investors would not risk capital if the labor force were not reliable. Therefore, Doolittle concluded, "the government which authorizes the manufacture and traffic in ardent spirits, lends its authority to legalize corruption, and violates the first principles of political economy."[5]

Doolittle's essay accompanied a vigorous campaign by the USTU leadership to win over state societies to a broadened abstinence pledge. The union's executive committee, dominated by commercial capitalists Edward Delavan, Matthew Newkirk, John Tappan, and Samuel Ward, wanted to include fermented beverages because the committee realized that great quantities of fermented drinks were heavily adulterated with distilled liquor. At the same time, the USTU directorate sought endorsement from its constituents for its antiliquor campaign.[6] By 1836 the campaign had gained sufficient momentum to permit a general meeting of USTU affiliates to be held.

Of the two issues, the broadened pledge presented the most difficulty. Moderates opposed expanding the pledge because of their belief that wine and beer were healthful drinks for foreign laborers. Others feared the implications of such a pledge for the practices of the churches.[7] Eventually a compromise was reached: the delegates pledged themselves to "tee totalism," but left the wording of such pledges to local temperance groups. In the same fashion the problem of condemning state license laws was seemingly resolved. Finally the USTU was renamed the American Temperance Union over which Delavan's faction retained executive control.[8]

In the year following the Saratoga meeting, Delavan's committee published a revised pledge substituting the term "intoxicating liquors" for "ardent spirits." Since recognition and assistance from the national society depended upon endorsing its pledge, this action acted to purge moderates from the ATU. Along with the new pledge, the ATU's leaders named 1838 as a "petition year" during which state legislatures were to be lobbied to repeal their licensing laws.[9]

These actions had enduring consequences for the temperance reform in America. At the same time that the business elites, which dominated the ATU, politicized temperance, they deprived it of the unified class commitment they had done so much to establish. Although their social peers would retain and even deepen their commitment to reform, not all would see the efficacy of direct political action to obtain it, particularly in a society committed to universal manhood suffrage.[10] But in 1837–38 these differences were relatively muted. For the most part the state affiliates petitioned their legislatures to place restrictions upon the liquor traffic. In others, like Maine, where conservative temperance men opposed political intervention, pro-ATU groups formed new societies.[11]

The most significant of these campaigns occurred in Massachusetts, and it quickly revealed the pitfalls awaiting political activists. The ensuing controversy over the so-called Fifteen Gallon Law aroused popular emotions and, more important, deeply divided the state's temperance forces into pro- and antilegislation factions. On February 21, 1838, a statewide gathering of reformers demanded the abolition of laws permitting the retail sale of alcoholic beverages. They dispatched a select committee, including Walter Channing and John Pierpont, to lobby for their aim. In less than two months the state banned the retail sale of liquor in amounts of less than fifteen gallons.[12]

Public outcry was immediate, and the legislature was deluged with petitions for and against the law. In response, hearings were held in February 1839, but the law remained on the books.[13] Channing had endorsed legislation as a "useful" aid to moral reform, but George F. Clark opposed it, charging that the law in Massachusetts was a shelter for the rich.[14] The ATU's 1839 report summarized the objections of the conservatives: "it is a prohibition to one class and not to another [and] favors the rich to the injury of the poor."[15]

Throughout the controversy, the Massachusetts oligarchy confined the debate over the Fifteen Gallon Law to the question of whether such legislation would advance or impede a class interest. The leadership of the Massachusetts Temperance Society supported a legislative remedy, charging that the rich had thus far failed to set a proper standard for society's lesser orders. Responding to others' fears of the impact of partisan strife on the movement, one prolegislationist warned: "One bar room or grog shop would do more to rouse the partisan passions of the multitude, than the warmest [temperance] appeal of the most eloquent advocate of truth." Eventually the Massachusetts Temperance Union's legislationists overrode the carefully put objections of its conservatives that class issues be kept out of popular politics.[16]

The Massachusetts gubernatorial race in the fall of 1839 became the focus of the movement's pro- and antilegislation factions. Conservatives challenged the prolegislation incumbent, Edward Everit, with Marcus Morton, former president of the ATS. Morton had no trouble winning popular support for his repeal campaign, and, as promised, he revoked the Fifteen Gallon Law in February 1840. Morton's action, however, only reinforced the resolve of the Channing–Pierpont faction, which met in Boston to declare that it was "the duty of temperance men to vote only for those who supported prohibitory legislation."[17]

The efforts of ATU affiliated societies to use the state stirred up popular hostility among its allies in the middle and working classes. Such allies had been attracted by the reform's promise to increase the productivity of capital and labor. Anxious to share in this development, these temperance adherents were welding this promise into a platform of republican nationalism. According to Albert Barnes, for example, "To maintain our liberty, it is needful to secure independent industry." Barnes, however, warned the members of the Mechanics' and Workingmen's Temperance Society of Philadelphia that such independence would bring not only prosperity, but also immigration, which could undermine liberty through increased intemperance. Only temperance reform could insure "the right of suffrage" for native born and foreigner alike and so the continuation of majority rule.[18] To those who espoused Barnes' version of temperance, the ATU's pragmatic conviction that moral suasion had failed suggested that they, themselves, somehow lacked the capacities of intelligence, sobriety, and industriousness required of temperance men, and, thus, it inspired their opposition, not to temperance, but to the ATU.[19]

The Washingtonian movement became the first organized expression of this hostility toward the ATU. The movement, which had its strength in eastern cities, proved particularly attractive to small tradesmen and mechanics whose prospects and ambitions had been encouraged by temperance doctrines, but who had suffered severely through the depression that coincided with the Union's antilicense drives of 1837–40. Organized in Baltimore in 1840, the first Washingtonian group consisted of a tailor, carpenter, coachmaker, silverplater, and two blacksmiths who shared the opinion that temperance reform was being led by "a parcel of hypocrits."[20]

Despite their animosity to ATU politics, Washingtonians accepted the rationale of temperance reform, and by insisting upon divorcing it from issues of religion and politics were firmly suasionist. They provided the ATU with an ideal vehicle for disseminating a vital part of entrepreneurial ideology throughout America's laboring classes.[21] In large part, Washingtonians indicted America's capitalist classes for having failed to reform themselves sufficiently, and for having adopted inappropriate means for reforming the working classes. Thus, "the very men who rigidly insist on the strictest integrity in regard to the rights of property, look with cool indifference on the rapid spread of intemperance and licentiousness, with their kindred vices," particularly in cities like New Haven, where the development of the factory system had created new social conditions that separated young workers from the protective influences of the church, family, and employers. In this context, even if the state were necessary it was certainly not sufficient, and temperance reform required "other agencies . . . be enlisted in this cause, for there is work to be performed which the arm of the law cannot reach."[22]

The Washingtonians proposed to meet this need by organizing as a fraternity of reformed drinkers who, through personal testimony, would persuade workers to abandon drinking not because it was immoral, but because of the harm that inevitably attended habitual drinking.[23] Thus, for leaders of the ATU, like Baltimore merchant Christian Keener, the great advantage of the Washingtonians was that "they have reached hundreds of men that would not come out to our churches.[24]

Thus encouraged, the New York Temperance Society, the backbone of the ATU, arranged to meet a delegation of Baltimore Washingtonians in March 1841. Fittingly, this meeting was presided over by Anson G. Phelps, senior partner of Phelps, Dodge and Company, a pioneer developer of Pennsylvania iron and Lake Superior copper mines. Phelps and the NYTS hoped that the delegation would provide reformers a means for bringing temperance to workers and others who lived their lives beyond the reach of the churches.[25] The Baltimore group, led by journeyman hatmaker John H. W. Hawkins, whose first business venture had failed in the depression of 1837–40, agreed to spread the temperance message for the ATU through Washingtonian societies, and in the spring of 1841 the union's leadership was optimistic that it had discovered a means for developing required popular support. Following their New York meeting, the Baltimore group was invited to Boston, where Deacon Moses Grant, a leader of the prolegislation faction of the Massachusetts Temperance Society, introduced Hawkins to the society. Hawkins obtained the support of Grant's followers because of his ability to "secure the attendance of drinking men [i.e., working men]" at temperance rallies.[26] The following year the Massachusetts Washington Total Abstinence Society was formally organized with Channing, a leader of the pro-legislation faction, as its president.[27]

But the ATU's optimism was soon dampened. Although Washingtonianism attracted a widespread popular following, and Hawkins publicly advocated prohibitory legislation, the union's secularist and fraternal elements, which it had viewed as a means of gathering working-class support, militated strongly against the union's political program. In the summer of 1842 John Marsh noted "an evident depression in the moral state of the reformed . . . and a painful unwillingness . . . to connect the temperance cause, as now seen, with religion."[28] Although Washingtonianism's official position regarding both politics and religion argued that support for these would follow personal reform, those who flocked to it from the working classes refused subsequently either to join the older temperance societies or to endorse their policies.[29]

Nevertheless, the ATU's leaders did not abandon their search for a viable fifth column within the working class. Indeed, they could not do so and reasonably hope to obtain a permanent legislative solution to the liquor problem. Washingtonianism's emulation of the suasionist wing of capitalist temperance sentiment had to be countered as did its repudiation of a role in the reform for organized religion, still regarded by the ATU as the best means of coercing the nation's elites. The situation that the ATU now confronted could best be met by working-class representatives who could help convince both capitalist and middle-class suasionists of the need for legislative reform and the working-class of its compatibility with personal reformation.

Early in 1842, the Massachusetts Temperance Society organized a speaking tour of eastern cities where Washingtonianism flourished. Its featured speaker was John B. Gough, a journeyman bookbinder whose efforts to begin his own business had failed disastrously during the depression years. Throughout 1844 and 1845 Gough tirelessly and with sensational results preached the ATU line that while "moral suasion *alone*, and in its fullest extent, too, in the case of the drunkard" was admirable, nevertheless the rum seller was at the root of intemperance; hence "different and more stringent measures should be adopted," and the law should prohibit the liquor traffic.[30] In the midst of this success, Gough was asked to carry the ATU message to the disaffected of the "religious and wealthy classes" and he concluded his tour in Albany where he addressed "the very elite of the city."[31]

But Gough was chiefly valued in his role as a working-class man redeemed from drunkenness who could counter the secular orientation that class had given to Washingtonianism. John Marsh and the ATU feared "the open infidelity and radicalism, and the abuse of ministers" preached by some Washingtonian speakers.[32] It was Gough's seeming ability to persuade the rank and file that religion and temperance were not only compatible, but mutually reinforcing, and that men of wealth and social standing should not be pushed aside and excluded from the temperance reform that made him an asset to the reformers' cause. Gough continued to tour major eastern cities for ATU and to receive extensive coverage from the press. In January 1845 Lyman Beecher urged Marsh to arrange for Gough to carry the ATU message of moral reform and legislative action against the liquor traffic to the western states.[33]

By this time, however, Gough had become engulfed in public controversy. He was accused of being "the tool of others in attacking Washingtonianism." He became a further liability to the ATU because of his recidivist social behavior and his steadily increasing speaking fees.[34] With his usefulness now questionable Gough's star plummeted as quickly as it had risen, but the ATU's concern to extend its message to the middle and working classes did not abate. In the spring of 1849 the ATU arranged for the tour of the Irish temperance reformer Father Theobald Matthew, who began an ambitious schedule that lasted until November 1850. Besides advocating temperance, Father Matthew, whose visit had been opposed by New York City's Roman Catholic Bishop John Hughes, urged the Irish to migrate to the West. Like Hawkins and Gough before him, controversy soon dissipated Father Matthew's impact.[35]

The efforts of the ATU leadership to exert its influence over the Washingtonians accomplished little more than to extend the divisions that characterized the established movement. Essentially Washingtonianism was an expression of middle- and working-class hostility toward the coercive impulses that dominated ATU temperance strategy. On the other hand, Washingtonians accepted the utilitarian basis of temperance and the conservative idea that self-reformation among the upper orders would produce a similar change within their own ranks—as they claimed their own experiences attested. But Washingtonians could not organize politically to oppose the ATU. To have done so would only have given the appearance of endorsing the liquor traffic.[36]

Yet the eclipse of Washingtonianism should be attributed to forces larger than its own political dilemmas. Washingtonianism is best regarded as an enthusiasm, rather than a movement. That it lacked the means to sustain itself lies not so much in its ideology as it does in the historical forces then shaping American society. Essentially the Washingtonians comprised those artisan and working classes caught up in the maw of entrepreneurial industrialization. Its challenge to the politics of the established temperance reform was quickly and easily surmounted. In the last analysis, however, such workers were being swept from America's social landscape into the dustbin of time.

Self-reformation—the heart and soul of Washingtonianism—had not been a strategic objective of temperance leaders. From Benjamin Rush onward the reform sought to eliminate customary drinking from the interstices of the workday. Absentee owners and entrepreneurial investors constituted its driving force. The churches of the established order were quickly and easily employed to arouse the class consciousness of those "who looked to the emerging industrial society" as the harbinger of progress, even as it was candidly recognized that "those most in need of reform would not come out to our churches."[37]

The eruption of Washingtonianism among those "most in need of reform" reflected both the hopes of those who might aspire to the "middle class" extolled by reformers, and the anger of those displaced from honorable and respectable employment by the factory system and other forms of capitalist enterprise. Such workers might calculate that self-reformation, undertaken as investment of moral capital, could or should carry them to economic and social safety. But self-reformation implied maintaining the status quo so as to offer the means whereby personal worth might be demonstrated—much as well-rendered tallow or finely turned barrel staves demonstrated the value of a chandler or cooper. A world devoid of the liquor traffic would be a world devoid of yet another opportunity to establish one's social value. Here, then, lay the Scylla and Charybdis of Washingtonianism, and here is where it foundered.[38]

Even as ATU's hopes for Washingtonianism were waning, yet another approach to the problem of temperance reform was being developed. In September 1842 two New York City businessmen, John W. Oliver, a printer, and Daniel H. Sands, "a highly respectable paper manufacturer," concerned by "the waves of popular excitement" accompanying the spread of Washingtonianism, organized a society "to consolidate and combine the discordant materials of the movement." Correctly perceiving the class animosities underlying the religious and political action debates, Oliver and Sands sought to create a fraternal organization that would "invest [temperance reform] with a social character."[39]

The Sons of Temperance, as the new organization was called, ostensibly sought a reconciliation of Washingtonians whom they depicted as "reformed men over flowing with zeal" and "almost to an individual, poor, dependent upon their daily labor for support," and "the old temperance man" who favored "calling in the aid of the civil power to put down the evil."[40] The Sons eschewed taking any public position on the questions of political action and the role of the churches. Describing their society as merely "another link in the chain" of reform, the Sons promised to provide members with mutual assistance and the means for elevating their character.[41]

The innocuous purpose of the Sons of Temperance, however, when combined with its stringent membership requirements, precluded any such reconciliation by effectively excluding many who would be Washingtonians. In addition to forgoing public debate on matters of politics and religion, prospective members had to possess what the Sons regarded as "a fair moral character." They had also to submit to periodic health checks and support tests. A "black book" was kept on the membership; backsliders were libel to expulsion. In such circumstances the Washingtonian practice of seeking out drinking men for conversion could not continue: the Sons of Temperance effectively was open only to those whose employment and values permitted them to pay dues and support a mutual insurance program.[42]

Organized in the midst of the Washingtonian controversy, when conservative reformers insisted that "Our law makers should not license men to . . . furnish that solvent which so greedily absorbs the wages of the mechanic," the formally noncommittal Sons did not escape suspicion at first. The order's essentially middle-class orientation was not fully appreciated by those who feared for the movement's future at a time when immigration was introducing yet more drinkers into the labor force.[43] The ATU's leaders feared that the Sons would enable "the zealous and influential [to] be drawn from their operation on the masses, and fritter away their enthusiasm in the private meetings of the Order."[44] But when the nonsectarian and nonpolitical stances of the order were recognized for what they were, prominent temperance capitalists like William Earl Dodge endorsed and supported it.[45] In fact the Sons of Temperance defined its success in terms of the decline of Washingtonianism, and by 1848 the new organization's leaders, the product of a rigidly hierarchic selection process, assured ATU's John Marsh that there was nothing in the temperance reform they espoused which suggested that "its chief glory consists in picking up drunkards and reforming them." Rather, the elimination of the liquor traffic by "moral and legal means" was their objective. By 1851 the Sons of Temperance boasted that its membership was a quarter of a million "men only, 21 years of age, nearly all legal voters."[46]

The Sons of Temperance was the first of a number of middle-class temperance fraternities to develop in the wake of the Washingtonian enthusiasm. Their formal stance of neutrality opened them to middle-class temperance reformers of all political persuasions, with resulting factional splits and proliferation, but they supplied the temperance movement with an infrastructure of cadres, capable of mobilizing for political action.[47] By viewing themselves merely as links in the chain of temperance reform and asserting that they did not "design to interfere with, or oppose in the remotest degree, other organizations in the glorious cause of temperance," the Sons and similar organizations assured the continuing domination of a divided capitalist class over the reform. These latter were entitled to this deference because, as one reformer put it, "By arousing enterprise, by rewarding labor and encouraging effort, wealth forms the great balance wheel of the social system."[48] What temperance reform required of wealth was, first, its example, and, second, its financial support. But, of greater importance, these fraternities signaled the end of the public debate between capital and labor over the means and objectives of temperance reform. The Washingtonians—fraternities of working-class men—had rejected political and religious coercion; the capitalist leadership of the ATU and the middle-class fraternal orders insisted upon both measures of restraint. Hereafter no serious effort was made to engage the working class politically in temperance reform.[49] Reform was now confined to those committed to using the state to eradicate social habits deemed inimical to increased productivity, and, by 1850, there had emerged in the state of

Maine a political temperance movement that promised to achieve this goal in the foreseeable future.

Neal Dow and the Advent of the Maine Law

The history and significance of the temperance movement in Maine has been obscured by the legendary career of Neal Dow, the Portland manufacturer who devised the legislative remedy for prohibiting common drinking that the ATU endorsed in 1851.[50] Dow himself has been misleadingly depicted as a moral fanatic driven by a conservative heritage of moral stewardship.[51] But an organized antiliquor sentiment antedated and informed Dow's own sympathies, and his career merely reflected the early history of the movement everywhere it appeared. Dow's Maine Law was a practical solution to the problems faced by the entire prolegislation wing of the movement.

According to Dow, organized antidrink sentiment originated in Portland around 1815. At that time a group of sixty-nine "leaders of every legitimate business enterprise in Portland" and two "diverging" clergymen established a society committed to total abstinence from the use of distilled liquor.[52] Initially, Dow records, the group ran into sharp opposition from Portland's "leading citizens," who were drawn from the city's commercial oligarchy whose business centered on distilling West Indian molasses into rum for domestic and foreign consumption. Writing some eighty-five years after the fact, Dow characterized the total abstinence society as a rebuke against established society by its peers, which is precisely what the initial reform was designed to be even as it sought in the long run "to correct the intemperate habits of the masses."[53] Thus, by the time Dow came of age a well defined antiliquor sentiment animated Portland's business community and Dow merely subscribed (however enthusiastically) to it.[54]

Dow did not attribute the need for drink reform to his moral or religious inheritance, but to the need to develop the state's enormous natural resources.[55] He believed the state's population had become "demoralized" during the War of 1812. Drinking, combined with the conditions of labor, particularly in farming, lumbering, and fishing—the state's largest economic activities—encouraged, he argued, intemperance by the men from whom Portland's manufacturers filled their labor supply.[56]

The quality of Portland's labor supply was beyond the control of the local temperance society, which began to foster similar antidrink organizations throughout the state in the mid-1820s.[57] In 1824, at age twenty-two, Dow, by now a partner in his father's tannery, branched out to banking and real estate. But it was not until four years later, in 1828, that he began to see that the approach of Portland's business community to temperance reform was deficient, and that "the great evil was in something besides drunkenness."[58]

The evil Dow perceived was the custom of master mechanics supplying journeymen and apprentices with liquor rations at midday and again in midafternoon. In 1828–29 the Maine Charitable Mechanics Association began to boycott the practice in the manner already long established by reformers. In addition, the Charitable Mechanics Association futilely sought the cooperation of Portland authorities by asking them to stop announcing midmorning work breaks.[59]

After their rebuff by the Portland town council, Dow moved to redirect the city's temperance enthusiasts toward total abstinence. He also challenged the right of the city's commercial oligarchy to exercise hegemony over public policy to the detriment of other property interests. In so doing Dow was claiming for the city's manufacturers the social position that had been sought for them by temperance reformers in Massachusetts, New York, and Pennsylvania after 1820. Since most of the city's work force found employment through the employers' association, Dow told their July 4 assembly that "the influence which the Mechanics' Associations can exert in the promotion of temperance is greater than that which other societies possess," but he did not initially extend his own analysis beyond the prevailing boycott tactics.[60]

Portland's manufacturing community kept abreast of temperance reform in the rest of the country, by adopting the total abstinence pledge from the use of hard liquor as a requisite for membership in March 1833. Dow attributed the society's difficulties to the dominance of the area's commercial distillers: "In business their capital was needed. . . . In politics their word was law. . . . In society their houses were the rendezvous of the '*elite*.'"[61] But by this time Portland's manufacturers were developing sufficient surplus capital to act independently. In 1834, when Maine's first statewide temperance society was being organized, Dow had enlarged his local capital investments to include holdings in a canal, a cotton mill, and several banks.[62] More important, he was seeking investments to develop the state's natural resources, and an 1835 trip to Bangor in search of investment opportunities in timber lands convinced the prophet that reform "involv[ed] something beyond the reformation of the victims." It was necessary to secure "the relief of society from the burdens resulting from that vice."[63] Moreover, he recognized the ultimate inefficacy of the employers' boycott to effect such relief. As the capitalist leaders of the ATS had already discovered, Dow decided that the state's license was a sanction for those engaged in the retail liquor trade, one which provided them with a sense of moral justification as well as a prerogative.[64]

Dow, of course, had not arrived at this insight in total isolation or guided by an inner moral light. In fact, temperance reform in Maine was, if anything, a case of arrested development due in large part to a lack of resident capital resources devoted to investment. But once Maine capital had achieved sufficient development, its social vision caught up with temperance reform elsewhere. In April 1834 the newly organized state temperance society debated the problem of the state's license laws as a sanction for, rather than a limitation upon the liquor traffic.[65] Again in 1837, the year following the decision of the ATU's executive committee to broaden the pledge to include total abstinence from all intoxicating liquors, Dow and his supporters, who included "many who were prominent in business and political circles of the state, or who afterwards became so," forced the issue within the state society. When they were defeated, Dow, James Appleton, another Portland manufacturer, Lot M. Morrill, Samuel Fessenden, and others of equal stature broke away to organize the Maine Temperance Union and, as elsewhere in the ATU's "petition year," submitted a demand to the legislature that the licensed retail liquor trade be severely restricted. A special committee of the Maine legislature endorsed the ATU's proposals and prepared legislation similar to that which the Massachusetts legislature adopted. Maine's "Twenty-eight Gallon" law received the support of Governor Edward Kent as well. According to Kent, moral suasion was "ultimately" the object of reform, but nevertheless temperance "'may yet receive aid and support from legal enactments.'"[66] Unlike Massachusetts, however, Maine's legislature remained unconvinced and rejected the measure in 1838 and again in 1839.[67]

Thus, by 1837 Maine's temperance capitalists were operating fully within the orbit of reform delineated by the ATU. If there was a distinction between events in Maine and other states, it lay in the fact that capital diversification had not yet developed there to the extent it had elsewhere. Consequently, conservative temperance advocates whose property interests were yet overly concentrated in the West Indian molasses and New England rum trade, and who feared also the class nature of the liquor prohibition sought, were able to delay the advent of legislative restrictions in the state. Moreover, when working-class opposition to the ATU's political objectives developed in Maine as elsewhere in the form of Washingtonianism, the response of Dow and the Maine Temperance Union was similar to capital's response everywhere. Dow and the Maine union warmly encouraged the development of the Washingtonians and successfully set out to win them over to political support.[68]

At the height of the Washingtonian revival, the Maine union reopened the question of antidrink legislation. Headed by Joseph C. Noyes, a former Congressman and "business man of large experience," the prolegislation temperance forces triumphed in 1846 with a ban on licensing retailers who sold liquor in amounts less than twenty-eight gallons. According to Dow the sole object of the law was "effectually to close up the drinking houses and tippling shops." In fact this piece of class legislation—identical in purpose to the earlier Massachusetts law—represented a compromise of the state's capital interests made possible by the growing strength of Maine's manufacturing community. The large-scale production of alcoholic spirits was not affected by the 1846 legislation, but dram shops, which had sprung up in response to employers boycotting drinking on the job, were prohibited.[69]

The 1846 Maine Twenty-eight Gallon Law remained at the heart of the legislation which became famous as the Maine Law after 1850. In the intervening years, Dow's experience as mayor of Portland had convinced him that the 1846 Maine Law lacked adequate means of enforcement since such lay outside the hands of local authorities. Dow's Maine Law placed both the licensing authority and enforcement power under local control. The law's major innovation—the one for which it received its acclaim as prohibitory—required manufacturers as well as sellers to obtain a license.[70] Thus, the Maine Law neatly evaded the thorny problem of confiscatory legislation that was implicit in the prolegislative temperance party's position. Although neither Dow nor his hagiographers record it, there is every probability that the state's larger distillers warmly greeted Maine Law prohibition. It certainly posed no threat to them. In fact Dow's measure passed the legislature with unseemly speed; in effect a majority of the various representatives of Maine's property interests had determined that legislation designed to prohibit ordinary and working-class drinking was a viable solution to the liquor problem, and that local property interests were in the best position to enforce the new morality.[71]

Maine's temperance reform, as led by Dow, illustrates the emergence of manufacturing enterprise playing an important role in temperance reform. It was Dow who encouraged the Maine mechanics' associations to spearhead legislative reform because "through them most of the laboring men of the town found employment," and it was these, "our mechanics, our yeomanry, and all the laboring classes of the community [who] are the principal sufferers."[72] What stimulated Dow was his close observation of conditions in areas where he sought to develop his capital. In Maine he recognized that "her territory was rich in material resources," but one where "the nature of the employment of a large portion of the male population . . . exposed them peculiarly to temptation to excess in the use of stimulants."[73]

Equally significant for the long-range development of temperance reform was Dow's attempt through the Maine Law to suppress the proliferation of tippling houses or grog shops, which sprang up in response to the concentration of manufacturing in urban areas and the concomitant separation of workers from the tools of production. The full title of Dow's legislation was "An Act for the Suppression of Drinking Houses and Tippling Shops." The proper use of political authority to repress these institutions would consume the time and energies of a generation of reformers, and divide the movement over questions of tactics and strategy before a political solution was contrived in the last years of the nineteenth century. Ultimately this approach, too, would fail as drinking institutions matured apace with the industrial capitalism that gave rise to them.[74] Nevertheless, it was Dow and his manufacturing allies who called attention to the problem by recognizing the concrete limitations of self-restraint and employer boycotts.

Following Dow's victory and subsequent endorsement by the ATU, five eastern states adopted similar legislation.[75] In addition statewide measures like the Maine Law seemed to answer the needs of western businessmen as well. Iowa provides a striking case in point.

From the beginning of its territorial existence, Iowa's politics was marked by conflict between its semiliterate small farmers—largely émigrés from the South—and migrants from innumerable New England and Mid-Atlantic towns and hamlets. The farmers opposed temperance out of habit and because alcoholic spirits constituted a significant item of production. On the other hand, at a time when "money was scarce and dear" local businessmen found themselves compelled to keep a stock of whiskey on hand to attract customers and laborers.[76] In 1847, Hiram Price, a native of New Hampshire, took the lead in organizing a division of the Sons of Temperance. A "radical and determined opponent of the use and sale of intoxicating liquors," Price led a successful drive for local option legislation in the state's cities and towns in the same year.[77] There matters rested until a New England syndicate of railroad investors headed by Henry Farnam and Joseph E. Sheffield approached Price in August 1853 to ask him to raise local capital for an extension of the Chicago and Rock Island railroad to open up the state's coal deposits.[78]

Railroad construction—like canal building—required large gangs of unskilled laborers drawn from immigrants and laborers in surrounding agricultural districts. Labor troubles were endemic to this work, and frequently began or ended in violence, and often were said to be associated with drinking. According to one authority, "One of the most annoying difficulties" faced by early railroad companies "was that of obtaining sober, law abiding labor."[79] During the construction of the Baltimore–Washington branch of the B. & O. Railroad, for example, the superintendent of construction claimed to have discovered "riot and disorder as a result of drunkenness" to be so endemic that after 1829 all maintenance contracts (futilely) banned the use of liquor "on the work."[80]

Farnam and Sheffield had been promoting railroad development since 1845 with mixed results until the success of the Chicago and Rock Island Railroad in the early 1850s. Farnam, who drew no distinction between the ethics of the countinghouse and those of the home, was alert to the need for sober employees and was not reluctant to dismiss them if his own efforts to reform them failed.[81] But the problems of extending successfully across the Mississippi to Council Bluffs through territory inhabited largely by "an idle, shiftless class" were beyond suasionist reform and local prohibition. Shortly after Price and a combination of local entrepreneurs set out to subscribe capital for the road by promising farmers it would raise their land values by up to 100 percent, the Davenport speculator–social reformer sat down in his office with two colleagues to draft Iowa's first statewide prohibitory legislation. Utilizing the Sons of Temperance and a State Alliance, Price began to agitate for his prohibitory measure, which was modeled after the Maine Law.[82]

At the height of Price's antidrink campaign the Farnam group successfully completed its capital subscriptions. The amity of temperance and railroad development was symbolized and propagandized during a six-day extravaganza organized by Farnam, who led a contingent of one thousand supporters up the Mississippi in an atmosphere in which "alcohol was not suffered to poison the union that was effected between the waters of the Mississippi River and Lake Michigan."[83] Six months later, in December 1854, Price's Alliance confronted Iowa's Democratic legislature with his prohibition legislation. Backed by Governor James W. Grimes, himself a railroad promoter and temperance man, Price's supporters saw conventional party distinctions dissolve as the state's legislators mandated prohibition effective July 4, 1855.[84]

In Iowa, prohibitory legislation was the political objective of those most closely associated with capitalist development of the state's natural resources. Temperance—that is, a liquor-free social environment, was the desideratum of those men who confronted the assumed incompatibility of profitable development, and a laboring class drawn almost exclusively from preindustrial farmers and agricultural workers. Temperance ideology, which imposed upon capital the moral obligation to increase the productivity of labor by establishing a liquor-free social order, crossed formal political boundaries with investment capital, as the case of Farnam and Price shows. State-enforced prohibition became the specific remedy for laboring conditions beyond the control of absentee owners wherever they appeared, and so foreshadowed the movement's culmination.

The Failure of Reform, 1850–1860

Capital's assumed obligation to create a liquor-free society had been weakened by the dispute that arose over the efficacy of using the state for this purpose. However, the suasionists were unable to convert their convictions into effective political action and thus could play only a negative part in defining the character of the state's role in reform. In large part, suasionists were precluded from political opposition to the prohibitionists because they shared the prohibitionists' ultimate convictions and objectives. Political opposition to temperance legislation on the other hand was tantamount to sanctioning the traffic, and it required the arousal of class animosities to be effective. After the debacle of the Massachusetts Fifteen Gallon law, suasionists ceased direct confrontation on the issue of prohibition; and the sweeping legislative triumphs of the "Maine Law men" attest to how weakly suasionists played the negative political role their convictions had assigned them. Henceforth the movement debated the questions of "what kind and how much" prohibition and not whether the state should be employed to accomplish that goal.

Yet the so-called first wave of prohibition dissipated in the partisan turmoil of the 1850s even as it became the "'breaking up plow of the Democracy.'"[85] The reason for this demise is partly attributable to partisan politics. But more important was the underlying class nature of the reform itself and the response of the movement's leadership to the much greater political crisis of the Union during those years. What differentiated the temperance reform from other aspects of what was to become Republicanism was its presupposition of a social structure that—regardless of individual effort or political arrangement—entailed the property relations of owner and worker, employer and employee mutually engaged in production for private profit. Indeed, temperance ideology is meaningless when divorced from this context. On the other hand the major issues that sundered the old political order in the 1850s—including slavery—and brought together the Republican coalition were issues that reflected intraclass factionalism. Maine Law men initially benefited from these divisions, and prohibition was regularly passed into law with support coming from all of property's factions. But the exigencies of obtaining popular support quickly made the Maine Law a rallying point for opposition to the emerging order, and even in Maine Neal Dow's law became the victim of new partisan coalitions.[86] Similarly, in Iowa, Hiram Price was unable to obtain support for prohibition at the state's first Republican convention, even though he headed the largest county delegation.[87]

The response of the ATU's leadership to this crisis was to reiterate the importance of the state as an instrument for reform and the efficacy of the Maine Law principle, which, it bears repeating, was the suppression of tippling houses and dram shops by local property interests. The ATU rejected the coalitionist tendencies of partisan politics by defining temperance as an objective that was above politics and hence nonpartisan. Nonpartisanship became capital's response to a political situation which it believed threatened a fundamental social reform, one which bore immediately and directly on the relationship between classes. As early as 1850 the ATU's national convention placed temperance beyond politics and in so doing ignored Reverend John Pierpont's objection that this reform had never been either a religious or a moral movement, but one that required the support of the electorate. The convention agreed instead with former Connecticut Governor William A. Buckingham that "voting absolutely for temperance men to promote objects that do not pertain to temperance had nothing to do with the questions before the convention." The convention called upon all temperance men to begin working to educate public opinion to the point where there would be a widespread nonpartisan demand for "the speedy and universal enactment of the strongest prohibitory statutes."[88] Implicit in the convention's position was the idea that the substratum of politics—the ideology that gave it meaning—was temperance ideology, and that all political convictions were to be informed by a moral conviction that a liquor-free environment was a social necessity and that the state was the proper instrument to establish it. Those men like Pierpont and Gerrit Smith who disagreed with the ATU majority's version of nonpartisanship shared this conviction, but doubted the capacity of politicians to use the state effectively unless temperance men themselves comprised the nucleus of popular parties.[89]

In 1853 the ATU's executive committee, which now included Anson G. Phelps and William Earl Dodge, published *An Appeal To The Public* which succinctly argued the basis of nonpartisanship and the efficacy of the Maine Law.[90] Temperance implemented by the Maine Law principle, the pamphlet argued, "has greatly added to the amount and availableness of human labor. Intemperate, indolent and vicious men have . . . become sober and ready and willing to go into the field and the work shop; and the money that was wasted . . . increases the demands for goods and provisions." The ATU pamphlet backed this contention by citing the testimony of a contractor who had worked on the Atlantic and Saint Lawrence Railroad connecting Portland with Montreal. Employing thousands of Irish and Americans along the way he reported that the unavailability of liquor meant that "his men on the average worked more days in the month, have been better able to perform their duty, and have had less 'sprees.'"[91]

Another basis for the nonpartisan appeal of temperance reform was its alleged sanguinary effect upon "lumber men and river drivers and raftsmen" who were described as "the most noisy and contentious class" in Bangor. No liquor meant more than "safe and quiet" streets: it meant an improvement in civic life necessary to the safe conduct of politics.[92] These themes formed the basis of the ATU's appeal, which was in fact a call for class unity in the midst of partisan strife. The ATU did not succeed in the 1850s in obtaining that unity, nor in decades following the Civil War when relations between property and the propertyless became more urgent, but nonpartisanship became the hallmark of the most class conscious of temperance's advocates.

The ironic denouement of the ATU's efforts to preserve unity in the midst of political crisis came in May 1853. In that month the union itself was sundered by a partisan dispute arising out of the "Woman Question." At a strategy meeting called to plan a temperance convention that would be concerned with enacting Maine-type prohibitory laws throughout the nation, the planning group became involved in an acrimonious dispute over Thomas Wentworth Higginson's attempt to have Susan B. Anthony named to the proposed convention's business committee. Arguing that "revolution was one thing and reformation another," Higginson's opponents forced a walkout of Anthony's supporters who included William Lloyd Garrison and Wendell Phillips.[93]

Both factions of the disintegrating ATU held their own "world's temperance convention" in New York the following September. On the crucial points of temperance reform, nonpartisanship, and the Maine Law principle, there was no disagreement.[94] The Higginson-Anthony faction chastised their colleagues that a moral reform like theirs knew "no distinction of creed, caste or sex"—as indeed it knew none of "section, party, or condition."[95] The conservatives contented themselves with recognizing the "absolute necessity" for cooperating with women.[96]

Ignoring the reality of its own division, the ATU's leaders chose

Neal Dow as the presiding officer of its World's Temperance Convention. In his keynote address to the delegates, Dow said that the sole problem confronting the reform was to determine the "best means" available to achieve prohibition. To this end the convention reaffirmed that prohibition "is above sect as it is above party" and that "the platform of this cause should be confined to as few and simple principles as possible." This meant that "the cause of Temperance is a question entirely separate and apart from the questions of '*Woman's Rights, Abolition, Land Reform*,' or any other, and that is must stand or fall upon its own merits." That is to say, however the holders of property regarded such questions, they nevertheless were to stand together on temperance—the one question that distinguished them from the propertyless.[97]

Thus, the response of the ATU to the political crisis of the 1850s was conservative. With the eventual outcome of that crisis uncertain and unpredictable, the union sought to maintain class unity in the face of partisanship and adopted a strategy it hoped would weather the storm of threatened disunion. But since it could neither keep temperance men out of partisan politics nor partisan politics out of its own house, the ATU became isolated from both its constituents and the emerging Republican party. Commanding neither a party nor a unified organization, the old leadership of the ATU, dominated by eastern commercial capitalists, was in a weak position to implement its nonpartisan reform in a society soon to be divided by Civil War and enduring factionalism.

The legacy of the early temperance movement was a mixed one. It had succeeded in arousing class-conscious responses to its cause in all parts of American society. It had forged an ambiguous union between expansionist capitalists and an emerging middle class committed to such expansion. Its boycott tactics were readily incorporated into the developing factory system where worker opposition could be outflanked, if not overcome with higher wages and a shortened workday. On the other hand, the temperance movement's political organizations were susceptible to factionalism, and its moralism and religiosity—originally intended to energize and coerce the upper classes—had aroused popular suspicions and animosity towards this radical reform. Moreover, while patterns of drinking had been altered and a sharp decline in per capita consumption of hard liquor became apparent, immigration continued to introduce large numbers of people who did not share the socioeconomic goals of the temperance reformers into a social order becoming characterized by a rigorously organized workday, but which nevertheless entailed large amounts of unorganized leisure time.[98] These latter developments would eventually undo the ATU's antiliquor strategy; but in the 1850s they were merely portentous.

Following the disruptions of the Civil War, a revived temperance movement once again confronted all these difficulties in much more acute forms. The dynamics of capitalist industrialization heightened the conflicts between capital and labor, and aggravated tensions within America's class of property holders. These tensions were manifest within the divided ranks of the temperance movement, and it was not until their resolution that a unified political assault on the liquor problem resumed. Between the Civil War and the turn of the century a generation of reformers expended itself upon internecine dispute and the development of a practical approach to reform.

3

"Practical Temperance": Reorganization of the Temperance Movement, 1865–1870

The result of a class-conscious analysis of property's needs in a society "where population is sparse and the demand for labor . . . great and incessant," the temperance movement fell victim to the centrifugal forces of Northern politics in the decade preceding secession. The conservative business leadership of the ATU had been unwilling to associate its reform with other issues, and its more radical allies had failed to gain acceptance of temperance by the emerging Republican party. In the two decades following the Civil War both factions of the movement continued their internecine struggle to provide a strategy and suitable tactics for establishing a liquor-free social order.[1]

Increasingly this struggle reflected differing perceptions of political economy that in turn mirrored differing expectations about the nature of the industrial society that appeared in these years. The political struggles of the postwar years raised a host of questions about the nature and purpose of that social order, and temperance reformers—no less than others—were compelled to address them, if only to devise a way to achieve their specific goal. It would not be until the presence of an urban proletariat was accepted as the defining problem of the antiliquor movement, however, that a unified approach to the liquor problem developed. And it would not be until this proletariat had become a truly national one that national prohibition by constitutional amendment became a serious political prospect. Throughout these years the cautious and pragmatic politics of the old ATU and its conservative, but expansionist, capitalist political economy repressed sundry middle-class efforts to move both temperance reform and American society into broader, more popular and democratic modes of social organization. In large measure the ATU's prevalence was due to the leadership supplied to its immediate postwar successor, the National Temperance Society (NTS), which carried on the conservative temperance tradition under the direction of William E. Dodge, financier and industrialist, whose Phelps-Dodge corporation became an early conglomerate industry.

William Earl Dodge and the Utilitarian Foundation of Temperance

William E. Dodge's concern for temperance reform was neither strictly benevolent nor peripherally related to his business affairs. It dated from his acquisition of 25,000 acres of Pennsylvania timberland and four sawmills in 1836 and continued until his death in 1883 at which time he oversaw from his Pearl Street offices an industrial empire that spanned both Western Hemisphere continents and a diversity of interests that included cotton, iron and copper, and timber. Following his 1836 acquisition, Dodge soon became active in the ATU. He supported the Sons of Temperance as a viable alternative to Washingtonianism even when the Sons themselves aroused conservative suspicions. Eventually Dodge became a director of the ATU, along with his principal business partner, Anson G. Phelps.[2] In all this work a fellow reformer remembered Dodge as "One of the busiest men, manipulating gigantic affairs [who] found the time for a thousand interests outside his counting room; and these instead of interfering with his commercial enterprises, worked into them, tempered them, and, in turn, caught from them something of the method and exactitude of the business habit."[3]

Dodge's temperance convictions deepened as his business interests expanded, and both activities eventually led him to the conviction that the business community had not played as active a political role as its importance warranted. In 1852, he criticized the merchants of New York for their failure to oversee the city's administration, charging that "the men who pay the bills" must assume responsibility in such matters.[4] Dodge believed that political authority should be used to establish social conditions conducive to business expansion. But, while he rejected slavery because he thought it destructive of slaves and masters alike, he rejected "Abolitionism" as well.[5] Only at the eleventh hour did he throw his support to Lincoln, reacting to "the stagnation which has now settled upon the business and commerce of New York." That done, Dodge next served at the abortive Peace Congress that sought to stave off civil war by holding the border states for the North. Dodge approached both sides at the Congress "as a businessman, a merchant of New York." He and his allies feared that a confederacy of free trading states would compel a similar response in the North, and "all our vast interests must be completely paralyzed." In attempting a compromise to avoid war and "a disasterous financial crisis," Dodge offered the South noninterference with slavery where it existed, strict enforcement of the Fugitive Slave Act, or reparations from the federal government.[6] Unable to avert the war, Dodge devoted his efforts to the chamber of commerce's Union Defense Committee and to the Christian Commission, a quasigovernmental effort to police the conduct of Union soldiers. Here Dodge personally oversaw the dissemination of temperance propaganda to the troops.[7]

In 1864, at the request of the New York business community, Dodge decided to take his views of political economy to Congress in the "hope to serve somewhat the commercial interests with which I have been so long identified." Dodge was committed to continued economic expansion. He viewed the Orient and a revived South as logical markets for the North's increasing production. He saw the federal government playing an important role in this national economic program by continuing to service the national debt, subsidizing railroads, establishing uniform bankruptcy laws, and, in the case of the South, stabilizing social conditions conducive to private economic growth.[8]

Upon assuming his seat in the Thirty-ninth Congress, Dodge displayed his single-minded devotion to business interests, and he demonstrated a spirit of cautious compromise (so characteristic of businessmen become politicians) to advance those interests. He warned his fellow legislators that the protracted debates over reconstruction had had an adverse effect upon "the men who control the money," and that their hesitation was having a negative effect upon those "carrying on the enterprise so necessary for the development of our country."[9] Dodge disagreed with radical proposals: his vision of a revived South assumed there were sufficient "loyal men" to trust with political power. As for the freedmen, social reform was what they needed:

> I feel that we are now in great peril, and ought not to look simply to the immediate enfranchisement of the negro race. . . . We need today measures which shall improve their condition, which shall render them most valuable as citizens. We want to place them in such a position that their labor will be sought after as a matter of interest.[10]

Dodge believed that the principal responsibility of the government with respect to the freedmen was to make them "more capable of intelligent labor," and he became a strong supporter of O. O. Howard's Freedmen's Bureau, which, under the General's direction, integrated temperance work into its programs. Thus Dodge incorporated the Freedmen into his general vision of labor for whom he advocated compulsory schooling in order to inculcate the social habits of "frugality, industry, [and] temperance."[11]

Dodge did not neglect temperance reform while he served in Congress. In February 1867, he revived the moribund Congressional Temperance Society with Hiram Price of Iowa, House Speaker Schuyler Colfax, and J. B. Grinnell, the Iowa clergyman turned railroad promoter. The group chose as president Henry Wilson, a shoe manufacturer from Massachusetts.

Dodge took advantage of the society's inaugural ceremonies to emphasize the utilitarian purpose of the reform. Temperance was not to be associated with sectarianism of any sort. Its purpose was to suppress the habitual use of intoxicating drinks. Dodge himself disclaimed that drinking itself led inevitably to drunkenness; rather the intemperate died prematurely "from disease superinduced by the use of intoxicating drinks." Dodge also disavowed that there was any biblical warrant to condemn drinking as sinful. Finally, he alluded to the recently returned Union armies—the backbone of the nation's work force—who would face the threat of "Drunkard's graves" if intemperance were not stayed.[12]

Dodge's deprecation of sectarianism, biblical authority, and extremist assertions was in keeping with temperance reform's secular origins and utilitarian purposes. Nevertheless, Dodge viewed the churches—all churches—as valuable adjuncts to reform. His theological and doctrinal indifference enabled him to offer financial support to church temperance work on a nondenominational basis. As one of his admiring biographers put it: "He made religion of business and business of religion."[13]

Dodge was equally pragmatic in his approach to political temperance reform. Because he regarded this issue as a class issue requiring widespread, nonpartisan conviction of its moral necessity, Dodge did not look to the forum of national politics for its resolution. Moreover he continued to focus his attention on the working-class drinking shops as the principal target for reform efforts. "I am for prohibition of the dram shop," he declared to an associate, "but I am willing to work with anybody who is honestly trying to curtail their number." To this he added, "If I cannot get all I want, I will get all I can."[14]

Yet another instance of Dodge's practical approach to liquor reform can be discovered in his attitude toward the federal government's excise tax. Since 1862, this tax on a wide variety of commodities had been used principally to pay the federal government's bonded indebtedness—an obligation paramount in Dodge's scheme of political economy. He urged Congress drop the tax altogether on cotton because "we must not forget that cotton is the basis upon which our chief importations are to be made in the future, and on any provision we make for the payment of the public debt we look to the duties on imports [and] we cannot have large importations unless we have some large article to export." Contrarily Dodge, who resigned from the Union League Club of New York because it served liquor, voted to retain the excise tax on distilled and malt beverages as a supplement to import duties, a move that contradicted the abstract temperance principle that the state ought not in any way encourage or sanction the legitimacy of the liquor traffic.[15]

Clearly, temperance reform was for Dodge and men like him an integral part of their world view of a private capitalist social order bounded by established social relations of capital and labor. Dodge, himself, exemplified in his life the highest motives and ideals to be found in the corporate business community of his day. Ultimately concerned with a vision of society, Dodge described its principal goal shortly before his death in 1883. He called upon those "who believe in the support of our own manufactories and in sustaining the laboring interests of this country" to disabuse workers of the idea that capitalism was an exploitative social system. "The truth is," he maintained, "that in this country capital is the best friend of labor."[16] Some years earlier he had told a House select committee investigating the depression of 1877 that "much of labor's suffering was due to the sale of intoxicating liquors," and that his workers had avoided the worst of the depression's evils because of the rigorous antiliquor policies employed by Phelps-Dodge.[17]

For Dodge a temperance regime—a no-liquor social environment—produced harmonious class relations, and established "a working man's paradise . . . in which the moral order is even more conspicuous than the material prosperity." He cited St. Johnsbury in Vermont, where he had several investments, as a town where "the tone and the sense of respect of the working people is much greater than of hands generally." There, according to Dodge, even though wages were not so high as elsewhere, nevertheless, working people were better off materially because there were no drinking houses.[18]

Yet however much temperance reform was integral in Dodge's scheme of things, it was not his sole concern. It had to be developed as a part of a general program. In short, the temperance spirit epitomized by Dodge was not fanatical or zealous. It was a rational and mundane part of the work-a-day world that was building an industrial capitalist social order. Dodge's peers recognized his leadership qualities and sympathized with his social goals. Upon his death in 1883, the New York State chamber of commerce, to which he had been elected president for nine consecutive terms, expressed its appreciation for his public spirit and philanthropy.[19] Businessmen from around the country paid similar tributes, remarking on how successfully he had integrated "the privileges and duties of a well rounded business and Christian life."[20]

The National Temperance Society: The Continuing Tradition

The old American Temperance Union had been established by reformers who believed that the moral regeneration of men of property was the key to their cause's success. As their movement grew they enlisted the churches whose sanctions they hoped would assist the general progress of regeneration of the propertied, and carry the message of reform to all elements of society. Finally, they sought to use the state to withdraw its sanction of the liquor traffic, and, at the same time, to institute progressive restrictions (prohibition) on the manufacture and sale of intoxicating liquor. Throughout the antebellum years, the ATU's tactics sought to realize the reformers' conviction that a liquor-free environment would increase productivity and stabilize class social relations.

Those who met with William E. Dodge in August 1865 to revive the temperance movement were deeply imbued with the spirit of the ATU. Among those attending were Edward C. Delavan, the wealthy Albany businessman, who helped spearhead the ATU, John Pierpont, grandfather of

J. P. Morgan, Charles Coffin Jewett, whose family founded General Electric, and William A. Buckingham, prominent Connecticut businessman and member of Congress. By styling this meeting as the fifth national convention, the old reformers emphasized their ties with the past.[21]

Two problems confronted the old ATU leaders: the need to achieve internal unity, and to integrate temperance reform into national politics in a way that would not disrupt other social and economic goals of a victorious and expansionist capitalist society.[22] Neither of these difficulties hinged upon the strategic objectives of the reformers, but they were tactically interrelated. Internal unity depended upon a satisfactory solution to the question of temperance's relation to other goals of political economy. The approach to this question, in turn, depended upon the degree to which the reformers clung to the movement's initial insights. Reuben Hyde Walworth, for example, pointed out that the first national temperance convention established the principle that reform should be undertaken by societies that had no other purpose, and he urged his colleagues to continue that tradition, citing the self-defeating characteristics of partisanship and sectarianism that had in his view divided the movement.[23]

Walworth expressed the conservative mood of the convention. Others were more extreme. Henry Dutton, former governor of Connecticut and a vigorous Maine Law man, condemned "zealous men [who] identified Temperance with politics, and [who] therefore gave a handle to the enemies of the cause who stated that it was a mere political movement." Accepting the notion that there was "a class of men who cannot be reached by moral suasion," Dutton urged "men of money" to make a strong show of supporting prohibitory legislation by contributing funds with which to enforce the laws with private means.[24] Theodore Cuyler urged the delegates to return to "the old truths of Beecher, Delavan, Barnes, Sargent, and Jewett," and cease quibbling over marginal issues like communion wine.[25] Representative James Briggs simply asserted "We must go back to the old ways."[26] In the face of this sentiment talk of a temperance party was muted and radical activists like Gerrit Smith of New York found little or no support.[27]

Conservative opposition to more activist politics had both ideological and practical roots. On the one hand the prior conviction that men of property had the primary moral responsibility for society's condition mitigated the impulse to seek popular electoral support. One delegate, noting the gradual increase in moderate drinking, claimed that prohibitory laws were being ignored because of the erosion of the moral commitment to total abstinence. Prohibitory legislation, he concluded, "can only be sustained by a strong moral sense in the community in favor of practical Temperance."[28]

The implication of this position was that a revived temperance organization should devote its efforts to renewing the moral spirit believed necessary to enforce the law, rather than to agitate for popular support of prohibition. The conservatives' practical objections to activist politics were presented by General J. S. Smith of New York who pointed out that "the friends of freedom and Temperance" had, in 1858, a higher obligation "than to throw away their votes on a Temperance ticket . . . and [thereby] insure the election of a pro-slavery candidate for Governor." For Smith the issue boiled down to the fact that temperance men were not "*one idea* men," and that "We can not sustain equal rights and a republican form of government with a pledged suffrage to vote only for candidates pledged to total abstinence."[29]

The conservatives' ideological convictions and practical orientation posed dilemmas for the future. The conviction that the moral strength of society resided in men of property sooner or later required that the state be used against those who could not be persuaded to stop drinking. The realization that temperance reform was but one aspect of capitalist political economy held out the hope that "Temperance men need not make a political party, but they could hold the balance of power."[30] The achievement of the former objective required, minimally, the attainment of the latter hope. To attain that hope at least one of two conditions would have to be met. Either the power structures of the orthodox parties would have to reach a procapitalist consensus on other matters of political economy, or they would have to experience a sense of class-imperative so great as to allow them to lay aside, if only temporarily, intraclass differences. In the burgeoning capitalist society of post-Civil War America, rife with conflicting property interests and committed to universal manhood suffrage, neither condition was likely to be fulfilled, although the second was a greater possibility than the first.[31] Nevertheless, the cautious policy of expediency urged by William E. Dodge appeared more realistic than the alternative of seeking a popular political decision for a major piece of class legislation.[32] It was the course to be followed by the National Temperance Society.

In addition to resolving superficially the question of the temperance movement's political role, the convention appointed a committee headed by Dodge to draft an organizational plan for the new national organization.[33] A committee under James Black of Pennsylvania reported on the need of the new organization to establish a publishing house and depository.[34] In doing so the committee sided with clergymen reformers like

John Marsh and Theodore Cuyler, who proclaimed "I don't want a thousand dollars from Delavan now and another thousand again from W.E. Dodge. . . . We want to build Temperance as Rome builds cathedrals, by a great number of small sums flowing in through rivulets."[35] It authorized a $100,000 fundraising drive to launch the publishing house, and prudently called for operations to begin as soon as $10,000 had been raised.[36] So ended the fifth national convention of the temperance forces with the conservative political faction of the old ATU firmly in control of the new organization. Committed to a pragmatic pressure politics and to the moral regeneration of property, the National Temperance Society, under William E. Dodge, turned its attention to establishing its corporate structure. In the fall of 1866 the society and publication house were merged into a single corporate entity at Dodge's Pearl Street offices. Dodge became president and chairman of the finance committee.[37] The initial subscribers to the society's permanent endowment were Dodge and his son, Anson G.P. Dodge, Edward C. Delavan, financeer Jay Cooke, and businessmen William B. Spooner, J. R. Sypher, and J. W. Lester. Their combined gifts totaled $30,000. The rivulets alluded to by Theodore Cuyler at the Saratoga meeting amounted to $1400—a long way from Rome's cathedrals.[38]

At its July 1868 meeting the NTS directors set forth their policy. The society's "primary and main work consists in creating and preparing a sound, pure and able temperance literature and in securing its circulation as extensively as possible." This literature would not be distributed gratis, but made available "at about the cost of manufacture, thus educating the people to purchase and read a temperance literature." The society would not spend its efforts and money soliciting donations from the churches; such work was properly left to local and state organizations. Instead the NTS would concentrate on obtaining the best possible writers to author its temperance tracts. In the political field, the society would petition Congress to prohibit the sale of drinks in the District of Columbia.[39]

The Prohibition Party: An Alternative to Tradition

The dissidents attending the fifth national temperance convention left Saratoga Springs outvoted, but not persuaded that all the reform needed was the moral rearmament of property holders and nonpartisan pressure on elected officials to enforce antiliquor legislation. Underlying their discontent was a mixture of experience and theoretical insight into the nature of party politics. There had, of course, been the searing political experiences of 1856–65 when temperance men found themselves in the vanguard of those forces breaking up the old Democratic and Whig alliances only to find their cause eventually excluded from the Republican party's program. Currently they witnessed the Democratic party's commitment to license laws and Republicans weakening at every chance what prohibitory legislation remained on the books.[40] Spurred on by these developments a rump session of prohibition activists at the national convention of the Independent Order of Good Templars called for a national convention to establish an independent temperance party.[41]

The rationale for an independent political party was set forth at the sixth national temperance convention sponsored by the NTS. Detroit clergyman-journalist John Russell offered the pragmatic view that the community of interest that underlay temperance was "scattered through both existing parties . . . unable to act in concert . . . estranged . . . by an intense party spirit, and . . . absorbed with minor political questions." As a consequence the temperance press was unsupported and ignored just as the regular press ignored the temperance movement. In addition temperance men found themselves "compelled to vote for license men . . . and accept and support the unparalleled absurdity of a license law, with a view to restricting the iniquitous traffic which it authorizes." A third party would rally the diffuse property interests of the country, and place prohibition in the mainstream of national politics.[42] Russell's argument appealed to those like Neal Dow who had always viewed temperance as part of a general social reconstruction largely achieved by the Civil War. Dow endorsed the new party because "the distinctive political issues that have for years past interested the American people are now comparatively unimportant, or fully settled."[43]

When the estimated two hundred delegates, drawn largely from the country's manufacturing states, met in Chicago they assented readily to the proposition that "the liquor traffic in intoxicating drinks greatly impairs the personal security and personal liberty of a large mass of citizens and renders private property insecure."[44] The convention characterized the liquor traffic as "a political wrong of unequalled enormity," and after an acrimonious debate agreed that neither of the major parties was willing or able to protect liberty and property by suppressing the traffic in alcoholic drinks. Hence, the delegates resolved that "we are driven by an imperative sense of duty to sever our connection with these parties and organize ourselves into a National Prohibition Party."[45] In proposing a single political party to defend property in this manner, the reform's spokesman denied that they sought to involve the government in a "moral reform [or] religious enterprise." Whatever personal decisions an individual might make with regard to drinking, the "anti-dramshop" party called upon the government merely to "be faithful in the discharge of its great duty to protect person and property" from the practical consequences of the grogshop.[46]

In all save one crucial respect this analysis of the liquor traffic's deleterious effects was identical to that of the movement's original, capitalist leadership. Both condemned the traffic because of its alleged social and political effects rather than on the grounds of an a priori moral or religious dogma.[47] Both saw political partisanship as the major obstacle to the passage of prohibitory legislation and its subsequent enforcement. Both saw the suppression of the liquor traffic as part of a general scheme of social reconstruction. And both focused on the working-class saloon as the major source of the drink evil. But conservative capital did not want this defense of property undertaken by a political party. Politics in the eyes of men like Dodge and the community of interest he represented was the basis for resolving differences arising out of the management of propertied interests; it was not an arena for arraying property against the unpropertied, particularly since the latter, as the principal "victims" of the liquor traffic, were viewed as a distinct threat to the security of property itself.[48] Implicit in the antidramshop position was yet another potentially divisive presupposition: a popular political party defending the interests of property necessarily presupposed a widespread distribution of property. Eventually, the drift of American economic development would bring this presupposition into the foreground of the antidramshoppers' concerns. But for the moment the appearance of a third party was the product of dissatisfaction with the strategy and tactics of the temperance movement's leadership and not of middle-class discontent with the direction of American society.

As might be expected, what little public reaction there was to the new party was at once dubious and hostile. A *New York Times* editorial written after the 1869 fall elections was highly critical of pressure tactics designed to break up the two major parties which are "formed for different purposes."[49] E. L. Godkin's reform-conscious publication, *The Nation*, had noted with approval the general revival of the political temperance movement after the reorganization of the National Temperance Society by Dodge and others. In resuming "the war against alcohol," *The Nation* observed that temperance arguments now followed a "perfectly utilitarian" line of reasoning, and were therefore "legitimate." But in as much as such reasoning sanctioned "political action," Godkin's magazine warned that "the gap between legislation and enforcement is real," and that the new party ran a grave risk of "bringing politics and law into greater and greater contempt."[50]

Following 1869's November elections, *The Nation* and the *New York Times* criticized the Anti-dramshop party's campaigns in Massachusetts, Maine, and Minnesota, although the reformers' impact was negligible. Yet, for all they opposed the new party, neither publication could find a way out of the temperance reform's continuing dilemma. *The Nation* assumed legislative remedies were necessary, and reduced its readers' choices to high license or prohibition, while, at the same time, admonishing that it doubted that the "mass of voters drew many refined distinctions on the subject."[51] Seeking a way out of this difficulty, Godkin's magazine proposed that "in some way a board composed of men of ability and character, who will give the subject their undivided attention," be established to deliver both the voters and politicians from the tentacles of the liquor traffic."[52]

Thus, by the close of the 1860s the antebellum temperance movement had been revived and reorganized. The tradition of the older movement, first established by expansionist mercantile capital and elaborated into Maine Law prohibition with the aid of emerging manufacturing capitalists, was secure within the National Temperance Society guided by William Earl Dodge, and supported by gifts from Cornelius Vanderbilt, John D. Rockefeller, Sr., John Wannamaker, Andrew Carnegie, and James H. Kellogg.[53] On the other hand, the new temperance party provided a vehicle for those like Samuel F. Carey who, as early as 1851, had voiced his suspicions of such leadership. In that year Carey eulogized Billy Clarke as the true founder of the temperance movement, and recalled that once, following a temperance address, a man remarked that Clarke seemed "a man of talents, but he is engaged in a small business." Concluded Carey: "There are men who thus speak of us all over the country [and] this aristocracy of wealth and fashion, I abominate."[54] Over the ensuing fifteen years this intraclass animosity would develop into a problem as serious as the liquor problem itself. To defuse it would be the task of another generation of antiliquor reformers.

Part II

The Middle Years: The Tradition Fails, 1865–1890

4

Ends and Means: Temperance Confronts an Industrial World, 1870–1884

The social order that emerged after the Civil War was neither expected nor desired by a considerable portion of the American middle class, including Prohibitionists. The "petty bourgeois" animosity toward established wealth expressed by the Sons of Temperance national Grand Worthy Patriarch, Samuel F. Carey, lay at the root of the divergent temperance movement. At first muted by expediency, it became more overt as America became characterized by business paralysis, industrial depression, and violence towards labor in the years 1870–1884.

If resentment towards the conservatism of established wealth nourished the Prohibitionist impulse, a rationalist critique of two-party politics provided the intellectual means to challenge the conventional wisdom both of temperance reform and traditional politics. Following the Chicago convention, Gerrit Smith, the millionaire abolitionist, published his "Address to the People of the United States," which set forth the new party's philosophy. Described as "the first official document of the new party" by a party historian, Smith's address attacked the ideas that government was a neutral authority and Prohibition an issue of individual morality. Government, he insisted, was the consequence of partisan strife in which political parties historically substituted their own welfare for that of society. Parties could not be expected to change radically until they were broken up. According to Smith: "No other but temporary parties are justifiable." Only thus could a democratic society assure itself that the government met its obligation to secure individual liberty and private property. As the Prohibitionists saw it "both of our existing parties are in such bondage to the interests and policies which cluster around and uphold the dramshop [that] neither of them will ever consent to demand its suppression."[1]

Smith also transformed intemperance from a moral defect of individuals or their social character into "a political wrong of unequalled enormity." The party did not quarrel with those who believed that government should not aid the temperance movement. On the other hand, Smith argued, neither should government do anything to hinder that reform. By licensing the grogshop and liquor traffic, he charged, the government not only hindered temperance, but involved itself in the failure to protect life and property. The Prohibition party's "war," he claimed, was not against personal drinking, but the grogshop and "rumselling."[2]

Smith did not specify the particular "interests and policies" that supported the grogshop. To have done so would have involved a critique of the very institution for whose protection he claimed the government existed, that is, private property. Such a critique, in turn, would have exposed private property as a political phenomenon advocated by parties for particular interests. But Smith's exposure of government as a mask for political interest provided a basis for breaking with the status quo and establishing alliances with other disaffected elements in American society. Such would require a broad review of the economic bases of those who supported grogshop politics. The direction in which the party would move and the reaction of conservative temperance forces soon became clear, and were based upon a conflict over the development of America's industrial order.

In 1870, the Prohibition party in Massachusetts united with the Labor–Reform party of that state to support Wendell Phillips' campaign for the governorship. This movement was an antimonopolistic combination of small manufacturers and skilled workers committed to Phillips' belief that: “We all know that there is not war between Labor and capital; that they are partners, not enemies, and that their true interests on any just basis are identical.”[3] What Phillips' prohibitionist-labor reform combination sought was to “crumble up wealth by making it unprofitable to be rich.”[4] That is, the new party sought to use politics to redistribute capital and establish social conditions thought to be conducive to investment and permit broader access to capitalist enterprise. In doing so it argued that politics was the basis for Massachusetts' current economic misfortune.

Phillips' party charged that a corrupt political alliance controlled the state for the benefit of outside capital. The “dramshop policy” of the established political order was a crucial factor in diminishing production, increasing the state's expenditures, and subjecting “wages to the will of the employer.”[5] The notion that under the existing party rule the state's government was limiting the productive capacity of the area's manufacturers, was central in the Massachusetts campaign.[6] Although the Phillips candidacy was not successful, the conservative prohibitionists' reaction was sharply critical of the effort to make a political issue of what they termed a moral and nonpartisan consideration.[7]

By the time of the 1872 national elections, the third party's orientation displayed a decided shift away from the expedient policy of remaining silent on other political issues. The party's standard bearers, James Black and John Russell, campaigned for legislation to reduce railroad and shipping rates and the end of “all monopoly and class legislation.” In addition the party's platform called for state-supported education and a liberal immigration policy that would treat newcomers on an equal basis with native-born Americans. The party endorsed universal suffrage as a right which “inheres in the nature of man.” Black and Russell campaigned for national prohibition on the grounds that it would “emancipate labor and practically thus promote labor reform.”[8] Said candidate Black: “And what branch of business or industry will reap a greater reward [from prohibition] than will the laboring class. . . . is there any measure of a practical character that could more certainly throw open wider the door to success and ensure to every man who labors a just recompense for his labor?”[9] For the Prohibitionists in 1872, the moral capital that prohibition would impose could yet be translated into material capital.

The Prohibition party's threat in the 1872 elections was, of course, negligible. Black received scarcely 5,000 votes. But the new party had unsettled state politics in many areas, and provoked a conservative reaction that sought to maintain the stability of the party system by removing “temperance” from democratic politics. In May 1871, E. L. Godkin, who was seeking an impartial board to decide between high license and prohibition, criticized the third party for failing to recognize that the root of the liquor problem was to be found in "the habits and character of the political class, which are too low to make effective dealing with so corrupting a question possible." The political class Godkin had in mind was the mass of voters and party regulars. Temperance reform, he argued, must be preceded by political reform and reform of the civil service. Until that happy day temperance reformers ought to support those "other moral and social agencies" which, Godkin claimed, have "so far been responsible for such progress as had been made."[10]

William E. Dodge's National Temperance Society also moved to thwart the third-party impulse. In spring 1873, the society's board named Vice President Henry Wilson, a Massachusetts shoe manufacturer, second in command to Dodge. In an additional effort to bolster its claim to reform leadership and political orthodoxy, it added Freedmen's Bureau head, O. O. Howard, and clergyman Henry Ward Beecher to positions on the board.[11] Later, in August, the board sponsored a resolution calling for the creation of an independent government commission to investigate the liquor traffic. With this measure the society's board hoped to place effective control of political temperance reform beyond the arena of popular politics, and, at the same time, establish the compelling necessity for national action on the problem of drink reform.[12]

Backed by a nationwide petition campaign organized by the society, Timothy O. Howe introduced the commission legislation in December 1872. Senate finance committee chairman, John Sherman, brought a substitute bill to the floor in February 1873.[13] The Senate bill proposed a five-man presidential board to "investigate the alcoholic liquor traffic in its economic, criminal, moral and scientific aspects, in its connection with pauperism, crime, social vice, the public health, and general welfare of the people; and also inquire and take testimony as to the practical results of license and restrictive legislation for the prevention of intemperance in the several states." The commissioners could not be holders of a political office and would receive no salary or other compensation for their work.[14]

The strategy behind the bill was deceptively simple. The exclusion of office holders and salaries limited the pool of investigative talent to the wealthy interest group that had sponsored the bill and petition campaign. In the course of debate, Roscoe Conkling, a thorn in the side of New York's mercantile community, conceded Congress's power to establish the commission, but insisted that its work could be accomplished by a Senate committee. But John Sherman reminded his colleagues that the bill's supporters wanted an independent commission and not another Senate committee. Carl Schurz observed that the bill's supporters favored prohibitory legislation in the states and were attempting to commit Congress in the same direction. Skeptical that the proposed commission would obtain more reliable information, Schurz concluded that its real purpose was to cloak its findings in the robe of governmental authority, and thereby achieve "a peculiarly impressive demonstration and special effect . . . by this unusual proceedings."[15]

Schurz's perspicacity did not sway the Senate. The commission's mandate was expanded to investigate fermented liquor and the manufacturing of alcoholic drinks. In March 1873 the amended bill was passed by a vote of twenty-six to twenty-one and sent to the House.[16] The House Judiciary Committee extended the term of the commission to two years, recommending it on the grounds of the "intrinsic gravity and importance of the temperance reform." An additional reason for recommending the bill was found in "the high character and great number of the petitioners."[17] The House committee went further than the Senate in hoping that the commission's governmental warrant would produce restrictive legislation, particularly in the territories: "the information thus obtained . . . clothed with the robe of more official authority . . . and less liable to challenge or contradiction than the individual efforts or statements of private philanthropists" would lead to more comprehensive restrictive legislation.[18] The committee pointed out that the concerns of these philanthropists were shared by "the most intelligent and respectable classes of our citizens" and that "the [intemperance] evil is national in extent and magnitude," and therefore required only a decision concerning "the best method of promoting temperance reform."[19] Despite this exhortation, the House killed the commission bill by refusing to suspend its rules to vote on it, and this effort of the National Temperance Society to rationalize and contain the reform movement ended in failure.[20]

The significance of this initial attempt by the National Temperance Society to control the political direction of temperance reform lies not so much in the ease with which the Forty–third Congress evaded it while endorsing and probably supporting its aims. Nor is it to be found in the degree to which such proposals could outflank the opposition, which could not oppose them without seeming to give support to the liquor traffic. Rather it is to be found in Carl Schurz's contention that what the reformers actually sought was the mantle of governmental authority to condone their activities. The commission proposed by Dodge and "private philanthropists" could not have been impartial on its face; it would have constituted a privately controlled mechanism that would have excluded popularly elected "political managers" and their constituencies from a determining political role in its activities. The success of such a venture, in turn, depended upon the cultivation of a popular attitude of reverence and respect for the state's authority as well as conventional political stability. On both counts the Prohibition party was inimical to the creation of such a climate, contending as it did that the state was merely the consequence of partisanship and so could not be morally superior to such strife.

The financial and economic crisis of the 1870s widened the division within the temperance movement. The Prohibitionists increasingly reflected a general middle-class concern over the social and economic directions of American society. In 1876 the party added the term "Reform" to its name, emphasizing this broader set of concerns.[21] In addition its platform revealed middle-class reliance upon a foreign labor supply—a dependence that made national prohibition appear all the more urgent. The party called for "a friendly and liberal policy to immigrants from all nations," one that would "guarant[ee] to them . . . ample protection and . . . equal rights and privileges." Other planks promised free public schooling, freedom of religion, and universal suffrage. The party indirectly supported a six-day work week by calling for "national observance of the Christian Sabbath, established by laws prohibiting ordinary labor and business." The platform also urged the abolition of "class legislation and special privilege in Government." Prohibitionists demanded the end of speculation in land, gold, and commodities, and called for legislation to regulate the developing national transportation system.[22] In short the new party by 1876 was promising temperance reform at the high price of a general political reform, which sought a more equitable distribution of the nation's capital resources. The prohibitionists' critique of the established order implied that the nation's economic crisis was at its heart a political crisis, just as it maintained that the liquor problem was a political problem.

In contrast to the perceptions of the Prohibition Reform party stood those of William E. Dodge and the supporters of the National Temperance Society. Just as the Prohibition party's stance reflected a larger sociopolitical milieu, so too did the conservatives'. They developed a nonpolitical explanation of both the liquor problem and the national economy, one that envisioned government support of big business and social reform aimed at increasing labor productivity.

In 1878, following the savage railroad strikes of the preceding year, *Bankers Magazine* called upon congressional investigators of depression and labor unrest to "lay on a broad basis of facts as a foundation of all enquiry as to the best remedies for the industrial troubles from which this nation is suffering in common with other nations." The journal questioned the supposition that the high wages paid to U. S. workers were offset by greater productivity. The magazine wanted data collected from other countries concerning hours and wages and the social habits of various working forces.[23] One House committee, under the direction of a Greenback–Labor Democrat, Hendrich B. Wright, drew the editors' fire for its penchant for gathering political opinions about the causes of the country's economic woes, but a second committee began to lay the foundations for the investigation the New York publication sought.[24]

The latter committee was chaired by New York manufacturer Abram S. Hewitt, a life-long personal friend of William E. Dodge, whose testimony the committee quickly sought.[25] In August 1878, Dodge and two National Temperance Society functionaries, J. N. Stearns and Aaron M. Powell, gave the Hewitt select committee their views on labor depression. Intemperance and not low wages lay at the heart of labor's difficulties, Dodge and his colleagues maintained. On the other hand business stagnation resulted from the uncertainty created by declining prices, which were, themselves, an indication of overproduction. Dodge proposed three remedies for the nation's predicament. Congress should appoint an independent commission to investigate the liquor traffic; the tariff structure should be modified, and the government should resume specie payments to restore business confidence.[26]

According to Dodge, American workers were highly paid, and had become accustomed to a high standard of living which they were unprepared to give up in the face of a downturn in the business cycle. This life style involved spending "large sums" for drink, a practice that stemmed from intemperance and its related vices, profligacy and dissipation.[27] Thus high wages and the social vice of intemperance mutually explained labor's troubles and overproduction: the national market had consumed to its limit because intemperance braked the economy by depriving other commodities of the wages that went for drink and added a surcharge on the cost of production that made competition with foreign enterprise disadvantageous.

In making his argument, Dodge cited the example of workers employed by some of his companies. Living under a company regime, Dodge's workers had survived cutbacks in operations and wage reductions. In turn, Dodge had been able to avoid shutdowns in his operations. Reduced to its essentials, Dodge's program echoed the first employers' boycotts of liquor. His companies acquired as much land surrounding their operations as required to isolate the population from grogshops. Thereafter Dodge introduced savings banks, churches and schools, and otherwise exercised "every moral influence that we could bring to bear on the good order of the community." The latter included encouraging the purchase of company-owned homes and the threat of dismissal for drinking.[28]

Given the ability of his capital to so control his employees' social environment, Dodge saw local prohibition as a viable political strategy, but neither he nor the National Temperance Society opposed national prohibition.[29] What Dodge and the NTS did oppose was the politicization of the temperance movement because its attack on the state and national politics appeared to threaten capital in other fundamental ways. Hewitt's committee heard testimony from many who shared Dodge's conviction that intemperance was the source of labor's difficulties, but who propounded the prohibitionist notion that "underconsumption" was the cause of the nation's economic troubles. Such people were particularly susceptible to prohibitionism, as the underconsumptionist analysis became associated with criticism of monopolistic enterprise and the continual failure of the government to halt or regulate such practices.[30]

Reduced to its essentials the division within the antiliquor movement involved middle-class concern over the economic and social costs of the liquor traffic on America's general economy, which sharply contrasted with conservative concern over the impact of drinking on the productive efficiency of the industrial laboring classes. The latter concern became more evident during the crisis years of the 1870s as America's divided property owners groped for an explanation of the nation's industrial disorders. By the end of the decade, however, the analysis of intemperance and overproduction that William E. Dodge offered to the Hewitt select committee became one approaching the level of an official explanation of reality.

In April 1878, Secretary of State William M. Evarts, a New York corporation lawyer and staunch opponent of the grogshop who had joined Charles C. Bonney's antisaloonist Law and Order League following the Chicago railroad strike, issued a circular letter to the department's consular offices.[31] Evarts asked his consular officers to gather hard data on hours and information about the social habits and attitudes of European workers. Evarts believed, as did Dodge, that American workers enjoyed higher wages and a higher standard of living than Europe's working classes. He concluded that "if the working people of the United States lived on the same quality of food . . . they could live as cheaply as the working people of any country in Europe."[32]

The Evarts report was both a plea for American workers to cooperate with American capital in the expansion and stabilization of the industrial order and a warning of dire economic consequences should they fail to do so. Evarts' report placed popular drinking among a trinity of shibboleths betraying capitalist apprehensions about the world they were making. Despite the evident hardships caused by the depression, Evarts maintained: "more misery is caused by strong drink . . . than by dull times, and . . . more misery is caused by strikes than by strong drink."[33] The remaining shibboleth was communism.[34] Yet the mere avoidance of these dangers by American workers would not be sufficient to remedy periodic crises of the business cycle.

In addition to inculcating the disciplines of abstemious temperance and frugality, American workers would be compelled by the exigencies of the times to acquiesce in business decisions, while endlessly increasing production, convenient theories of overproduction notwithstanding. Survival itself, the report warned, was at stake:

> The question which now preemptorily challenges all thinking minds is how to create a foreign demand for those manufactures which are left after supplying our home demands. We cannot stand still for the momentum of increase will soon become so great that it will push us out anyway; to push us safely and profitably is of so much importance as to almost overtop all other public questions of the hour. The question appeals equally to the selfishness and patriotism of all our citizens, but to the laborer it appeals with tenfold force, for without work he cannot live, and unless we can extend the markets for our manufacturers he cannot expect steady work, and unless our manufacturers can undersell foreign manufacturers, we cannot enlarge our foreign market.[35]

In urging American workers to go the last mile with American businessmen in search of foreign markets, the Evarts report insisted: "Under no consideration must we have strikes; under no consideration must our facilities lie idle. If our manufacturers cannot run their establishments profitably . . . and pay the prevailing wages, our working people must help them to make profit by consenting to a reduction in wages."[36]

Given such moral imperatives as outlined by Evarts, intemperance was disfunctional in at least two respects. First, there was its obvious connection with industrial inefficiency. Second, and perhaps more important, was its connection to social instability. As we have seen, Dodge and like-minded temperance advocates believed that American workers' own profligacy—manifested by drinking—dissipated their high wages, and thus left them with no reserves to set against downturns in the business cycle. In turn "necessary" reductions in wages triggered in such workers discontent, which in turn led to strikes for higher wages. As this line of argument went, abstemious temperance, as an instance of frugality, would prepare workers for recessions, thereby eliminating the need to strike. This view of temperance presupposed a permanent class of proletarian wage earners, a notion foreign to popular thought, prohibitionist and otherwise, and foreign also to the idea that temperance functioned to provide a capitalist stake, or means of egress, from the laboring classes. As if to emphasize this latter distinction, the Evarts report announced that "the days of sudden fortunes . . . are gone."[37]

Evarts urged American workers "native and naturalized, [to] read these reports in that national spirit with which I have endeavored to point out some of the principal features therein, and drive from their midst communism, strikes and drink." In return for this effort and for "chok[ing] down all demagogical attempts to divide the American people into hostile ranks as capitalists and laborers," Evarts stressed the reciprocal obligation of the employer to "look upon his workman as morally one of his family."[38] Should these mutual obligations be respected, the secretary was confident that the nation would prosper because "the advantage [belonged to] those who soonest accept[ed] the situation and show[ed] the most sensible continuity in the new paths of success."[39]

House Executive Document No. 5 of the Forty-sixth Congress did not explode over the political scene of Victorian America. Neither did it alter the currents within the temperance movement. Its importance lays in its revelation of the strength of the hold that the idea of temperance had upon America's fledgling industrial and manufacturing capitalists. While Evarts' report is suffused with an earnest rhetoric of moral exhortation, it is not a temperance tract. Much of its argument is implied; the requirement of temperance is merely taken for granted.

Similarly, while American politics had not reached the degree of rigidity that it would, the Evarts report, nevertheless, propounded a version of reality that was not widely accepted. The report ignored the suggestion that America's economic woes were caused by "underconsumption" in the domestic market, a condition believed to arise from monopolistic concentrations of capital. In doing so it avoided Prohibitionist contentions that the liquor traffic—not drinking per se—played a central role in the formation of such concentrations. It also avoided the connection between drinking and depressed working conditions that pro-temperance workers readily made in the late 1870s.[40]

Secretary Evarts' report marked the beginning of a long-term effort to construct a program in which "the fostering, the developing, and the directing of our commerce by the government should be laid down as a necessity of the first importance."[41] Its success required the repression of class consciousness, or, rather, its absorption into a vague nationalist doctrine of common republican citizenship. As Evarts expressed it: "We are not a nation of capitalists and laborers; we are a nation of republican citizens. Let us, then, ignore these dividing lines, and . . . work upward and onward in the scale of respectable citizenship, doing that which is best for all."[42]

One of the major obstacles to a cooperative industrial order was the failure of the national government to establish authoritatively what industrial conditions were. Carroll D. Wright, who would soon direct this effort for the federal government, told Senator Henry Blair's committee of his conviction that such impartial investigations would greatly reduce class tensions.[43] Like William E. Dodge, Evarts, and other corporatist temperance advocates, Wright believed that American workers would accept the legitimacy of practical capitalist hegemony provided capitalists demonstrated sufficient "moral character" in their conduct towards their employees to insure workers of their concern for their welfare. Such treatment, he testified, would reveal that workers "are usually loyal, and . . . are content and industrious under reductions when reductions are essential."[44]

In testifying for the creation of a national bureau of labor statistics, which impartially would inform both capitalists and workers concerning industrial conditions, Wright ignored underconsumptionist analyses of those conditions. At the same time he assumed that the liquor problem was one involving the moral character of the working class, and, as such, fell within the province of capitalist social reform. Here, Wright believed in the ultimate efficacy of the factory system: "The experience of the past twenty years clearly proves that in all factory centers where the manufacturers themselves have taken an interest in the [liquor] question, and have insisted upon employing men of sobriety, there has been a vast improvement." Improvident habits caused pauperism, and their most effective check was a "sentiment that shall say to a man that without sobriety there is not employment."[45]

By 1883, the year of William E. Dodge's death, the divided temperance movement reflected two distinct and conflicting analyses of the course and direction of American society. These analyses placed differing emphasis on the nature of America's liquor problem, and consequently upon remedies for it. From within the ranks of corporatist capital, temperance advocates viewed the problem of drinking as primarily one of the moral character of the working class that required both restraints and guidance on the part of employers. On the other hand, middle-class temperance advocates cited the role of the state in legitimizing the liquor traffic that "robs us of clothing, robs us of shelter, robs us of bread."[46] To such critics America's economic and liquor problems were mutually intertwined and required a national political solution beginning with prohibition. But the temperance movement's corporate protagonists rejected democratic political agitation for reform. Such partisan strife would undermine social efforts to bind employers and workers into common republican citizenship, and weaken the authority of the state to act as a neutral arbiter of reality in matters of national economic policy.

In the ten years between the time the National Temperance Society first moved to thwart the third-party movement and William E. Dodge's death, he and his followers continued to work for an accommodation of reform to two-party politics. The congress faced continued proposals and petitions for a commission of inquiry and constitutional prohibition. Third-party advocates could not oppose such tactics without seeming to support the liquor traffic and their coopted support weakened seriously their attempts to break away from the old temperance politics of nonpartisan pressure.

Yet if the movement's conservative capitalist wing had the tactical advantage over its middle-class opponents, its strategic objectives were a long way from realization. Certainly William E. Dodge recognized this. In his will he left twenty thousand dollars in trust to the NTS "for the gratuitous distribution" of society publications to the nation's workers, "particularly among railroad employees."[47] Although he genuinely believed that his approach to temperance reform was responsible for the "remarkable change . . . in the habits and customs of the people" in all parts of the country, he also recognized that the nation's urban metropolises had not undergone that change.[48]

In the decade following his death, Dodge's conservative temperance heirs would endeavor to develop a solution to the problem of the urban saloon in harmony with their assumptions and political priorities. Third-party activists also struggled to put their priorities into focus and develop a broadly based national reform effort. These efforts sharpened the divisions within the movement all the more, and led, ultimately, to the triumph of the view that the liquor problem was a problem of social class requiring nonpartisan attention from all sectors of American society.

5

The Beginning of Conservative Reaction: Liquor Control and the Critique of the Industrial City, 1880–1890

The rapidity and extent of commercial industrialization after the Civil War profoundly affected the development of American cities and the consciousness of its putative beneficiaries. Between 1860 and 1880 America's urban population grew from just over six million to more than fourteen million people.[1] The mass of this increase found itself toiling in factories and sweatshops, and living in dehumanized and disfunctional social conditions. At the same time, these city dwellers joined political parties, voted, and created what pro-business reformers termed "the problem of democracy."[2]

To cope with this extraordinary development urban critics associated with the eastern metropolitan corporate community undertook to reassess their social order's basic institutions in light of the dominant institutions of the maturing industrial order: the division of labor and the divorce of owners from laborers. Political parties, the churches, family, and state were all scrutinized to discover the impact of industrialization upon them, and their potential for furthering a system of capitalist social relations. As expressed by one such reformer, their critiques sought to "offer . . . a society composed of many grades, with easy transition from any one grade to the next higher or even the next lower."[3] At length the urban saloon—itself the product of the rationalization of production—became the focal point of their concern, and was seen to be at the core of a galaxy of problems impeding a successful transition to a mature capitalist social order. The analysis of this set of social problems provided the basis for a massive, class-conscious assault on this bastion of working-class life and leisure.[4]

The conviction that the urban masses were incapable of rational political activity lay at the heart of these reformer-critics' analysis. As such they interpreted the outcome of popular party politics as determined by a rootless mass whose votes could be purchased for the price of a drink.[5] This criticism of the urban masses was connected to what was taken to be the indifference of the business community whose "personal interests are directly involved" in successful municipal government, to explain the apparent random confusion of party politics.[6]

Two other factors were isolated as contributing to the difficulties of governing the cities. New York's Tilden Commission pointed out the interconnection of partisan strife and the intrusion of state and national political issues onto the local scene. The second factor the commission noted was the dependency of local governments on state legislatures for much of their legislation.[7] The Tilden Commission, led by William M. Evarts, Oswald Ottendorfen, and E. L. Godkin, condemned this situation on the grounds that "there is no more just reason why the control of the public works of a great city should be lodged in the hands of a democrat or a republican [sic], than there is why an adherent of one of another of the great parties should be made the superintendent of a business corporation." With respect to the dependency of municipalities on state legislatures, the commission acknowledged that what had once been considered a major reform had proved to be a failure.[8]

In brief, the Tilden Commission held that cities were analogous to business corporations, providing goods and services to consumers. As such they ought to be run like businesses by businessmen. Since by far businessmen had the greatest stake in the provision of these services, they should assume responsibility to provide responsible political leadership.

In the words of Godkin, cities ought to be run "by the kind of men one would make directors of a bank or trustees of an estate, or else by highly trained officials."[9]

In the years following the publication of the Tilden Commission's report, the views and concerns of these probusiness urban reformers expanded, but their basic suppositions remained unaltered. In January 1890 Godkin published an essay, "Criminal Politics," that revealed the interrelation of metropolitan capital's position and the problem of liquor control. According to Godkin, the most fundamental question confronting the modern world was "the government of great cities under universal suffrage." Modern cities, he claimed, attracted "nearly all the poor, the improvident, the disgraced, the criminals, all the adventurers of both sexes, [who] are consumed with the passion for city life."[10] Even workers were inordinately affected by the enticements and allurements of the city—"luxuries which seem to be within every man's grasp gratis."[11] "Without respectable natural leaders," the urban masses were manipulated by "political adventurers . . . with no standing in the business community." This leadership found its strength "in the control it exerts over the ignorant, criminal, and vicious classes through its liquor dealers."[12] Godkin argued that the business community was responsible for this situation, failing as it did to recognize the importance of political organization. Instead, businessmen had contented themselves with devising schemes of government they hoped would serve their purposes without requiring their constant supervision.[13]

The failure of this approach was manifest for Murray Hill's sounding board. Moreover, if universal suffrage were the real problem, it was a permanent one, and "complaining of it is like complaining of a stormy sea as a reason for giving up navigation."[14] It fell upon those of "superior intelligence" to guide the masses. Such could be found in either political party, and Godkin pointed to the successful campaign of Abram S. Hewitt against Henry George as an instance when business leadership and the superior intelligence of both parties had successfully combined to defeat mobocracy.[15]

If the success of the campaign against Henry George inspired Godkin and his followers to hope for eventual success against the urban masses, then surely the performance of the Prohibition Party in the 1880s caused them to despair. If the power of the saloon element were to be curbed so as to permit urban industry to flourish, the force of the third party's appeal had also to be broken. For it was to prohibitionism and other antimonopoly parties that increasing numbers of disaffected middle-class voters were turning. As Robert D. Marcus has noted, in the fragile ecology of nineteenth-century politics, a handful of votes made all the difference.[16]

Fortunately for the urban reformers the party was about to reach its high water mark of supporters. This fact would eventually compel the party's division into "broad gauge" supporters of an antimonopoly platform and "narrow gauge" proponents of constitutional prohibition. It was the focus of corporatist urban reformers upon the saloon as a social and political institution that laid the basis for reclaiming prohibitionist narrow gaugers for nonpartisan, antisaloon reform.

In 1881 the national leadership of the Prohibition party undertook a reorganization in light of its steadily increasing statewide voting support. Completed in August 1882, the party's national committee included two prominent defectors from the nonpartisan ranks of the National Temperance Society, Samuel D. Hastings of the Good Templars and Frances E. Willard, national head of the WCTU With a strengthened national organization, the party dramatically increased its voting strength in the 1882 elections. In New York, for example, the party's gubernatorial candidate received more than 25,000 votes due to an aggressive campaign and "the dissatisfaction of temperance Republicans with the attitude of their party."[17]

In 1884 the full force of the party's impact on national politics was felt for the first time. The party gained the support of a publisher capable of subsidizing its literature for national distribution. Isaac K. Funk of Chicago allied himself with the party and published its principal newspaper, *The Voice*. Frances Willard had finally persuaded the bulk of her followers to support the third party, and when the Republican party's platform committee refused to endorse constitutional prohibition, she went to Pittsburgh to hand over her organization's support to the "Prohibition Home Protection Party," lineal descendant of Gerrit Smith's 1869 party.[18]

The party's 1884 platform excoriated James G. Blaine's proposal to remit to the states the national government's revenue from the excise tax on liquor as one that would permanently legitimize the liquor traffic. In this election year, the Republican's proposal would have meant the remission of almost 78 percent of the federal government's revenues in a year when the government taxed 7.6 million gallons of distilled beverages and 1.9 million barrels of fermented beverages. As one businessman noted: "the navy floats on beer—when we have any navy to float—and a surplus over."[19]

Yet, in recognition of so many disaffected Republicans swelling its ranks, the third party's antimonopolist, prolabor planks were reduced in number and weakened in content. Suffrage for women was left up to the states, and political rights and educational benefits for immigrant workers were glossed over. In addition, the party dropped the term "Reform" from its title. Finally the party muted its underconsumptionist stance, merely observing with respect to prohibition that "no . . . other legislation can so healthily stimulate production, or increase the demand for capital and labor . . . as would the suppression of this traffic."[20]

The party realized it would not win the election, but thought itself strong enough "to strike a crushing blow at one wing of the liquor army," the Republican party.[21] To do so it had so diluted its platform that a splinter party fielded a national ticket which attracted fewer than ten thousand votes.[22] This group, the American Prohibition National Party, denounced "all secret lodges," prison and foreign contract labor, "land and other monopolies," and polygamy. It demanded prohibition, woman suffrage, and the extension of the protection of the Thirteenth, Fourteenth, and Fifteenth amendments to Indians and Chinese.[23] The regular party's candidate, John P. St. John, former governor of Kansas, concentrated on the large eastern urban areas, and garnered more than one hundred and fifty thousand votes. Prohibition had become a national issue with serious ramifications as a Democrat entered the White House for the first time since 1856.[24]

The response of urban reformers to the party's electoral gains was to stress the problem of obtaining electoral support in urban areas with a large "foreign element," and to develop practical limitations on the urban saloon. In 1886, for example, *The Nation* proposed a policy of high license to restrict the number of saloons, and to "make every licensee from self-interest alert to the breaking of the law." The reform journal's position was endorsed by the *New York Times*, which also called for local option legislation.[25]

The urban-oriented temperance reformers also worked within the Republican party to secure temperance planks of a similar nature. In May 1886, Albert Griffin formed the Anti-Saloon Republican Conference in an effort "to win back to the party the Prohibitionists." Griffin sought to commit the party to "a definite line of policy, teaching the temperance cause, having for its avowed object the destruction or greatest diminuation of the business of dramselling." Griffin's efforts were ultimately unsuccessful, and he complained to his financial supporter, John D. Rockefeller, Sr., that the "bitter opposition" of Prohibitionists and "timidity" of regular Republicans had "bankrupted" temperance reform.[26]

Despite such efforts the Prohibition party continued to gain support, particularly in states such as Iowa where the party won support from fusionists in the Greenback and Union Labor parties. In 1886 the party's combined statewide vote increased by some three hundred thousand votes, and by no means were all of these mere defectors from the Republican party.[27] Nevertheless, this assumption continued to prevail among conservative temperance men and urban reformers seeking to establish "a Breakwater against the extreme and *unwise* efforts of wellmeaning temperance men and women who strive to run everything into Politics & very narrow exclusive politics also."[28]

In 1889 a small group, closely identified with this concern, organized to present to the middle-class reading public "certain sociological questions at present engaging attention, or of consequence to the well-being of the community." Terming itself the "Sociological Group" its members published a series of papers in *Century Magazine* that they commissioned and reviewed. It was their hope "to bring scientific methods with a Christian purpose and spirit to the study of the questions to be addressed."[29]

The men comprising this self-constituted authority were leaders in the eastern, urban–industrial community: Charles W. Shields, Henry Codman Potter, Theodore T. Munger, Seth Low, Richard T. Ely, William Chauncy Langdon and Samuel W. Dike. Shields taught theology at Princeton from 1865 to 1903, and specialized in the "harmony of science and religion." Potter held pastorates at the socially prestigious Trinity Church of Boston and Grace Church of New York, and had been appointed Assistant Bishop of New York in 1883. Low, whose family fortune was based on the China trade, was prominent in New York's municipal reform movement. Langdon foresook a career as a patent lawyer in 1858, and became an organizer of the National Young Men's Christian Association. Dike, a Congregationalist, specialized in studying the family as a social problem. All epitomized devotion to the social role of promoting interclass harmony that temperance reformer Lyman Beecher had defined for the churches some seventy years beforehand in connection with temperance reform. The reformers soon expanded their group to include lawyer and diplomat Edward John Phelps, former comptroller of the United States Treasury and minister to Great Britain; William Mulligan Sloane, Seth Low Professor of History at Columbia University; Charles Dudley Warner, journalist and essayist; and two more exponents of applied Christianity, Washington Gladden and Charles Asa Briggs. Francis A. Peabody, William F. Slocum, who became president of Colorado College, and Hugh Miller Thompson completed the group.[30]

The group's first essay addressed "The Problems of Modern Society."[31] It reflected the class conscious concern that formal political power had passed to those "who seek and find their support in the more ignorant and lowest classes," and affirmed that the abuse of this power was responsible for the widening gap between the rich and poor. Enchoing themes earlier expressed by Beecher and William E. Dodge, the essay called upon the churches to reconcile society's disparate elements by establishing "a deeper sense of mutual responsibility and trust" among them.[32]

The key to social reconciliation, argued William Langdon, lay in the employment of "sociological knowledge" to be derived from the study of "three divine institutions, the Family, the State, and the Church," which he termed "the generator," "The organizer," and "the regenerator of society" respectively.[33] Sustaining these institutions, according to Langdon, were both devine and natural laws "beyond the reach and competence of the laws of man." This condition, in turn, gave rise to a "Christian Sociology . . . which no human legislature can repeal nor human willfullness escape." Such a sociology, properly studied and taught, would reveal the correct order of social relationships and thereby heal the divisions characterizing modern society.[34]

From these suppositions Langdon proceeded to critique a "purely political conception" of social problems that he held was inimical to family and state alike. In the case of the family this corosive idea took the form of a belief that "there were no other than bodily differences" between men and women. The consequence of such a belief would be "the moral elimination of the family," and with it the destruction of "the sense of joint responsibility" and "mutual dependence" that should guide the sexes.[35] Contemporary political notions also impeded the state's function as "organizer" of society because those who adhered to them were committed by their party to uphold them. Such *idees fixès* were both a cause and consequence of leaving the resolution of "great political problems . . . too largely to the platform." Langdon called for contemporary social problems to be "studied in a calmer and more scientific temper" than that provided by party politicians. The results of such study, he concluded, "will be given to the country, not as party [doctrine] but as abstract principles."[36]

Ultimately Langdon and his associates looked for the definition and resolution social problems by extrapolitical means. Social technicians, versed in Christian Sociology, would formulate answers to pressing social questions, and the churches as divine "regenerators" of society would serve as agencies for dispensing the new knowledge and new politics. "Ecclesiology" would define "the true relation of organic religion to the family, to society, and to the state." Thus the Sociological Group's practical problem was to determine "How can Christianity be brought to bear, as an intermediate, to coordinate in one the now antagonistic and seemingly irreconcilable forces of the modern monied and working classes?"[37]

The Sociological Group also discussed the family.[38] In its view, as expressed by Samuel Dike, the family was fundamental to social and political stability. The modern family, however, had become corrupted by a rationalistic individualism, affecting both men and women, that viewed marriage as merely a contract between two disposed persons. Consequently, "the family had surrendered its early political functions" establishing a trend culminating in the women's suffrage movement—a "final step" that would "secure the completed substitution of the individual for the family as the ultimate and only true depository of the perrogatives of the political power."[39] If the family could be restored to its former corporate unity, Dike believed it could be used to "return to our advantage the greater reproductive powers of certain classes against which we now contend with doubtful success."

Dike's concern to "return to our advantage the greater reproductive powers of certain classes" is sufficiently murky to fend off most attempts at analysis. Nevertheless, at least two mutual but conflicting concerns of the urban establishment do emerge. One is persisent concern over the scarcity of labor and thus high wages. The other concern is that an expanded labor pool, in a regime of universal (manhood) suffrage, would create political problems that would more than offset gains based upon a surplus of labor. On the other hand, the sort of family implied by Dike could have many workers, but only one voter, about the best that could be hoped for in a Christian Republic. In any event, Dike urged that the family and its connections with "the saloon, the brothel, the almshouse, and the prisons" be carefully reviewed. Such study would bring attention to the magnitude of the problems posed by individualism given way to "licentiousness [which] corrupts the physical basis of the family."[40]

In its most ambitious study before turning to the liquor problem, the group argued for social reform focusing on the working class as necessary to achieve industrial supremacy for the United States.[41] More than ever before "still greater efforts must be made to promote the intellectual, moral, and physical welfare of the masses." In doing so, the reformers contended, Americans must give up popular notions of equality and success:

> Our ideal is a social state, not of equality, but of equal opportunities. . . . Not the self-made man—that is the self-made millionaire—can ever be a model for the masses, but the contented and really prosperous artisan, gradually getting ahead in the world, enjoying life, developing all his powers and living worthily with his family, partaking according to their [*sic*] capacities of the blessings of civilization.[42]

Despite forsaking so much of the nation's popular republican heritage, the Ely and Low report did not regard the future as bleak. On the contrary, a "golden age" lay ahead; its principal obstacle—and the cause of the labor problem—lay with the masses whose "rude and uncultured mind is averse to change."[43] Among such changes singled out as "definitive" was the separation of workers from ownership and control of their tools in the course of industrial development which had made "[e]xistence now for the masses . . . insecure."[44] Yet it was not so much the insecurity of the urban masses confronting "an uncertain and even capricious world market" that concerned the sociological reformers as it was the condition of "irregularity of employment and of income" which led to "enforced idleness in our modern cities." Such conditions were "almost devoid of opportunities for innocent and wholesome recreation," and conducive to "intemperance and vice, both wasting the scanty savings of labor." Equally feared by the reformers was "a roving labor population" not subject to traditional constraints.[45]

What gave the reformers hope was their conviction that industrial development had brought to the working class an absolute increase in the amount of wages. This improvement, they argued, no matter how unevenly distributed, provided the basis for upgrading the industrial work force because, in their eyes, "increasing civilization means increasing wants of the most legitimate kind." According to Ely and Low the means to achieve this end were at hand, and "while we may lament the kinds of wants too often experienced by the masses, we ought to rejoice in the fact that wants do increase." The problem for reform would be "to give the right direction to expanding nature."[46]

The guarded optimism and reform strategy of the Sociological Group proceeded from twin assumptions: "the division of labor is a necessity in our present industrial life" and "one department of life—the industrial fields—had attained perfection."[47] Thus it fell upon collateral institutions to insure social stability for the perfect institution in the new era.

Prominent among the disfunctional elements the reformers faced was "the liquor saloon [which] presents never ending temptation to those who live in labor quarters, while the modern city is almost wholly devoid of opportunities for wholesome, life-giving recreation for the poor."[48] It would be up to modern reform to implement social strategies that would divert the darker impulses of laborers into more constructive channels, enabling them to prosper and remain contented within the new industrial order.

Chief among the ancillary institutions to be involved in this reform effort were the churches. Their task would be "to establish legitimate authority over the minds and wills of men," and to inculcate "individual and social moral virtues [against] indulgence and luxury." In order to achieve this objective, however, the churches themselves would need to change. The direction would not come from scripture, but from "instruction from the best minds of our time. Social science should be pursued in every seminary for the training of ministers of religion."[49]

The state, too, had its role to play in the scheme of the sociological reformers. It should redirect education by establishing manual training and industrial schools, which would provide workers' children with "an enormous advantage . . . in the competition for life, and above all train them to the habits of industry and mental application."[50] The state should also encourage labor organizations, and the Ely-Low report further urged "a frank recognition of their necessity [and] an encouragement of all that is good in them, and repression of the evil." Similarly the state could encourage savings banks as a means for inculcating frugality and developing a sense of a "stake" in the social order, which itself would "produce excellent political effects."[51]

However much the new industrial order might represent the perfection of social organization, the Sociological Group recognized that it had been accompanied by a political order that had given rise to a popular resentment that "nourished revolutionary and even anarchistic sentiments." The state, in their view, had to encourage "diverse kinds of remedies," which, however, stopped short of "further restrictions for agricultural or manufacturing corporations." Nevertheless, without labor reform "a successful national struggle for existence is otherwise out of the question."[52] As recent political developments had shown, the reformers argued, "the masses have been left to themselves to work out the problems of industrial civilization and they are not equal to the task." A new leadership of political reformers, sensitive to the needs of the masses and composed of the those fitted by culture and wealth for the role would have to take up their cause, and the reformers were confident that workers would follow them.[53]

The reports of the Sociological Group, published between 1889 and 1891, drew together into a coherent whole a number of elements characterizing the procapitalist and proindustrial reform sentiment that had developed within the eastern corporate community in the preceding ten years. First and foremost among these was the notion of an urban proletariat unable to understand the depth and permanence of the changes affecting their working lives. Consequently, what economist Francis A. Walker had termed their "brutish conservatism" manifested itself in the pursuit of chimerical political remedies that had all but handed over political authority at every level to irresponsible politicians who pandered to their grossest instincts. Chief among such was licentiousness, a proclivity for self-indulgence that most often took the form of intemperance and which the "enforced idleness" of the modern industrial system aggravated in the absence of more wholesome alternatives. In the reformers' eyes intemperance closed a vicious circle that condemned society to lagging productivity interrupted by useless but dangerous spasms of political unrest. The concentration of industrial workers in large urban areas—itself taken to be a sign of the natural and inevitable progress of industrial organization under capitalist auspices—merely exacerbated workers' social predisposition to dissolute individualism and rebellious conservatism.

Convinced that democratic politics would never, under such circumstances, provide the framework for continuous industrial expansion, yet mindful of the impossibility of revoking universal manhood suffrage, reformers called upon the middle class electorate to abandon political parties and to adopt nonpartisan tactics as a means to leverage formal political authority.[54] In addition they propounded the view that government itself was analogous to a business corporation, and should be made less vulnerable to the decisions of popularly elected officials.[55] Ultimately this analysis of politics reduced itself to a search for class conscious rulers—preferably businessmen or technicians schooled in the rhetoric of Christian sociology—and citizens providing mutual support in the flux of electoral politics.[56]

The third element in the urban reformers' program was a form of social reform carried out under the auspices of institutions ancillary to industrial corporations. Chief among these were the churches and the state, once the latter had been purged of its partisan orientation. Essentially the task of social reform was to tame working-class hostility to the industrial order and channel working class energies into procapitalist modes of behavior. According to the Sociological Group, "the labor problem was by no means a class problem" requiring a political solution based upon partisan politics. Rather the problem required "the harmonious working together of all classes" under a leadership composed of "the highest and best."[57] The churches, informed by the latest sociological precepts, were obvious institutions to "necessarily advance the interests of all society" by developing programs that would "truly advance the interests of wage earners."[58]

Within the analysis of nonpartisanship, the so-called liquor problem played a complex and central role. As a substantive social issue, drinking was alleged to influence the irrational passions of the masses, and lead to social disintegration in the form of work stoppages and strikes, while it created political disorder in the form of a manipulated "liquor vote" centered in the urban saloon. Since 1884 at least, this view had been the official position of William E. Dodge's National Temperance Society, the leading conservative political temperance reform organization in the nation. Aaron M. Powell, the society's executive secretary, told the Senate Committee on Education and Labor: "that as affecting the industrial interests of America unfavorably there is no single influence to be compared with the dramshop system of the nation."[59] Before the same committee, William Daniel, president of the Maryland State Temperance Union, argued that the "liquor traffic . . . is a constant and growing menace to the very perpetuity of government itself."[60] Finally the liquor problem had been enormously complicated by its existence as a partisan issue following the emergence of the Prohibition party as an important factor in the nation's politics. On the one hand it signified the alienation of a substantial portion of the middle class from the politics of the two-party system, while on the other hand it enabled political authorities who were unacceptable to the corporate business community to control the votes of a constantly increasing urban proletariat.

By the conclusion of the 1880s, disaffection of the middle class intensified the liquor problem as a central concern in the corporate business community. During the next ten years it sought, through nonpartisanship and municipal reform, to crush the impetus of the Prohibition party and reclaim the crucial balance of votes needed to implement progressive reforms, which included destruction of the saloon as a step towards establishing an urban, industrial environment to be characterized by a politically docile proletariat that accepted the stringent discipline of industrialism.

Yet another aspect of the Sociological Group's "Christian Sociology" merits attention. In sharp contrast to radicals in the third party antiliquor movement, Dike, Low, Ely, et al. shifted the locus of the liquor problem from a state-supported apparatus of the traffic in alcoholic beverages to the habits and culture of the urban masses. It was their "Ishmaelitish proclivities" and "brutish conservatism" that impeded both industrialization and the ability of the state to provide the means to that goal. The identification of the working class's diverse culture as the source of the manifold liquor problem decisively transformed that class from a potential ally in social reconstruction into an object to be reformed. This elitist view of the liquor problem came into increasing vogue, and as it did, third party efforts to bridge the gap between labor and middle class became progressively weaker. In the end a full blown progressive, nonpartisan antisaloon movement would absorb middle-class political energies. But from the perspective of the late 1880s the Christian Sociology of the Sociological Group was merely an idea aborning.

Part III

The Climactic Years: The Emergence and Failure of Antisaloonism, 1890–1914

6

The Collapse of Third-Party Prohibition and Emergence of Political Antisaloonism, 1890–1900

Temperance Politics and the Committee of Fifty

As American society entered the last decade of the nineteenth century evidence of its structural instability continued to be of concern to all who hoped capitalistic development would provide a foundation of social stability and progress. Concerned critics, such as state department secretary William Evarts, focused on the crucial role the working class had to play in fostering such development. Others, like E. L. Godkin, analyzed the role of the working class in the political system and concluded that urban workers constituted a major obstacle to the politics required to achieve Evarts's goal of international industrial supremacy for the American economy.

The Sociological Group was yet another important expression of corporatist concern for the advancement of a capitalist society. Formed in the late 1880s, the group, as we have seen, reiterated Evarts's objectives and stressed the necessity of social stability as a necessary precondition to industrial progress. The group sought to devise proper integrative roles for the family, the churches, and the state in establishing industrial harmony. Believing that the intemperance and "brutish conservatism" of the urban masses had, under universal suffrage and the prevailing mores of individualism, disrupted the political system, the group and other corporate-minded reformers asserted that control of the government had fallen into the hands least capable of appreciating or achieving industrial progress.[1]

Overt opposition to nominal democracy was not possible, but the Sociological Group's approach to reform offered the possibility of neutralizing the political power of the urban working class.[2] Such reform would require the recruitment of cadres of political activists from outside regular party structures. Henry W. Farnam, who was to play an important role in devising an antiliquor alternative to the Prohibition party as one way of obtaining these recruits, described the situation to Horace White, editor of the *New York Post*. "In our country wealth seems to be a positive bar to holding public offices, instead of an aid, and it should be the duty of public-spirited citizens to try to induce men of independent means to work for the public."[3] The social class from which such public-spirited citizens were to be found was the middle class. Here reformers confronted a class strongly attracted to third-party politics of a more or less radical nature. Throughout the 1880s the liquor question in its manifold dimensions provided a basis for expressing middle-class discontents with the consequences of industrialization, and the Prohibition party attracted increasing numbers of those opposed to regular party politics.[4] Before conservative reform could hope to succeed, such third party activists and supporters would have to be reclaimed to the political system they abjured.

In 1888 over a quarter million such voters cast ballots for the Prohibition party's presidential ticket. That year the party ran a Pennsylvania banker and railroad executive, Clinton B. Fiske, and his candidacy attracted some seventy percent more votes than had that of John P. St. John, the Kansas agrarian, in 1884.[5] Clearly middle-class discontent was not abating. Rather, it challenged the Prohibition party to extend even farther the basis for independent popular support. In so doing the party's leadership debated the merits of a so-called broad gauge platform that would place other issues along with prohibition before the electorate. At the same time a faction of the party's left wing sought a modus vivendi that could bring the party into a viable alliance with other dissident political elements in America.[6] To attract such dissidents the party's national executive committee called for "a new party, a people's party, not an office-seeker's party" that could "dethrone the grog shop," and recommended that more attention be given to the economic ramifications of the liquor traffic.[7]

Efforts to bring the party into a broad coalition peaked in January and February 1892 when Frances Willard and other "fusionists" met with representatives of the Farmers' Alliance, Greenback, National Reform, and People's parties in Chicago and St. Louis. Although the meetings elicited diffuse support for both prohibition and women's suffrage, Willard and her supporters failed to obtain a platform plank that suited their needs on either issue.[8] In attempting these fusionist efforts the Prohibition party's radicals acted consistently in the tradition of the Gerrit Smith-Wendell Phillips style of middle-class radicalism that had inspired the party's foundation in 1869.[9]

Shortly before the fusionist conferences, for example, Edwin C. Pierce, writing in *The Arena* magazine, called for a union of prohibitionist and labor parties to achieve "more nearly an equal distribution of wealth, not so much of the wealth already amassed by society as of wealth that is to be produced in the future." Pierce criticized conservative prohibitionists for their failure to endorse prolabor legislation on the grounds that such action would entail supporting "class legislation," which, he argued, was precisely what labor needed. Pierce also demanded a "broad-gauge" platform calling for land reform and government ownership of railroads, telegraphs, and anthracite coal mines. The party should also support municipal ownership of public utilities and public education. Finally Pierce cited Phillips, himself, in his opposition to those prohibitionists who opposed universal suffrage or who advocated political means tests as prerequisite to vote. Such measures were "too easy a repose for the conservatism of wealth," he claimed as he urged the party to "stand with Jefferson for Democracy and education, not for education first and the ballot afterwards."[10]

Pierce also gave voice to the economic radicalism of fusionist prohibitionists. The extension of American industry into overseas markets would make labor reform impossible: "No large extension of our market for manufactors [*sic*] in Spanish America or other foreign countries is possible if we are to reduce hours of labor, abolish child labor, call married women from factory to home, and raise wages in America, regardless of the effect upon the cost of production." In place of a national economic policy directed at the expansion of overseas markets, Pierce called for a program grounded on "reliance upon the home market." This program would operate "by suppressing the saloon, by shortening hours, [and] by increasing wages we can indefinitely increase the capacity of our own people to consume."[11] Pierce concluded that the economic program he described would encourage democracy while it promoted prosperity. Thus, "the ultra-conservatives, the cormorants of society, the panderers to vice, the white-liners of the South" would be left to support the discredited "anti-national idea" of overseas economic expansion. Because he believed those elements constituted an electoral minority, Pierce was confident a fusionist "popular party" would attract a democratic majority.[12]

So too were the party's other fusionists and broad-gaugers whose differences were matters of tactics. John P. St. John, for example, opposed fusion but endorsed a broad-gauge platform like the one Pierce outlined. His naive economic radicalism was similar to Pierce's. St. John held the liquor traffic responsible for the decline in capital investments directed at the home consumer market. By 1891, he maintained, the liquor traffic was drawing off one and a half billion dollars of potential capital. According to the former Kansas governor this capital could be used to build 1.5 million houses. Such construction, in turn, would mean for example "more axes for our men to go out and cut timber, more cross-cut saws, [and] more men to hand them." The abolition of the liquor traffic would also solve the problem of declining wages: "Today we find two men hunting one job; that is what makes wages low. Blot out the liquor traffic and there will be two jobs hunting one man, and that is what makes wages high." Characterizing the present system as one of "legalized robbery," St. John urged prohibitionists to adopt a program that would "[g]ive the poor man a chance to get a little house for himself and family [and] hold the big fellows down and lift the little fellows up and thus equalize opportunities to get along in the world."[13]

Such sentiments were not, of course, confined to radicals of the Prohibition party. They were characteristic of much of the political rhetoric of third-party dissent in the latter decades of the nineteenth century. The agrarian agitator, Tom Watson, for example, termed the middle class "the mainstay of life" and argued that the equitable distribution of productive labor and wealth would complete a revolution that would see, among other things, the barroom disappear.[14] If the Georgia populist did not openly concede that the liquor traffic was central to the political system he opposed, he nonetheless accepted along with prohibitionists that it was inherent in the system itself.

Besides the conviction that America's political economy had to be adjusted for a more equitable distribution of wealth, prohibitionists shared with other third-party elements the belief that permanent reform could come only at the hands of a popular party. After 1890 the Prohibition party largely abandoned nonpartisan efforts to achieve state constitutional amendments in order to strengthen party organization.[15]

Contrasting sharply with views of conservative antiliquor forces that the masses were corrupt was Neal Dow's belief that "the people are virtuous, courageous, and intelligent."[16] By linking popular democracy to the idea of economic reform, both broad-gauge and fusionist prohibitionists sought to expand the base of the party's appeal. In their conception the liquor traffic corrupted both, and enabled a few to prosper at the expense of the majority.

In the long run, however, the tactics of fusion and the broad-gauge platform failed the party's efforts to build a truly popular reform party. Fusion was rejected by those whom the party approached. Fusionists could not agree on a specific prohibitionist platform or on a way to address the equally vexatious question of women's suffrage. Fusionist prohibitionists complicated their task by the seeming opportunism that motivated them.[17] Beneath the surface, however, lay the party's long history of ambivalent cooperation with established parties to achieve limited antiliquor legislation. The return of its radicals to a stance of political independence and a platform of broad appeal could not obscure its collaborationist reputation and links to the status quo. These efforts also had obscured the party's critique of the central role of the liquor traffic in sustaining the established order.

Following the collapse of Frances Willard's fusionist efforts in 1892, the Prohibition party met in Cincinnati to select a presidential candidate, and the resolutions committee presented the broadest platform the party had been asked to approve.[18] Terming the liquor traffic the "citadel of the forces which corrupt politics," the platform charged those forces with thwarting the popular will and with delivering the nation "into the hands of rapacious class interests." The platform included a scheme to have the government regulate the money supply on a per capita basis that would increase the supply as the population increased.[19] The party demanded tariff reform that amounted to reciprocity and called for a revenue system that would tax possessions rather than consumer goods. As did populists, prohibitionists called for government control of railroads and other such corporations. The party also expressed its hostility to the investment of foreign capital in land, and demanded that the government reclaim all unearned grants of lands from railroads and other corporations. Despite this seemingly radical orientation, however, the party abandoned its previous liberal attitude with respect to immigration and naturalization, thereby indicating its ambivalence with regard to the working class that was developing in America.

Notwithstanding these and other specific antimonopolist criticisms, the main thrust of the party's attack was against the two-party system.[20] The party charged that it exploited the "toiling masses" even as it subserved the interest of the "money power." According to the party platform "the competition of both old parties for the vote of the slums, and their assiduous courting of the liquor power" went hand-in-hand with their covert alliance with capital. The result was to make all three the "practical arbiters" of the nation's destiny. Such a broad-gauge critique stood as a classic expression of the resentment felt by a class of small owners-producers toward the dynamics of modern capitalism's political economy. It could not provide the basis for an alliance that would incorporate the urban proletariat into a democratic mass movement. The party's broad-gauge view of America's political economy depicted the urban masses either as victims of or collaborators with the money power. Besotted by drink and manipulated by saloon keepers, urban workers could only be redeemed by state-enforced prohibition.

In the last analysis the Prohibition party's radicals lacked a critical economic theory to match their insight into the political nature of the state. Frances Willard, John St. John, Edward J. Wheeler, and their supporters could not forgo a society based upon capital and labor. They could only interpose themselves as moral arbiters between two classes they could not control, and then only as advocates of an inherently procapitalist ethic, since prohibition essentially reflected the need of an acquisitive class to increase production cheaply. If American workers did not take prohibitionists seriously it was at least in part because prohibitionists failed to take them seriously. Thus, even as broad-gauge sentiment developed in the crisis of 1893–96, it was doomed to fail as an expression of democratic politics.

But if radical prohibitionism was irrelevent to the development of modern American society, it did present a challenge to others whose hopes for a dry utopia were more closely tied to the emerging economic order. Such prohibitionists operated both within and outside of the party. Conservatives within the party were unable to stem the populist insurgency in 1892 when the party nominated an antimonopoly California grower, John Bidwell, and an eccentric Texas journalist and entrepreneur, James B. Cranfill, to carry the broad-gauge message to the nation's electorate.[21] As vote-getters both candidates were disappointing. They could not stay the appeal of populism in the West, while their brand of prohibition had powerful opponents in the party's northeastern strongholds.[22] Nevertheless, in an election which saw the greatest defection to date of voters from the two-party system—some eleven percent—the Prohibition party held its share of defectors and increased its total vote.

It was against this background of general middle-class insurgency and increased Prohibitionist sectarianism that supporters of conservative temperance reform moved to redirect middle-class discontent, and thereby to create a coalition of capital and middle class that could suppress working-class drinking by concentrating upon capital's long-standing objective of eliminating the saloon rather than by pursuing efforts to eradicate either the drink habit itself or the entire liquor traffic. Specifically this task of redirecting middle-class antiliquor politics was undertaken by the Sociological Group, originally formed to analyze the problems of "labor reform and the government of the cities," but which in early 1893 determined to "concentrate [its] attention on the drink problem in the United States."[23]

The reorganized Sociological Group called itself the Committee of Fifty for the Investigation of the Liquor Problem, and selected its new members "chiefly from eastern cities, in order that it might be possible to procure large meetings of the committee in New York City twice a year." A few men from Milwaukee, St. Louis, and Los Angeles were also asked to participate. The committee's finances were "privately subscribed, mostly in Boston and New York."[24]

The composition of the Committee of Fifty leaves little or no doubt about the seriousness of the eastern corporate community in the matter of the political control of liquor.[25] Among the more prominent of its business leadership were John H. Converse, owner and president of the Baldwin Locomotive works in Philadelphia, Col. Jacob L. Greene, president of the Connecticut Mutual Life Insurance Company, and William E. Dodge, Jr., son of the late organizer of the National Temperance Society. Jacob H. Schiff, the head of Kuhn-Loeb bankers, was chosen from the New York banking community.[26]

From the world of politics and law the committee recruited Charles J. Bonaparte, a wealthy member of Baltimore society and active in municipal reform, and James C. Carter, the head of the Wall Street law firm of Davies and Schudder. Carroll D. Wright, the United States Commissioner of Labor, was invited to serve on the committee as well.

The eastern academic community was represented by such men as Henry Pickering Bowditch, the leading American physiologist of his time, who had married into a Leipzig banking family. Felix Adler, who taught political and social ethics at Columbia, was asked to serve the committee, as was W. O. Atwater, a pioneer in scientific agronomy and the founder and chief of the experimental stations of the U.S. Department of Agriculture.

The committee was distinguished by another characteristic that set it apart from the ordinary: numbers of its members moved in and out of important government service from positions equally high in business and the professions. A typical example was William Bayard Cutting, a director of the American Exchange National Bank, the Southern Pacific, and the Norfolk and Southern Railway companies, who also served on the United States Civil Service Commission. Another such was John S. Billings, who established the library of the United States Surgeon General's Office. A third political service figure was Z. R. Brockway, pioneer in the field of penology, who had been named Special U.S. Commissioner to establish a military prison in 1873. The committee also recruited publisher Richard W. Gilder, who had served as the chairman of the New York Tenement House Commission and on the council of the National Civil Service Reform League.

The committee drew heavily upon prominent clergymen from major denominations. Conspicuous by their absence from such a large proportion of the committee's composition, however, were representatives of evangelical sects. The presence of so many prominent members of the clerical hierarchy was not surprising when considered in the context of the original composition of the Sociological Group, and the social role that the group had proposed for the churches. The clerical representatives were nevertheless relatively atypical persons who had strong backgrounds either in church administration or university teaching. The Reverend Charles A. Briggs, for example, a Presbyterian theologian, agreed to serve. Church administrators such as Right Reverend Thomas Conaty, rector of the Catholic University of America, and the Reverend William Reed Huntington, who was instrumental in founding and building the Cathedral of St. John the Divine, helped to guide the committee's work. In its total composition, the Committee of Fifty represented a cross-section of the eastern corporate community chosen according to a standard of institutional social action outlined by the Sociological Group between 1888 and 1890.

The Committee of Fifty's investigations of the liquor problem spanned a twelve-year period, during which time it expended, apart from personal expenses, some twenty-one thousand dollars, published five books, and numerous articles in journals such as *Atlantic Monthly* and *Forum*, examining different aspects of the liquor problem as it defined them.[27] The Committee of Fifty created four subcommittees to consider the liquor problem as physiological, legislative, economic, and social and moral problems. Charles W. Eliot, James C. Carter, and Seth Low were chosen to head the investigation of the legislative aspects of the problem. Peabody, Elgin R. L. Gould, and Columbia University's William H. Sloane directed the efforts of the subcommittee on the social and ethical aspects of drinking, which resulted in a study of "substitutes" for the saloon. The subcommittee on economic aspects of the drink problem was headed by Harvard economist Francis A. Walker, author of the notion that the masses were possessed of "Ishmaelitish proclivities." Z. R. Brockway, John Graham Brooks, and E. R. L. Gould also served on Walker's subcommittee.[28] The physiology subcommittee was also composed of experts, including Billings, Atwater, and Russell H. Chittendon, professor of physiological chemistry at Yale University.

The personnel of the committee was chosen in order "to bring together a body of opinion, so comprehensive and competent that it may be received as an authority in the most various communities and circumstances."[29] Four years later, when the committee made a public statement about the nature and purpose of its undertaking in a printed circular letter, the committee explained that it hoped its findings and recommendations would obtain "a measure of confidence on the part of the community which is not granted to partisan statements."[30] Thus the committee sought for itself the supposed neutrality of nonpartisanship as the basis for its authority. Elsewhere, the committee stressed the central importance of a nonpartisan investigation of the liquor problem: "No subject affects more profoundly the economic and moral life of the nation, and yet in no subject is the evidence so likely to be colored by prejudice, or limited by inadequate knowledge." The committee disavowed any effort to "radically change the habits of the world." Rather it believed that "wise and practical efforts can mitigate almost any evil [and] can produce a public opinion that operates in the right direction."[31] The direction in which the committee hoped to move antiliquor sentiment was away from partisan politics and toward a cooperative nonpartisan effort to suppress the working-class-saloon by "providing a starting point for a rational and trustworthy method of action."[32] Thus, however much the committee described itself as a neutral agency devoted to the collection of facts, it was and remained a political body representing the historical position of corporate capitalists on the liquor problem in its origins, conception, and execution of its activities.

This fact the committee itself recognized. In elaborating upon its activities, Francis G. Peabody explained that its "limitation of purpose, however, may on the contrary suggest new ways of applying the spirit of reform." The committee's leading moral theoretician went on to explain:

"The cause of temprance has been much obstructed . . . through dissensions among those who should have been allies." Peabody identified such potential allies as those usually given to issuing "missionary tracts or moral appeals." Such efforts impeded the cause of temperance, as they led to "intemperate speech and exaggerated statement." Peabody further explained that as much as the social order was threatened by intemperance, "excessive statements which experience soon discovers to be unsupported by facts" equally endangered that order.[33]

Peabody pointed out, moreover, that the committee's disclaimer to be one more disinterested reform group should not be construed to mean that its investigations would be of little practical value. "An investigation, therefore," he observed, "which disclaims didactic intention may not be without didactic results." To illustrate the point, Peabody cited the Committee of Fifty's conclusions that liquor drinking can, under severely restricted circumstances, have a "judicious use," and, further, that no single piece of legislation could be demonstrated to be more successful in limiting drinking than any other. While such conclusions might be rejected peremptorily by "those accustomed to inflammatory appeals," the Harvard moralist stated in an indirect but obvious reference to prohibitionists, such conclusions "will to other minds open the way to a more tolerant and judicious application of law as a means rather than an end, and will suggest a cautious opportunism which adapts methods of law to variations in local condition, racial tendency, and density of population."[34]

In effect Peabody and the Committee of Fifty proposed the traditional objective of the conservative party of political temperance reform, which sought to use the state as an instrument to achieve the maximum amount of political restriction (prohibition) on drinking consonant with political order. State action was to be supplemented by that of other quasi-political institutions—church, industry, and social agencies. A program of varying legislative restrictions served this end better than did doctrinaire commitment to a single remedy.

The Committee of Fifty's approach to its work involved it in an ideological contradiction. As it sought to redirect the antiliquor movement, its tactics required it formally to ignore both the political ramifications and historical origins of its activities. Only by doing so could it present the liquor problem not as it was—a political problem—but as it was not, an "economic" or "legislative" problem. Nevertheless, such assumptions arose from the experiences of urban elites struggling in the political climate of Gilded Age America. In New York City, for example, temperance and urban reformers could not forgo support from middle-class Germans in their efforts to control whiskey-drinking Irishmen of the working class. Consequently, Abram Hewitt, who turned away Henry George's challenge with German support, altered the city's Sunday closing ordinances "so that beer may be sold in respectable places where music is performed," and also gave the mayor power to issue special Sunday licenses to cover ad hoc or seasonal "entertainments" requiring light alcoholic refreshment. It was such experiences as these that led the committee to suppose that "racial tendency" was important to understanding its liquor problem, and that the law was a means rather than an end.[35]

Such assumptions controlled the political tactics of the committee and reflected their social values. Consequently the committee could not accept the possibility of achieving its goals by engaging in popular or mass politics. This was so, argued Jacob Greene, because "the influences which here tend to operate disasterously are rooted in the social nature and relations of man." The proper tactics for the temperance forces to adopt were those of the "patient opportunist," particularly with respect to achieving legislative goals. What was needed was a flexible system of controls that took into account the exigencies of local conditions, including the race and temperament of those whom Greene described as "the great body of drinkers in saloons" on which his study focused.[36]

Nowhere is the class bias of the committee more evident than in Greene's discussion of the "ethical problem" of drinking. By virtue of Greene's efforts the committee recognized that the roots of the so-called liquor problem were buried in society's social relations and nature. These produced the supposedly disfunctional behavior of popular drinking. Notwithstanding this empirically valid observation—one that workers had called forcefully to the attention of Senator Henry Blair's committee on labor and education more than a decade before—the committee was bent on strengthening these relationships rather than altering them. Rather than tamper with the social relations of a capitalist society, the committee urged temperance men to devise for the working class a variety of liquor controls. Democratic politics could not achieve this goal, as the weakness of the Prohibition party revealed. The working class, supposed by the committee to be controlled by irrational forces of race and ethnic inheritance, would not voluntarily submit to the discipline of state-sponsored prohibition. Other controls had to replace the chimera of prohibition achieved by the democratic process.

The principal consequence of the committee's logic was its exploration of substitutes for the saloon.[37] Such an approach enabled the committee to avoid confronting directly the antidemocratic implications of its position by opening other avenues to attract the energies of third-party-temperance advocates. The aim of the investigation was to discover viable means of "offsetting and finally overcoming the social features of the liquor traffic . . . and that [political] system is commended which it is believed will reduce to a minimum the social possibilities of the saloon." The subcommittee, which was directed by Raymond Calkins, also undertook to devise activities "which shall be wholesome, educative, and contributive to a higher form of individual and community life" to replace the saloon, which "has had handed to it by the community the monopoly of the social life of the majority of American wage-earners."[38]

In its efforts to curb the working class's "morbid appetite for liquor," the Calkins subcommittee envisioned a total system of social control, one that employed the most effective legislative restrictions on the sale of liquor, and sought to utilize "the experience, the wisdom, and the wealth of those interested in social progress" in the development of social agencies that would provide the "right kind of social centers" for workers. The subcommittee's desideratum was a comprehensive series of agencies supervising the social development of the working class from childhood through married life. These agencies should not be sponsored by municipalities, the subcommittee argued, because such control "carried with it too much danger of political control." Instead the Calkins group urged that "this work can best be done . . . by individual or private philanthropic enterprise." But its desire to see that social controls remained under the direction of the community's wealthy did not prevent the Committee of Fifty's investigators from ascribing a positive function to governmental authority: the provision of the physical plant for the multifold activities which were to supplant the saloon and uplift the wage-earning class.[39]

The Committee of Fifty's program for reform called for enlarging the political role of the wealthy by establishing antiliquor institutions of their design, while demeaning or reducing that role for other classes. This position was, in turn, the consequence of the assumption that the "liquor problem" resulted from some ineradicable flaw in the social and moral character of America's rapidly expanding urban working class, the "Ishmaelitish proclivities" that Francis A. Walker had described in 1897 as the real cause of pauperism, which, inexplicably, it simultaneously held to be located in the social relations of capital and labor. The Committee never confronted this contradiction, probably because it never perceived it. As a political tactic, the committee's assumption also laid the basis for reclaiming middle-class defectors from the two-party system. By ascribing the liquor problem and, by extension, the larger social and political problems of American life to social defects supposedly inherent in urban workers, the committee precluded any justification for attempting to align politically with that class itself to destroy the liquor traffic. At the same time it presented an alternative political program which would not only not interfere with the larger direction of American society, but ideally render it feasible.[40]

As in its reflections upon the moral and social problems of instituting reform, the Committee of Fifty's investigations of the legislative and economic aspects of its problem revealed similar assumptions about the nature of the liquor problem. The subcommittee on legislation was particularly critical of statutory prohibition because it had not been as effective in restricting the sale and distribution of intoxicants from "districts where public sentiment has been adverse or strongly divided" as prohibitionists claimed.[41] Moreover, this sort of legislation, the Eliot subcommittee charged, had frequently led to a "general degeneration in public life" and other assorted evils which undermined respect for all political authority, making it, thereby, a "service less desirable for upright men."[42]

The committee looked to a modified version of Sweden's Gothenburg System to solve problems related to antiliquor legislation and enforcement. Committee member E. R. L. Gould, writing in the *Forum,* reiterated the committee's dictum that "the control of the liquor traffic is a moral and social question and has no place in politics." He deprecated most legislative remedies and pointed to the corruption wrought by liquor interests and "lower elements of both political parties" as impediments to legislative controls. The Gothenburg System, on the other hand, invested the state's authority in the hands of a private corporation that could be comprised (as it was in Sweden) of "private citizens . . . some of the very best known."[43]

Gould's *Forum* article summarized the results of a larger study of the Gothenburg System which he had undertaken at the behest of the commissioner of labor and fellow Committee of Fifty colleague, Carroll D. Wright. In addition to its capability of giving private citizens immune power over distributing liquor, Gould was impressed with the system's potential to rechannel the efforts of "the temperance party." If conducted properly, the system could turn such parties from popular agitation to the "reform in details" of the restrictive monopoly. Yet Gould was not so sanguine as to predict that middle-class temperance agitators would accept indefinitely a system based on the premise that, all things considered, "it is better to regulate [the liquor traffic] through the higher rather than the lower elements of the community," than to curtail the traffic altogether. Should prohibitionists "fear that the upper classes of society" would want to maintain the system indefinitely, they would not accept it readily. Despite these misgivings, the Gothenburg System's promise of a restrictive private monopoly of supply and distribution remained the committee's best hope to resolve the vexacious questions of legislation and enforcement.[44]

In the long run, the Eliot subcommittee and the Committee of Fifty generally were attacking the notion that law was the sufficient end of political action. "The influences of race or nationality are apparently more important than legislation," Eliot wrote.[45] Since this was the case, the subcommittee report, maintaining that "the law is best which is best administered," strongly preferred legislation adapted to local requirements and supplemented by informal political arrangements "to promote temperance." Among these latter, the Eliot report cited "the giving of a preference in certain employments to total abstainers or to persons who never lately [*sic*] drink while on duty" as among the "more promising directions" lately taken in reform-conscious circles.[46]

But the committee's methodological errors reveal a deeper flaw in its conception of society. By characterizing law as less than sufficient, and, at the same time, extolling the virtues of legal administration, the committee simultaneously exposed and reinforced its ideological conviction that men in general could not (and therefore would not) voluntarily behave appropriately. While there was ample evidence that such was not the case, the committee chose to fall back upon a vague ethnocentric determinism to justify expanding state authority, rather than confront directly the issue of *why* and under what circumstances human beings of every description, creed, and social order drink. To have done the latter, would have required the committee to address that which makes politics both possible and unachievable: human reason. (In this respect, however, the committee's failure is a general one.)

The economic subcommittee, under the direction of national labor commissioner Carroll D. Wright, arrived at similar conclusions. The subcommittee had at its disposal the full resources of Wright's Bureau of Labor. In fact the labor bureau's 1897 annual report, "Economic Aspects of the Liquor Problem," was undertaken in conjunction with the subcommittee's subsequent investigation.[47] Besides not wanting to duplicate efforts, Henry W. Farnum, the subcommittee's secretary, explained that the Bureau of Labor's study was to reflect "the credit side of alcohol's account" while that of the Committee of Fifty was to reveal the negative. While Farnum admitted the methodological difficulties accompanying these investigations, he also showed that the subcommittee was not above playing fast and loose with its data to arrive at its conclusions: the data of the two investigations "are not strictly comparable . . . but together they present an imposing picture."[48]

The conclusions reached by the subcommittee were supplementary to those of the other subcommittees. In addition to asserting that race and national origin were fundamental elements of the working-class liquor problem, the Wright committee suggested that knowledge of "the efficacy of economic ways and means" would enable reformers better to "be able to adapt our means to our ends."[49] Specifically, the Wright committee looked to the "very powerful economic forces . . . in modern industry" to supplement and even supersede the efforts of reform agencies.[50] These forces included labor unions "in spite of occasional lapses," and large-scale employers. The former frequently placed pro forma restrictions upon the drinking of their members because insurance and benefit programs required them to do so. On the other hand, major employers, the traditional source of antiliquor sentiment, were concerned with safety and productive efficiency. The Wright committee cited the 1897 labor bureau report to substantiate increasing concern of industry to adopt practical restrictive and preventive measures, and to justify its conclusions that "economic forces are already working in the direction of moderation which need but be stimulated and directed to become effective allies of the moral agencies which are attacking the evils of the liquor habit."[51]

Assuming that the forces of modern industrialization would eventually stabilize the industrial working class, the Committee of Fifty framed its political strategy to reorient temperance advocates away from democratic agitation for sweeping legislation toward the mobilization of religious, civic, and philanthropic agencies. These bodies would direct their reform energies toward circumscribing and suppressing the saloon.[52] Success in this endeavor would require cooperation from those whom the committee viewed as "influential people who . . . are intensely in earnest for moral reform," as it was they "who can help most in bringing about the change we want to see."[53] In addition the temperance movement's rank and file had to be persuaded to follow the committee's lead, while the credibility of the new agencies of moral reform had to be established.

Of these exigencies, credibility was paramount. The committee, for the most part, regarded the Prohibition party as "a pernicious mistake," but one involving "only a very insignificant minority of that vast body of people who believe . . . in the practice of total abstinence."[54] With respect to the latter, the committee recognized that it was dealing with a politically potent force whose ideological convictions concerning alcoholic beverages, per se, rested on increasingly untenable grounds, but which nevertheless provided a basis for opposition to the committee's objectives, even as it was being undermined.[55]

Nowhere was the issue of the committee's credibility raised more forcefully and challenged more directly than in its embroilment with the education department of the WCTU. Nowhere, also, were the larger issues of temperance reform more clearly delineated. The basis of the WCTU's program of temperance education in the schools lay in Frances Willard's conviction that rational enlightenment was the foundation of moral conviction. Willard denied that attributes of race, national or ethnic origin were necessary impediments to such enlightenment; all people could be persuaded to abstain once informed of alcohol's insidious and deadly attributes.[56]

The implementation of this view in the union's public education programs had been in the hands of Mary H. Hunt since 1880. Hunt's political instincts were matched by her considerable entrepreneurial talents, and by the mid–1890s she presided over the Scientific Temperance Association, founded to manage her own lucrative publishing ventures, as well as the WCTU's National and International Department of Scientific Temperance Instruction.[57] From the latter position Hunt and her state affiliates had secured state and national legislation requiring instruction in temperance hygiene in primary grades and high school. They gained a virtual monopoly over the adoption of required textbooks, one of which was Hunt's own *Pathfinder* series.[58] So great was Hunt's power in this area that publishers of unapproved textbooks were simply locked out of the market, and, it was rumored, others merely caved in, purchased her endorsement, and "put so much nonsense into their school physiologies."[59]

In November 1897, at the request of Jacob Greene's committee on ethics, the Committee of Fifty's committee on the physiological aspects of the drink problem took up the question of temperance education in the schools.[60] Greene's committee had already received a report critical of that instruction prepared by Princeton University sociologist Walter A. Wyckoff and Columbia University's William Mulligan Sloane, but turned to the physiologists recognizing that "the question as to whether alcoholic drinks are in any sense a food was one of very considerable importance."[61] Indeed, as the committee's involvement in this issue deepened, its members came to believe that "the key to the whole situation is in the physiology of the subject."[62]

The crucial importance of physiology lay in the nature of the temperance movement's perception of the drink "evil." Popular opposition to drink was based upon practical assesssments of its consequences in a capitalist industrial society. Neither religious belief nor abstract morality sustained this opposition. It was science, rather than the former that confirmed middle-class hostility to drink. And it was science, or the testimony of science about the pernicious nature of alcohol, that gave credibility to

Mary Hunt's operations, and organized WCTU educational strategy. Should the testimony of science fail with respect to the nature of alcohol, the entire edifice of organized antiliquor sentiment was threatened.

Hunt recognized this fact as did the Committee of Fifty; and when a committee of the Middlesex South (Mass.) Medical Society criticized the state's 1885 temperance education law, she protested vehemently to Henry Bowditch: "I cannot see by what stretch of the imagination the friends of Temperance Education . . . can conclude that the purposes of this Committee . . . are friendly." Hunt declared that Bowditch's medical society's committee was "arrogant" in its criticism of the state's temperance physiologies as being the work of "those who have had no experimental knowledge of the subjects treated." On the contrary, Hunt asserted, the books had been prepared with the assistance of prominent university-connected medical officials, and she added that the Massachusetts law was the expression of the will of "tens of thousands of the best people . . . among whom were a large proportion of the physicians of the entire State."[63]

When the Committee of Fifty's W. O. Atwater was reported to Hunt as having made a "very pronounced attack" on temperance physiologies at a Chautauqua meeting, Hunt demanded to know the particulars, informing Atwater that "as a scientific man" he had to realize criticism must be specific were it to be useful. Atwater's eleven page, typed reply to Hunt succinctly stated the Committee of Fifty's attitude with respect to the importance of the physiological evidence being "the key to the whole situation."[64]

Atwater argued that the physiological case against alcohol was not nearly so strong as Hunt and her supporters made it out to be. Moreover, as more experimental evidence accumulated, it was likely to become weaker still. Atwater cited examples of erroneous and misleading statements about alcohol's impact on human physiology that he found in the WCTU-endorsed "Steele's Physiology." To the informed reader such were merely "ludicrous," but to children they were "grossly deceiving." Temperance sentiment founded upon such misinformation would ultimately be discredited, and so too would the agencies that sustained it.[65]

In short, the argument for temperance had to be shifted to another ground. It was foolhardy to employ unsound pedagogy to advance scientifically false information, particularly as the physiological consequences of drinking were minor when compared to its "terribly demoralizing" impact upon "character." Finally, Atwater warned, the well-intentioned zeal of the WCTU required support from "those whose wisdom and influence makes their cooperation essential to the best success of moral movements." Among such he maintained, "there are many out of sympathy not with the purpose, but with the methods of your work."[66]

Hunt was hardly assuaged, and the sniping between the committee and her supporters continued for several years, culminating in 1904 with the publication of an elaborate "Reply to the Physiological Sub-Committee of the Committee of Fifty."[67] At the heart of the struggle was the committee's intention to shift the argument for total abstinence to other grounds, and yet avoid alienating popular temperance support. For this reason John S. Billings urged the physiological subcommittee to draft its position "so as to give less semblence of sanction to habitual drinking." The subcommittee had to endorse total abstinence, even if, as physiologists, its findings "do not of themselves suffice for affirming the necessity or even advisability of total abstinence." The committee must "avoid the danger of being misunderstood" particularly since "we are striking at the very foundation of temperance as very many of the best people understand it and we want to show that what we urge is really the surest ground on which it can rest."[68]

The ground to which Billings alluded was what he termed "the ethical side of the question."[69] The erosion of proabstinence arguments based upon alcohol's alleged effect on human physiology should not, in the committee's view, weaken antiliquor sentiment. What the committee regarded as the evils of intemperance, that is, the custom of popular drinking, abounded regardless of what effects a given amount of alcohol produced in an individual. People should abjure drinking, not because alcohol harmed them, but "because of their duties as citizens and to the community."[70] The committee feared that misplaced emphasis would weaken and discredit the antiliquor movement, the more so when school children could readily observe the discrepancy between WCTU temperance education and "the presence in every community of a large number of healthy and vigorous individuals for whom a small amount of alcohol forms a portion of their daily diet."[71]

The committee was also alert to the danger such misplaced emphasis represented to its long range scheme to reorient temperance reform to a program of substituting for and ultimately suppressing the saloon. As Atwater pointed out to Hunt, WCTU misinformation was disseminated from "the public school, the Sunday school, the pulpit and the promoters of moral reform to which not only the young, but the public at large look for the highest standard of truthfulness."[72] In the committee's view therefore, the instructional programs of WCTU were a direct threat to the viability of the temperance movement at the very time when the committee claimed the nation's social and economic forces had developed to a point at which they could be expected to deal effectively with the liquor problem.

The Committee of Fifty's own credibility was at stake as well, and in the course of its dispute with Mary Hunt, it had always to present itself publicly as disinterested and judicious, free of the spirit of partisanship.[73] At the same time it did not confine its activities to circulating internal memos and book publication. Over the years, members of the physiological subcommittee used their influence to obtain funds from the United States Treasury to carry on their work, and intervened in three northeastern states—Massachusetts, Connecticut, and New York—to secure changes in temperance education legislation.[74] The committee's relative successes in these forays bespoke its social power as well as the depth of its insight into the need of the antiliquor movement to abandon the tactics of democratic agitation for legislative objectives, and to focus reformist energy on attacking the "satisfaction of the social instinct" provided by the saloon.[75]

The investigations of the committee coincided with America's passage into the twentieth century as a major industrial power and emerging force in international politics. The committee's activities represented a significant part of a general response by the eastern corporate and business community to major social and political problems attending their efforts to establish a social order compatible with the long-term exigencies of modern industrial capitalism, a political goal that aroused continued and widespread antagonism from other classes in American society. Primarily, however, the Committee of Fifty addressed itself to the problem of implementing political temperance reform in a society characterized, by 1893, by increasing antagonism not only between, but even within, classes. At the time that the committee constituted itself, intraclass antagonism, which it characterized as "partisanship," was as much the committee's concern as was the traditional goal of a political temperance reform.

The Prohibition party had made considerable inroads into the middle classes, so much so that, as one critic noted, the Republican party lost the 1892 elections because it lacked the moral courage to deal effectively with the "three great issues [that] are discernible on the political horizon . . . Labor and Temperance and Equal Suffrage."[76] The Prohibitionist party offered to demoralized members of the middle classes a rational alternative to a party whose "moral instincts were becoming deadened." Their defection from the two-party system challenged politically the long-range goal of corporate Eastern wealth as defined by Seth Low, Richard T. Ely, and other members of the committee: industrial supremacy in a world market. Hence, the Committee of Fifty's immediate goal had been to "suggest new ways of applying the spirit of reform" to middle-class defectors; ways that took cognizance of the potential for social control which the "very powerful economic forces . . . in industry . . . possessed."

The assault on two-party politics by third-party prohibitionists made it increasingly difficult for the protagonists of conservative political temperance reform to control popular political authorities, particularly in urban areas. Consequently, their drive to restructure that authority had produced an analysis of a political machine which could be controlled provided that "good" men would work and vote in concert. The need to regroup and reorganize this demoralized class of citizens against the darker political forces of the city created an additional incentive to devise ways to implement political temperance reform that could employ the energies and enthusiasms of the middle class politically, while circumventing popular politics. In the end, the Committee of Fifty merely reiterated long standing principles of temperance reform that capital had developed before the Civil War: this reform was above partisan concerns (because of its class nature) and the suppression by the state of the social institutions that were the occasions of working-class drinking was the principal remedy for the liquor problem. The committee's posture of nonpartisanship was an effort to regain the middle class to these principles by assuring it that all of property's social institutions could be brought to bear upon suppressing the saloon as supplements to state imposed restrictions.

The Triumph of Antisaloonism

In summary, the political purpose of the Committee of Fifty was twofold: its program was designed to undermine the rationale of popular political agitation for temperance reform by demonstrating that the source of the problem was essentially social and not political; at the same time it aimed at attracting a demoralized middle class by suggesting that political liquor control could be established with limited state action undertaken in conjunction with social institutions largely controlled by private wealth—particularly large industrial corporations, churches, and philanthropic organizations. In support of these ideas, the Committee of Fifty also advanced the proposition that industrialization was itself in the vanguard of reforming forces even as it conceded the "drink problem" was a product of industrialization. As the experience of the Prohibition party had shown, united political action between the middle class and labor required a program not compatible with the proletarianization of masses of workers. Hence, another approach to liquor control was required.

The Committee of Fifty's work received editorial support from the influential opinion-shaping journal, *Harper's Weekly.* In an editorial the magazine criticized the temperance movement which it held had "resolved itself into a mere matter of politics." This blunder, *Harper's* maintained, had caused the movement to become "muted with blindness of intellect [*sic*] and ignorance of the webwork of sociological facts which complicate the issue." But *Harper's* editors held out hope for reform because of the committee's work. This work being carried out in "a sane and workmanlike fashion," would provide the answers to the complex problems of reform. Noting with confidence that the committee was headed by Seth Low, that it comprised "a favorable catalogue of names, and assures a many sided view of all the complexities of the question," *Harper's* promised its readers that "this will be a contribution to the resources of knowledge and suggestions from which should spring effective practical methods [of liquor reform], whether embodied in suasion or legal compulsion." What also recommended the committee's work to *Harper's* was "the self-imposed task" of these men who had avoided any publicity of their activities. Finally, the editors noted the committee's promise to investigate fully the use of stimulants by various nationalities and, in addition, to consider the effect of drinking upon "the industrial efficiency of our composite classes" as indicative of the proper approach to liquor control.[77]

To a considerable extent the Committee of Fifty's work was preserved from criticism by its prestige and by the failure of critics to perceive its larger implications. In a mildly critical anonymous review of the committee's study of liquor legislation, Edward T. Devine acknowledged that the committee had benefitted from "liberal financial support and unbounded public confidence," and "has had an unprecedented amount of co-operation [*sic*] from public and private bodies and much private voluntary assistance."[78] Devine's criticism was limited to an expression of his belief that the personal bias of Frederick T. Wines and John Koren was responsible for an unnecessarily harsh depiction of prohibitory legislation. In general, though, he felt that their work on the legislative aspects of the liquor problem "will probably stand as the beginning of our scientific work in this field."[79]

One extant theoretician of third-party political prohibition missed the main thrust of the Committee of Fifty's work, despite its entanglement with the WCTU. August F. Fehlandt, who in 1904 published a critical history of political temperance, *A Century of Drink Reform in the United States*, rejected the physiological arguments of the committee and disparaged the committee itself as "a self-constituted body . . . which hold[s] very conservative views, for the most part, in the matter of temperance."[80] But Fehlandt failed to see the antidemocratic purpose of the committee, and judged its work as not inimical to third-party politics, but as supplementary or, if not that, irrelevant.[81]

Neither the lack of wide publicity nor the failure of criticism contributed to the more or less full implementation of the Committee of Fifty's program, even before its formal existence had ceased, and to the coincident decline of the Prohibition party during these same years. In the latter case, cataclysmic depression and the great industrial strikes that followed the party's 1892 effort to win a broadly based following of workers and farmers did more to shatter middle-class confidence that such a political union was possible than did the meticulous investigations of the Committee of Fifty.

The response of Boston's Joseph Cook to the massive social unrest of these years provides a vivid illustration of the limits to which prohibitionists could go in effecting reform in alliance with America's industrial workers. Cook's reaction to strikes and strikers also affords insights into the limits middle-class values placed upon the Prohibition party. Cook was a popular lecturer who inaugurated the Boston Monday Lecture series at Tremont Temple to review various currents of political and social reform. He also published a journal, *Our Day*, featuring such writers and reformers as Frances Willard and David Dudley Field. An exemplar of middle-class social commitment, Cook was the sort of person the Prohibition party had to attract for leadership and, once attracted, one who would have to extend the hand of union to industrial workers if the party's democratic thrust were to succeed. Cook's small odyssey reveals the extent of his class's commitment to a capitalist social order.

In 1888 Cook abandoned the Republican party, claiming it was "now on its knees to the whiskey oligarchy" in much the same way he believed the old Whig party had been subservient to the legendary slave power.[82] Convinced that the major parties were "afraid to offend the whiskey vote in bondage to the saloon," Cook turned to the Prohibition party. But it was not so much the party—much less the ideal of a popular political party—that attracted him as it was its objective. "Until prohibition succeeds," he wrote, "average municipal politics will be kept in bondage to the criminal classes."[83]

In addition to fearing the underclass of urban workers, Cook was suspicious of immigrants, and by 1890 was suggesting other means to implement prohibition. Like the Committee of Fifty, Cook called upon churches and philanthropic organizations to play larger roles in the prohibition movement. He hoped the churches would ban "rum-sellers" and use Sunday schools to spread temperance propaganda. Cook urged the adoption of "other expediences," including educational tests for suffrage, to offset the immigrant vote on temperance issues.[83]

From within this conservative context, mistrustful of current political authority and suspicious of an immigrant-dominated working class that could vote, Cook responded to the crisis of 1892–93. In the midst of the approaching depression, fierce industrial strikes in the plants of the Carnegie Steel Corporation were followed by similar outbreaks throughout the nation, climaxed by the great labor struggles waged in the Idaho mine fields around the Coeur d'Alene. The crisis did not halt with the election of Grover Cleveland, and there was considerable fear that the following summer would witness similar outbreaks of labor violence. In February, 1893, Cook's *Our Day* reprinted an article by David Dudley Field, according to which, the slow progress toward industrial reconciliation was due to "the action of the workers themselves in resorting to violence . . . to gain their ends." While workers were a large proportion of American society, "they are a minority and a small minority, of the whole population," and ought to remember that their "surest alliance is on the sympathy of your countrymen, on prudent counsels and the rapid march of time," rather than upon direct action.[85]

In July 1893 Cook endorsed the WCTU's rejection of nonpartisanship and defended its "broad policy . . . to attack not only the chief foe [the liquor traffic] but its notorious and open allies." Cook's endorsement of the WCTU hinged on his belief that the union's program of scientific temperance instruction could provide the basis for a successful temperance party.[86] Although he did not identify the liquor traffic's allies in this article, it is clear from his other writings that the urban masses and contemporary political machines were the culprits. This conviction militated, in Cook's mind, against the possibility of a democratic solution to the nation's liquor problem. In his January 22, 1894 Monday lecture, Cook revealed how closely his views paralleled those of traditional conservatives in the prohibitionist movement. Cook told his audience that the nation had fallen from unexampled prosperity because of the working-class threat to the protectionist national economic policy. This threat caused employers to react with uncertainty and a lack of confidence in future business conditions. Cook explained to his listeners that poverty among America's workers resulted from their own intemperance which they aggravated by their inherent improvidence.[87]

Later in 1894 the formation of motley assemblages of itinerant laborers into "industrial armies" like that of Jacob S. Coxey further eroded the possibility of an effective union of reformers like Cook and a self-conscious working class. Disturbed that one such army was making its way eastward, Cook travelled to Ogden, Utah, to observe conditions himself. Appalled by what he learned Cook responded to demands for stable wages by insisting that workers' pay had to be geared to prevailing business conditions: workers could expect no more than a sliding scale of wages. Cook charged that "Kelley's army" wanted "paternalism in Government . . . not self-help." Cook's analysis of the situation sharply revealed his procapitalist bias. Recognizing that workers lacked the perceptions of reality that motivated property holders, Cook maintained that America's principal social problem was the flawed nature of its working class and stated: "what is needed today in providing for the wants of the unemployed is a sieve to separate workers from shirkers."[88]

The outbreak of the great railroad strike of Gene Debs' American Railway Union completed the disillusion of Boston's advocate of social reform via popular third party politics. Cook charged that the Debs-led strikers were seeking a "continental dictatorship," and complained bitterly that "the action of the authorities in repressing disorder was painfully slow."[89] Cook demanded "an impartial federal authority" to impose order on capital and labor alike. Nor was he reticent about granting the state the instruments necessary to be impartial. The one good which derived from the conflict, he asserted, was the clear demonstration of the worth and necessity of the federal government maintaining a well equipped standing army. The political challenge represented by the American Railway Union's strike forced Cook back within the political framework that the radicals within the Prohibition party challenged. To a considerable extent, however, the Boston reformer never really had escaped it, as he never gave any indication that he grasped the implications of the radical Prohibitionist challenge to the prevailing political order.

Cook's outburst against the strikers was carried in *The Independent, New York Times,* and *The Nation.* Each was associated with the cause of conservative temperance reform, and sought to rally middle-class sentiment from the strikers by asserting that Debs' strategy resulted from his drinking habits.[90] The willingness of these journals to accept a vague diagnosis of "dipsomania" as evidence that the union leader was a drunk suggests not so much malice aforethought as it does a prior ideological conviction about the cause of American society's political and social disorder.

The Prohibition party experienced these tremors of middle-class reaction to working-class unrest throughout the 1890s. As the party's radical wing continued to press for broader commitments to political change, an eastern-based opposition demanded that the party campaign upon the single issue of national prohibition.[91] At the nominating convention held at Pittsburgh in May, 1896, the conservative faction, led by Rockefeller associate William T. Wardwell and publisher Isaac Funk, named Pennsylvania manufacturer A. A. Stevens as temporary chairman. The radical "populist" faction succeeded in naming Oliver W. Stewart of Illinois as the convention's permanent chairman. The radical wing also controlled the Resolutions committee, which reported a broad-gauge program to the convention floor.[92]

The defeat of the free silver plank marked the beginning of the conservative's takeover of the convention. Robert H. Patton, a Springfield, Illinois, lawyer, offered a substitute for the broad-gauge platform, endorsing a single prohibition plank and allowing "every Prohibitionist the freedom of his own convictions upon all other political questions." Patton's substitute resolution won an overwhelming victory for the conservatives, a victory which split the party as the radicals walked out to hold their own convention.[93] Shorn of its radical faction, the conservative candidates for national office lost considerably more than fifty percent of the party's 1892 voters.[94]

The collapse of the Prohibition party between 1892 and 1896 was principally due to the pressure of the events of these years, which affected its components adversely. By 1896 the Dow–St. John Republican radicalism that had been nurtured in the pre–Civil War political crisis between entrepreneurial capitalist and skilled mechanic on the one hand and the Southern slave economy on the other, had largely been abandoned by a middle class which could see only proletarian revolution, which it ordinarily equated with anarchy, as the outcome of radical politics. Between progressive conservatism and revolution stood prohibitionists, which, as middle-class critics of industrial capitalism, saw too clearly and yet not clearly enough.

What they saw clearly was the political nature of government, and that law and social order were alike products of politics. What Prohibitionists did not see, although their doctrine pointed in that direction, was the political nature of society itself and, thus, of private property as well. Radical prohibitionism had indicted a national political policy for the maintenance of the liquor traffic, cyclical depressions induced by a scarcity of capital for the national consumer market and the formation of a rootless and, in its own eye, increasingly rum-soaked proletariat. At its height the Prohibition party represented an effort on a significant part of the middle classes to arrest these developments by destroying the liquor traffic, which it described as "the citadel of the forces that corrupt politics, thwart the will of the people and deliver our country into the hands of rapacious class interests."[95]

But selective insight into the political nature of society was not confined to prohibitionists. The eastern corporate community was equally possessed of it. This community since the Civil War had defined its political objectives in such a way as to require the formation of a large urban proletariat. It now offered to America's middle classes, particularly the urban middle class, a long range antiliquor program promising the formation of such proletariat, while avoiding the consequences of such a political development, by bringing virtually all the social institutions of property to bear upon the liquor problem. Faced by conditions in the early and mid-1890s, which seemed to importune a cataclysmic assault on property, the tenuous coalition that the Prohibition party attempted to represent collapsed. Unlike the pre–Civil War abolitionists whose heritage it claimed, middle-class temperance men now chose to stand for property and against its victims; themselves more the victim of their own ill-grounded fear of a rum-soaked, virtueless proletariat than of labor radicalism. Already prepared for their collapse, indeed prepared to hasten it along, was a politics of social class organized to continue the proletarianization of the working class in a liquor-free environment. This new form of politics would utilize quasipolitical institutions, whose ultimate foundation was property, to augment the activity of the two-party system, which, itself, would be limited by so-called nonpartisan tactics, that is, a politics of class interest.

The new politics of class interest devised by conservative liquor reformers is most aptly characterized as antisaloonism. These politics posited the continuing and inevitable concentration of both capital and labor in larger and larger urban areas that would afford nonpartisan politics the opportunity to develop a program of social reform, namely the creation of substitutes for the saloon to alter the habits and attitudes of the working class.[96] This narrow and parochial bias resulted in part from the immediate interests of the corporate communities of Boston, New York, and Philadelphia that had established the Committee of Fifty, to free the cities from undependable political authorities. But to a far greater extent it derived from their shared ambition to transform America into a mass industrial society.

7

Antisaloonism and Urban Reform, 1890–1915

Antisaloonism, as outlined by the Committee of Fifty, restated the conservative antiliquor position that all instruments of property should be bought to bear against the working class saloon and that local property interests should judge how best to employ political authority over it.[1] As an expression of class interest, however, antisaloonism was an integral part of a general concern to utilize political power to achieve a social order compatible with the expansion of business enterprise. To this extent, antisaloonism was motivated to quell middle-class partisanship by presenting an alternative to prohibitionism, as well as by the desire to regulate working-class social habits. The eastern metropolitan character of the conservative antisaloon strategy was evident from the personnel of the committee, and its desire for a uniform approach to the liquor problem was equally apparent from its cooperation with the national Labor Bureau chief, Carroll D. Wright.

Antisaloonism became an integral part of urban reform as it was defined and implemented by organizations such as the National Municipal League, whose first two presidents, James C. Carter and Charles J. Bonaparte, had played important roles in the Committee of Fifty's work. At the time of the League's founding in 1894 through the efforts of the City Club of New York and the Philadelphia Municipal League, nine members of the committee, including John H. Converse, were among those attending.[2]

The National Municipal League was not strictly an antiliquor organization, but antisaloonism was an integral aspect of its program for reforming American cities. Like the Committee of Fifty, the metropolitan and corporate character of the League's founders was its principal social feature. Although it proclaimed that it sought to "harmonize the methods and combine the forces of all who realize that it is only by united action and organization that good citizens can secure the adoption of good laws and the selection of men of trained ability and proved integrity for all municipal positions," the League had no representatives from either labor organizations or political parties at its initial conference.[3] Among those who fit the reformers' definition of good citizens were Marshall Field, the Chicago department store magnate, Anson Phelps Stokes, partner in the Phelps-Dodge commercial-industrial combine, and Lyman J. Gage, president of the First National Bank of Chicago.[4]

The results of the League's first conference pleased E. L. Godkin—in many ways the father of its thoughts and actions—because it had avoided discussing abstract plans of government and instead devoted its energies to practical schemes to promote his ideas of better city government. The League also sought to "prevent the success of incompetent or corrupt candidates for public office."[5] To this end the National Municipal League became a major forum of spokesmen for business expansion to work out a general rationale for urban social reform and suitable political tactics to implement it. The new urban environment envisioned by these reformers was to be liquor free and saloonless.

Before a general program could be implemented, however, the means of obtaining and securing political power had to be formulated. The delegates to the Philadelphia convention therefore stressed the need to utilize extra-political agencies like schools, churches, and women's clubs to implement reform, and considered the relative merits of forming independent political parties or infiltrating existing parties.[6] The long range goal of political activism was to bring business organizations into reform politics and influence regular political authorities.[7]

At the League's annual meeting in Louisville, May 5–7, 1897, Ryerson Ritchie, secretary of the Cleveland Chamber of Commerce, and Franklyn MacVeagh, the Chicago lawyer and banker who later became William Howard Taft's Secretary of the Treasury, discussed the objectives of the political activity of business organizations and argued that the crux of the urban political problem was the absence of businessmen in politics.[8] The problem to which each speaker addressed himself was how the business community could achieve the maximum possible political impact. Taken together these addresses may be considered as a statement of thinking which prevailed among the National Municipal League's constituents.

Ritchie used the Cleveland Chamber of Commerce to illustrate the political potential of business organizations. Its basic purpose "was to enlist public support in what it desired to accomplish," to ward off criticism, and to establish the view that the Chamber of Commerce acted on behalf of the entire city.[9] The Chamber of Commerce was peculiarly suited to this task, Ritchie explained, because it gave its members freedom to develop their programs and plans in secrecy. Its organization and prestige also made it possible for the Chamber's representatives to convince ordinary political authorities to implement long-range projects. Thus, "the relation which businessmen bear to the municipal government of a city is really much more intimate than one might judge from the lack of interest they seem to take in the management of a corporation in which, to use a commercial simile, they hold a majority of stock." Ritchie stressed the capacity of such business organizations to bring wayward businessmen into line and to sponsor reform and civic associations to achieve "direct and far-reaching . . . effect upon the voters of the community." Finally, he insisted that businessmen could no longer remain aloof from politics if urban commercial expansion were to be achieved.[10]

MacVeagh, on the other hand, rejected the idea of businessmen directly assuming public office. He discounted the possibility of providing the electorate with a choice between business and other parties because he thought the nature of the problem was such that formal political action depended too much upon arousing a spirit of altruism and voluntarism, qualities he thought were not sufficiently widespread in the business community.

Instead, he pointed to the persistent support businessmen had given to civil service reform, and argued that this trend should be encouraged so as to create an "expert" and "professional" government, which could operate without the direct supervision of businessmen, but which would function in the interest of "right-intentioned people and would look to them for its [the government's] essential direction," thus freeing the business community for other socially useful tasks.[11]

The importance of the National Municipal League attached to some sort of intervention of business organizations into politics derived both from a coherent critique of the social order and from the character and objectives of its membership. By 1904 the organizations that met the League's reform criterion included the boards of trade of twelve cities and the chambers of commerce or commercial clubs of fourteen other major cities, including Boston, Los Angeles, Dallas, and San Francisco.[12] These organizations were committed to political action for the attainment of their goals, which included social reform and antiliquor measures as well as the reorganization of governmental structures. In the words of the former president of the Pittsburgh Chamber of Commerce, H. D. W. English, their purpose was "suggesting remedies in civil matters which may effect commercial advance in a conservative and compassionate way without fear of criticism for doing so for partisanship advantage [*sic*]."[13] The League propounded as the "newest idea" in civil reform "the belief that if the administrative system can be perfected upon the basis of business economy, and properly safeguarded, it makes little difference which kind of men are elected."[14]

Yet all of this was but a means to an end which included "the welfare and regeneration of American cities."[15] The vagaries of popular politics placed an unacceptable limitation upon long-range prescriptions for business enterprise. Ordinary political authorities simply were "not capable of looking very far into the future and seeing benefits from money expended today which will come back, perhaps, to our children." For this reason political arrangements had to be subordinated to the objectives of the "men who are responsible for the substantial growth and progress of the city," a thought that had echoed through the business community from the time of William E. Dodge.[16]

At the League's 1897 annual meeting, Leo S. Rowe, a lecturer in municipal government at the University of Pennsylvania, endeavored to put the problem of political control for social change into a unified perspective. The source of America's instability was the conflict between "the *form* of city government and the *nature of city problems*."[17] Making the same distinction that had been made by the Sociological Group in the 1880s, Rowe argued that popular government could be sustained in the long run to the advantage of business enterprise if the political power to be obtained by business through the various city manager and commission forms of government recognized "the necessity of adapting individual conduct to such new [industrial] conditions" that business had created, and developed "a new concept of individual responsibility" to replace what had been forever lost. That responsibility and "the possibilities of organized action must be developed" or, Rowe concluded, "the marvelous increase in productive capacity during the century" would become a danger even as it was endangered.[18]

The source of danger to the productive capacity of society that Rowe saw lay in the demoralized middle class and in the general rise in incomes and the declining hours of work for the working class. As a result "leisure has become a reality to all classes." Thus, as Rowe saw it, industrialization and the accompanying proletarization of workers had created the potential for social collapse which only vigorous exercise of political power could remedy. Money and leisure, the material prerequisites for freedom, now supposed to be possessed by the laboring classes, coupled with a demoralized middle class, had created the "unfavorable environment [which] inevitably becomes the source of racial degeneracy and social disintegration," Rowe warned, and concluded that only the political control of leisure would safeguard the future of American industrial society.[19]

To achieve this end, Rowe urged the delegates at Louisville to undertake political action on the municipal level to create "a new *mode* of life, and with it a new *view* of life for the large mass of the community." Under these circumstances, parks and playgrounds, cheap urban transportation, and other recreational facilities had to be forged to replace "a monotonous succession of narrow and depressing throughfares . . . flaring signs . . . [and] saloon[s]."[20]

Saloons had long been recognized as the centers of working-class leisure activity; they were not condemned as the fruit of industrialization but rather as an obstacle to it. They, Rowe argued, should be replaced "through the ruralization of the city . . . the erection of imposing and inspiring buildings . . . a change in the immediate environment of the poorer classes, and finally, through the acceptance of the social standard in the performance of municipal services, a new conception of municipal activity, and with it of city life."[21]

The concern for the political control of the leisure activity of the masses was not a peripheral, academic concern. It was vital to the corporate community which viewed it as a requisite condition of continued economic growth.[22] As such it became a subject of permanent importance to the League.[23] In 1908, at the league's Pittsburgh convention, one business leader frankly admitted that it was no longer possible for a city to attract outside capital investments without a program of broad civic reform: "Allow the city to drift civicly [*sic*] upon the rocks and the commercial prosperity will soon follow [it there]."[24] Businessmen had discovered "that hundreds of thousands of dollars to equip modern mills must, to be a future success, carry with it [*sic*] other thousands of dollars for de-cent houses for working men to live in who can in turn give the full equivalent in healthy and effective service in these mills; that machinery that maims men and causes loss of time and extra expenses must be supplanted by protective machinery or it will prove a losing proposition commercially."[25]

The extent of the corporate business community's concern with the total social environment of the working class was revealed at the Pittsburgh conference. Robert W. DeForest, former tenement house commissioner of New York and vice-president of the New Jersey Central Railroad, told his audience that the Pittsburgh Survey, one of the most ambitious studies of urban social life ever attempted, had been undertaken "because to improve the social and living conditions of the working classes in our industrial cities we must first know accurately what and why they are as we find them." Pittsburgh had been chosen, he explained, because, as the home of the Carnegie Steel Works, it "was the typical industrial American city."[26] DeForest said that the undertaking's success was possible only because of an extraordinary degree of cooperation on the part of investigators, city officials, the Chamber of Commerce, and the Russell Sage Foundation, of which he was the head.

Working-class productivity underlay the concern for reform of Pittsburgh's city fathers and the Sage Foundation. But it was, as H. D. W. English put it, up to "the organizing genius of America [which] sets this polyglot mass to work, producing wealth which in magnitude, stands matchless in the history of the world . . . to champion this man." Raise him from "his dirt and beer," and "the reaction will be felt in the life of this thriving industrial center."[27]

Raising the working classes from dirt and beer for the sake of continued industrial expansion involved considerably more effort than simply altering the physical circumstances of their existence, important as these were. Equally important to the League was the need to alter workers' habits. Hence the concept of social control by business organizations through municipal agencies extending their dominion over all of workers' mundane affairs. But, of those affairs, the newly found "leisure" that modern industrialism had made possible, was the major concern to the League and the interests it represented. In 1904, Delos F. Wilcox, a business consultant for public utilities whose criticism of the League's model charter program had been incorporated into its final report on the subject, published his second book-length study of the American city problem in which he identified the use of leisure time as the principal obstacle to the continuation of industrial development and middle-class political institutions. In developing his analysis Wilcox cited the saloon's major role in shaping the leisure habits of the working class. And it was the working class, Wilcox argued, that was the key to the success or failure of American political and economic institutions.[28]

The impact of industrialization on the working class had created social dislocations that were clearly reflected in municipal politics. Here, according to Wilcox, only the working class maintained an active interest, but the conditions of labor had had a demoralizing impact on workers as evidenced by their insistence upon introducing what Wilcox saw as extraneous national issues into urban affairs.[29] Wilcox related this demoralization to the division of labor that had removed workers from control of the instruments of production. The result was "to make machines of men, to diminish their ethical responsibility, [and] to set up a fixed and artificial reward for labor without reference to its real social value." Wilcox called for "corporate action on the part of employers" to halt the continued alienation of workers, a phenomenon which he viewed as potentially "fatal to democracy and the future development of the race."[30] Wilcox believed that this sort of action by employers would enhance the "development of social capacity and ethical responsibility in groups . . . by dint of working together in industrial pursuits men may acquire a greater capacity for political cooperation."[31]

Against this background of concern for corporate action by employers to obtain the political cooperation of workers, Wilcox took up the implications of working-class leisure activities. Industrialization had shortened the hours of labor and thereby increased the amount of leisure time available to the working class, while at the same time it had altered the conditions of labor so that work no longer played a significant role in the formation of social character, and had become "a natural preparation for dissipation during long hours of leisure." Hence Wilcox saw "the right use of leisure" as crucial to character formation and the success or failure of American society, which he uncritically linked to the continuation of the very process of industrialization to which he had attributed the problems of modern life.[32]

Wilcox singled out "licentiousness, gambling and intemperance" as the major threats to proper character formation. Of these, intemperance was "the close ally of the other vices [and] a positive menace to social order." Wilcox's analysis of the saloon relied solely upon the work of the Committee of Fifty. As an occasion of intemperance the saloon was an institution that "defied law, create[d] anarchy, and destro[ied] reason." On the other hand, as the Caulkins report had shown, the saloon also provided "an immense service as a social center" that would enable it to survive the political attacks of its opponents "until some other means are devised to take its place."[33]

As did the Committee of Fifty, Wilcox ruled out "Puritanic legislation" as an effective method for dealing with the saloon, which he characterized as an un-American social institution responsible for "criminal collusion between the chosen representatives of the people and the powers that prey upon the people."[34] What was needed in this situation, the National Municipal League's theoretician concluded, was the enlargement of the scope of political controls "for the discouragement of vice and the direction of the uses of the people's leisure into channels consistent with and conducive to the welfare of democracy."[35]

In the remainder of this essay—by far the most extensive in his book—Wilcox discussed the forms this extension of political controls should take. These ranged from the establishment of parks to the staging of "municipal ceremonials." All these could avert "the apparently vicious tendencies of the majority of the people in cities like New York and Philadelphia, as evidenced by the frequent votes of confidence given to political organizations known to thrive upon the protection of crime and the encouragement of vice."[36] In other words, Wilcox's prescription for reform was the institutionalization of "substitutes for the Saloon."

Any analysis of Wilcox's thought will reveal its conservative intent. Although he pinpointed industrialization in its many ramifications as being responsible for the social discontent he saw about him, Wilcox called only for the enlargement of corporate effort on the part of employers and the expansion of political patterns of employer-employee cooperation in work and politics, where they had given way to patterns of social conflict. Wilcox's analysis supposed that the working class, because it suffered in obvious ways from the division of labor and the exigencies of business enterprise, had actually become dehumanized and incapable of self-government, which he described as cooperation between social classes that he himself perceived as having long ceased having any grounds for cooperation.

The National Municipal League and other progressive reformers did not seek genuine social harmony, but rather the continuation of industrial development characterized by distinct social classes. They recognized that industrialization had loosened traditional restraints on workers, and supposed that it had provided them with material increases in both leisure and money, the use of which the reformers sought to subject to political authority that would create new sanctions for their use. In the long run the objective sought by this reform was the formation of a working class whose "play spirit" and "pleasure instinct" along with its "social instinct" would be curbed and channeled by political authority in order to produce the habits of sobriety, abstemiousness, and obedience to authority that the temperance reform had always sought but had failed to attain.[37]

The saloon, both as an expression and as a determinant of working class conduct, became the focal point of a renewed effort of repression during the years before World War I. The supposed vice of drinking was secondary to the saloon's larger social role. Progressive reformers, upon close investigation of the saloons, professed to be astonished to find in industrial districts that there was only a "relatively small amount of drunkenness."[38] Looming larger in the total picture, however, was the fact that "the working man's club" permitted full and free expression of political opinion: "The names of Karl Marx and leaders of social and political thought," observed one investigator, "are often heard here." As such the saloon had become their "school for good and evil."[39] Indeed, as the Committee of Fifty discovered, the saloon enjoyed a virtual monopoly on the leisure time of the urban working class, and provided it with an extraordinary number of services, ranging from toilet facilities to labor exchange information.[40]

In this larger context, then, the saloon was judged disruptive to American political and economic life. Not only was it a haven for petty political officials and the focal point for the organization of the "vicious element" within society, but it created a climate of opinion and attitude of mind inimical to industrial harmony. Finally, it served as a counterweight to the need for political loyalty, a need which found expression in the reformers' efforts to inculcate civic pride in the masses through public education, while, at the same time, they set out to devise alternative structures of political power to permit business organizations to direct the evolution of industrial society.

The attention given to liquor control by business reform associations was logical and inevitable given the need to create a political order conducive to large scale industrialization. As designed by the National Municipal League's affiliates, liquor control was intended to satisfy two needs. On the one hand, the political reforms sought to establish "prohibition *in fact* [and] not only in name."[41] On the other hand it sought to unify divided temperance forces under the movement's traditional leadership: "Especially [the movement] needs the leadership of men with the brains and organizing power which give success to the great commercial and industrial enterprises of our time."[42] To achieve these ends, the Committee of Fifty had called for a program that would utilize the social power of a variety of agencies in cooperation with the state. In the words of John Koren (who was raised to the level of the antisaloon movement's theoretician by the National Municipal League), the hope of the temperance cause lay "in efforts for gradual betterment through ethical forces and general enlightenment plus progressive restriction."[43]

The origins of this antisaloon approach did not, in fact, spring entirely from the deliberations of the Committee of Fifty, nor was its implementation nationally effected by the National Municipal League as such. Rather, enterprising businessmen acting independently of both and largely, of each other, were the source of the urban antiliquor movement. A case in point was the development of the "Minneapolis Plan" for liquor control.[44]

At the second meeting of the League, D.F. Simpson, Minneapolis's city attorney, described the successful plan, which by then had been in effect for some ten years. City government had to be controlled "from day to day and year to year" by good citizens, whose first obligation lay in establishing conditions necessary to that end. Simpson maintained that it was crucial to circumscribe the city's saloons by proscribing their operation "outside the prinicipal business districts of the city." By confining saloons to the business district Minneapolis authorities had successfully excluded them from "practically the entire residential portion of the city and many manufacturing and business centers." This step had been taken in candid recognition that the city's saloons were "the total political center for people whose homes are in the vicinity and who make the saloon their evening loafing place." Such progressive restrictions were necessary, Simpson concluded, because of the "necessity of municipal elections being controlled by men who desire good government [and] such men must take steps to place and keep themselves in control . . . [because] no one else will do it for them."[45]

In the case of Minneapolis, the drive to restrict saloons had been led by the Pillsbury family, who were to flour processing what Carnegie and Havemeyer were to steel and sugar. Led by George A. Pillsbury, who at the time was serving as president of the city council, "all businessmen, and church and temperance people" supported the reform party's antisaloon platform in the municipal elections of 1884. Pillsbury and the city's business community had become aroused by the attraction of the saloon for transient harvesters and laborers who were said to comprise a large part of the "element of disorder" confronting the city. After his election, Pillsbury announced the details of his plan, which involved a transfer of powers from the city council to the office of mayor—a transfer effected by the city attorney, who was Pillsbury's nephew. Opposition from the saloon owners and "ward Republicans" was overcome with the support of Democratic businessmen, prohibitionists, and Roman Catholic Archbishop John Ireland, who later helped found the national Anti-Saloon League in 1895.[46]

To a considerable extent the success of Pillsbury's reform drive in Minneapolis was due to the family's extraordinary political power, not only in the city but in the state. Prior to 1884 the senior Pillsbury, Charles, had been governor. At the time of the 1884 municipal elections another Pillsbury was a U.S. Senator.[47] Such concentrated power over local and state conditions was not, however, the rule, and this fact probably explains the general difficulties that progressive reform programs experienced in this area: Nashville and, to a lesser extent, Chicago were among the "few cities" to implement this model of reform.[48]

The Minneapolis plan also failed to incorporate the wider spectrum of such controlling agencies as the churches and settlement houses into its program. In the presence of Pillsbury's power there was little need for them and there is no evidence that the business and church reformers recognized a positive role for them at the time. However, it is highly unlikely that such ancillary groups were prepared to play the role assigned to them by the Committee of Fifty. This was the conclusion reached by the committee's investigators after their study of conditions in Chicago.[49] Poor business management, lack of adequate financing, and—particularly in the case of church-sponsored activities—the obvious intrusion of ulterior motives had combined to defeat efforts to curtail the attractiveness and influence of the saloon. Above all, the investigators discovered that there was, as yet, no concerted well-directed effort by the community toward this end, and "the business portion has practically none."[50]

In one way or another this reform movement, which swept the nation before World War I, failed to meet the expectations of reformers like Jacob Riis, who anticipated a system of "rational controls."[51] Still, it remained the conviction of urban reformers and businessmen alike that such reform was not only necessary but feasible. So argued *Harper's Weekly* as it observed that the revived temperance drive was evidence enough that the "proper kind of legislation must vary" and that local political authorities must (and did) accept responsibility for "the weak and erring."[52] Such conservative hopes were raised considerably when New Hampshire and Vermont abandoned statutory prohibition for local option and high license fees.[53]

By 1908, when the National Municipal League formally committed itself to eliminating the liquor problem, the development of this reform appeared to have undergone sufficient "experimentation" for its advocates to realize that what was basically required for the success of liquor control was a means of conferring the political power to limit and regulate saloons directly upon local municipal authorities.[54] At the League's 1908 meeting delegates heard a professor of city government, the head of the Toronto Board of Liquor Control, the director of New York City's temperance forces, the chairman of the New Jersey Excise Board, and others discuss the problem of liquor control.[55] Raymond Augustus Hatton, who delivered the principal paper on the subject, argued that the developments of recent years had made it clear that the problem of liquor control was basically municipal: "Any solution which is offered must be based largely on urban conditions."[56] Hatton's colleagues agreed with this principle, although they differed on the question of appropriate means.

Underlying the insistence that liquor was fundamentally a municipal problem was the traditional aim of progressives to free the cities from their political entanglements with state legislatures, as well as the older temperance position that reform was best handled by local property interests. Reverend John P. Peters described the problem of New York City as one that involved the unwillingness of the state to surrender its prerogatives because "the liquor tax provided by the law is extremely profitable to the state and the greater part of these profits are [*sic*] derived from the cities." On the other hand, most states left enforcement in the hands of local authorities who, in turn, were sympathetic to local opinion: "It is for this reason that grand juries in New York City will not indict offenders against the law."[57]

More important than the problem of who should administer the law was that of what sort of law should be administered. The National Municipal League officially supported local option in combination with regulatory legislation designed to suppress the activity of saloons in those districts that would not support local prohibition. Statewide prohibition was anathema to the League as the sort of sweeping legislation that required too much popular support to sustain.[58] To deal with the problem of legislation Hatton told the Pittsburgh Convention that the League had authorized a national investigation of "the great variety in the methods dealing with the liquor traffic."[59] This decision led to the formation in 1908 of the League's standing committee on the liquor problem.[60]

Between the years 1913 and 1916, the widespread success of local option drives accentuated the problems of controlling liquor consumption within the nation's municipal jurisdictions. During that time the League and municipal authorities sought to implement controls that would limit liquor drinking without leading to defiance of the laws.[61] These efforts were largely failures, so much so that the League's expert, John Koren, who bitterly opposed prohibition because it would not, he asserted, "stem the unquenchable desire for stimulants," was forced to admit at the League's annual meeting in 1913 that "I believe that conditions are not only as bad as I have talked of, but really worse."[62] At the same convention, Cornelius G. Kidder, chairman of the League's Alcohol Committee, acknowledged that the group "has not gone far" in its efforts to advance the work of the Committee of Fifty. During the years since its inception, Kidder said, the problem of liquor control had been considered by the League "solely as an economic question and partly as a political one." But it could not answer authoritatively the one concern that had guided its work: "what authority should directly control the issue of licenses?"[63]

To some extent, a general solution to this problem was precluded by the Committee's basic conclusion, forced upon it by the bewildering events of the preceding fifteen years: "*The essential thing is to have authorities of the right caliber and trusted character.*"[64] This conclusion placed the liquor problem in the area of direct and continuing political control regardless of the scope of legislation involved. In turn, this sort of control required the kind of political intervention that urban corporate business communities had sought to avoid. In short, by 1914 the political reform envisioned for almost two decades by metropolitan capital had failed: liquor control, felt to be more necessary than ever before, was more remote than it had ever been. Convincing proofs of failure, wrote John Koren, "are the ominous figures of production and consumption of liquor . . . [which] of recent years have shown an unmistakable steady upward trend."[65]

Any explanation of the failure of the corporate community to achieve its goals of political temperance before 1914, despite widespread enthusiasm among its own ranks for that goal as well as the enthusiasm generated for liquor control among the middle classes, should look to the inherent limitations in the program of so powerful a social class. In the progressive scheme of reform it was assumed that liquor drinking "is essentially one of the social problems of labor, for the reason that the working people suffer more from the evil consequences . . . than any other class."[66] The two-fold ideological basis for this assumption was solely economic and partly political, as pointed out by Cornelius Kidder in 1913. The corporate community attacked the Prohibition party's analysis of the liquor traffic, which had persuaded a significant portion of the middle classes that the long-term goals of American society were out of harmony with the needs of its people, by asserting that the liquor problem was merely a class problem.

This problem was to be solved by the mobilization of other middle-class institutions to regulate and control what was considered to be, *because it was a class problem*, a problem requiring an indefinite yet flexible supervision by established authorities.[67] Such an interpretation required the cultivation of a new attitude of devotion to political order on the part of all social classes.[68] This order, expanded and coordinated by the larger goal of industrialization, and which political authorities would implement, was supposed to transform the working class from inefficient work habits and intemperate social and political attitudes by constant supervision and indirect control of all of its activities. But, in fact, this transformation proved to be beyond the means of the various civic and church agencies assigned these tasks in antisaloon strategy. The liquor problem, like industrialization itself, transcended the urban environment that had dictated the assumptions of the corporate community's antisaloon strategists. Nevertheless, industrial corporations themselves became involved in developing antiliquor industrial programs based upon similar premises. Eventually, however, persuaded that the liquor problem was a class problem, and that prohibition in fact could not be achieved at the political levels traditionally employed by expansionist capital, the reform was redirected towards a national political solution.

8

Antisaloonism and Industrial Development, 1890–1915

Conservative advocates of antisaloon liquor reform sought a social environment compatible with industrial expansion, which they described as the inevitable outcome of social evolution. Such expansion, they believed, would be characterized by ever greater concentrations of capital and labor in the nation's major urban centers. Indeed, it was this expectation that underlay their hopes for the eventual success of their reform movement—itself considered somewhat contradictorily to be both a necessary precondition for and an inevitable consequence of the world they described. As early as 1891 economist Simon Patton predicted the very nature of industrialization would compel a total ban on alcoholic beverages. Similarly, Henry W. Farnam recalled that for the Committee of Fifty, "there seemed reason to believe at that time that there were strong economic forces at work for moderation . . . so that there was reason to hope that natural forces would work out towards some kind of [prohibitionist] solution."[1]

Such assumptions guided both the Committee of Fifty and businessmen like Charles Francis Adams. They biased the committee's investigations and recommendations. Convinced a priori that labor conditions would be determined by the nation's largest employers, reformers were confident of antisaloonism's capacity to supplement business's ability to produce "the sober industrious working man."[2] Thus when Wright's labor bureau undertook to investigate employee drinking restrictions, it solicited information from "large employers of labor" only, and thereby ignored the much broader picture of the American economy.[3] Wright's interpretation of this evidence was also marred by his expectations. The bureau's report ignored the fact that 79 percent of the employers queried did not respond, and that of the 7,000 who did, 1,600 reported that they did "not take the liquor habit into consideration" as a condition of employment.[4] The report also failed to consider that the majority of responding employers were unable to evaluate the effectiveness of their efforts to curtail drinking.[5] Instead of pondering these sobering realities, the bureau took heart from the fact that its small percentage of respondents included railroad corporations like the New York Central and Hudson River and Boston and Maine, or industrial concerns like the Colorado Fuel and Iron Company and Carnegie Steel.[6] Such confidence colored Wright's own judgments about the proper course for liquor reform: modern industrial conditions, he wrote, would themselves inhibit working-class drinking, and reformers should encourage this tendency by establishing supplemental agencies to assist large corporations.[7]

As time would tell, the optimism of the antisaloon reformers was unwarranted. Industrial capitalism continued to be plagued by labor problems that eventually bankrupted antisaloonist programs. In explaining his conversion to national prohibition, Henry Farnam admitted "the optimism of my report was not justified"; per capita consumption of alcoholic beverages increased relentlessly in the midst of flourishing antisaloon work.[8] It was the failure of these programs to produce a stable, productive and liquor-free work force that led to the resurgence of prohibitionist sentiment.[9]

Corporate antisaloon programs emanated from the desire to increase production so as to increase profits. Capitalist production imposed on society what amounted to a binding law, according to Carroll D. Wright. Wright told the United States Industrial Commission in 1901 that it was "thoroughly understood . . . that it requires more capital to produce a given quantity of a product than formerly; that the margin of profit decreases; that the quantity increases, and wage earnings increase." Hence markets had to expand to guarantee profits.[10] In order to minimize the impact of labor costs on profits ever larger capital expenditures on plant and equipment were required. In turn, sophisticated machinery required ever more reliable workers. Here lay the grinding reality beneath the drive to establish a liquor-free social order. Here, too, lay the shoals upon which antisaloon programs eventually foundered, for corporate business proved incapable of holding or training its work force in the face of fluctuating demands for labor.

The railroads were among the first industrial corporations to experience the full burden of capitalist development, and as such formulated programs to deal with labor problems which became prototypes for industry generally.[11] In the decades after the Civil War the railroads, obedient to Wright's law, relentlessly expanded their operations, even in the midst of depression years, for as Charles E. Perkins put it, if they did not, "some other road may work out that way."[12] Expansion compounded the roads' problems.[13] Throughout the last years of the nineteenth century the number of men available for work on the railroads declined steadily, and only increased production could offset the unremitting increase in labor costs.[14] Yet as the steady rise in the number of fatalities and accidents revealed, the work force was not up to the task. By 1900 wages constituted 60 percent of all railroad operating costs, while in the same year almost 60,000 people suffered death or injury from the roads' operations.[15]

While each railroad ultimately had to deal with these problems as it saw best, a general approach, nevertheless, was worked out, emphasizing the need to retain men in service and increase their productive output. At its core, the railroads' programs incorporated a basic tenet of antisaloonism: a productive work force had to be sober and abstemious. The seriousness with which railroads pursued temperance can be judged from the number of dismissals from the service of the giant Burlington system, headed by Perkins. Between 1877 and 1892, the Burlington dismissed over twenty-three hundred men for using liquor. The percentage of employees involved—nearly thirty—was nearly twice as great as for any other single cause of dismissal. In addition, the company sought to blacklist its former employees and prevent them from working for other railroads.[16]

Perkins was adamant about the enforcement of the no-liquor rule, and vigorously opposed the efforts of lower-level management to obtain a more flexible enforcement policy.[17] Similarly, James C. Clark, president of the Illinois Central, informed his superintendents that while it was "not in the interest of the company to overtax the physical abilities of its employees," and that they had a right to "fair and even-handed justice," nevertheless, "every master mechanic shall be responsible if he keeps an engineer in service who drinks liquor on duty or is a drunkard or rowdy off duty."[18] In a similar vein, Alexander Hogg told delegates to the International Congress of Educators in 1885 that his road, the Missouri-Pacific system, was following the long-standing custom of the Baltimore & Ohio in prohibiting the use of intoxicating drink by employees both on and off duty. Another temperance measure that Hogg advocated was the practice of granting free transportation to temperance lecturers throughout Texas "to wage a ceaseless war against intemperance."[19]

The antidrink policy of the railroad companies became universal when the recommendations of the Committee on Uniform Train Rules and Telegraphic Orders were adopted as the standard code by the General Time Convention in 1887. The new general regulations called for the dismissal of intoxicated employees, banned the use of intoxicants on the road or around railroad property, and called for the promotion decisions to consider employees' temperance habits.[20] Formal declarations against drinking, however, could not eliminate the probem, since the ultimate sanction of dismissal ignored the pressing problem of the shortage of labor at a time when conditions of operation required increased skill and endurance from all workers.

The problem of upgrading the supply of labor was taken up by the American Society of Railroad Superintendents in October 1895. The society's Committee on Relations of Railroads with Their Employees stressed the need to conserve the existing labor force by providing employees with experience in many grades of railroad employment, in the course of which "the unfit or unworthy" would drop out. Promotions should be made on the basis of merit and not mere seniority. Discipline should be a "humane practice" aimed at education and correction, and dismissal should follow only in "cases of accumulated misdeeds, or in well-proven cases of drunkenness, gambling, [and] lying." The committee also urged railroads to develop liaisons with other antisaloon agencies like the YMCA's: "There can be no question as to their refining influence upon the men, who by their existence are deprived of plausible excuse to seek recreation at saloons."[21] Two years later, the committee on employer-employee relations urged the society to adopt the "Brown System" of discipline because it promised "the steady employment of regular men, consequently a greater percentage of experienced men," and created "a greater feeling of contentment" that supposedly led to the domestication of workers.[22]

The railroads' drive to increase the system's productivity by expanding its operations and improving the quality of its labor force had little effect on actual labor standards, as the rising accident rate indicated. In their analysis of this continuing problem railroad leaders placed increasing emphasis on the personal defects of their employees. At a meeting of the Central Association of Railroad Officers, Dr. J. H. Ford, surgeon of the C.C.C. and St. Louis Railway, argued circuitously that accidents were inherent in railroad operations because, despite all precautions, accidents in fact did occur. Hence they must be "charged up to the personal equation—some defect in some operator."[23]

Anticipating this line of analysis, a leading railroad journal, *Railway Age*, earlier had demanded active measures that echoed the recommendation of the Committee of Fifty: combat employee drinking with substitutes for the saloon. Only then would an era of higher labor standards and railroad prosperity begin. Progress, the editorial acknowledged, was possible and "the movement against the saloon is one of the most hopeful and laudable undertakings of American railway management."[24]

Typical of the railroads' efforts to upgrade and retain their labor force was the announcement by the Pittsburgh Bessemer and Lake Erie Railroad in August 1898 that employees would no longer be suspended for infractions of company policy. Instead, the company announced that it had instituted a merit and demerit system to evaluate worker efficiency and loyalty which, it was hoped, would result in an increase of both, enabling the company "thereby [to] secure better service." The only exceptions to the merit-grading system were drunkenness, either on or off duty, "frequenting saloons or other places of low resort," and other "serious offenses" like insubordination, dishonesty, and incompetency.[25] But whatever favorable publicity such programs received, they merely aggravated the basic problems of a shortage of reliable labor and a high turnover rate. A more comprehensive solution was needed and, by the turn of the century, the nation's largest roads were committed to the one that antisaloonist welfare programs seemed to offer.

In an effort to determine what measures would improve labor standards on the nation's leading railroads, the U.S. Industrial Commission issued a questionnaire to the sixty-two corporations that controlled 146,005 of the country's 189,249 miles of railroad. The commissioners received replies from thirty-eight of those companies which, themselves, controlled more than 100,000 miles of track.[26] All these roads had instituted some form of welfare program and had taken steps to reduce dismissals. Railroad executive A. B. Stickney explained that the older practices were harmful to the companies as they lost men who frequently did not know company rules. Stickney concluded that a "system of discipline, therefore, which will measure more accurately the degree of fidelity or incompetency which enters into every act of an employee is the only system scientifically justified." The system that approximated Stickney's ideal was the Brown System, which, he believed, offered three advantages: reducing the number of dismissals, enabling companies to undertake long-range evaluations of workers' performance, and reducing the number of days lost because of suspension.[27] In short, it kept more men on the job longer.

The need to keep more men on the job longer stemmed from conditions within the industry. In the decade of the 1890s the railroads expanded operations despite or even because of periods of depression. By 1898 the country's total track mileage had grown by 12 percent.[28] During the same period the average load hauled by each freight train locomotive in service increased by 25.6 percent. At the same time the number of ton-miles completed by each locomotive rose 27.3 percent from four to 5.5 million, while the average freight car carried a 24.7 percent greater load than it had at the beginning of the decade.[29]

Such productive gains, however, were not without their costs. At the end of the decade of increasing traffic, fewer than half of the cars in service were equipped with train brakes operated from the locomotive cab. Fewer than two-thirds had automatic coupling devices.[30] These inconsistencies were reflected in the annual toll of death and injury that plagued operations. While even here it was possible to measure gains of some sort, the railroads' increasing need for reliable, quality labor made such seem illusory at best. For example, in 1890 just over 2,400 employees were killed and more than 22,000 injured. By the end of the decade the figures, respectively, were 2,675 and 41,142. Given the industry's growth, some progress could be measured: one death per 67 miles of track operated in 1890 against one death for every 71 miles in 1900. The difference represents a gain of 5.7 percent, far lower than those logged in the productivity of other areas of capital investments. Similarly, the railroads were able to reduce all operations-connected injuries by only 6.3 percent over the course of the decade.[31]

In the all-important class of trainmen, death and injury figures were even more discouraging. In 1888 the railroads reported one death for every 117 such workers, with one in 12 injured. By 1901 the figures stood at one death for every 136 employed (a gain of 14 percent over 1888, but a drop of 17.6 percent from 1897), and one in 13 injured.[32]

The response of railroad management to these conditions had been to try to stabilize and upgrade its working force, particularly the "floating element," which was held responsible for the railroad's high cost of production. Managers realized that merely proscribing drinking was not a realistic solution to their problems, as they could ill afford to lose their limited supply of labor by dismissing drinkers.[33] In an attempt to reorient their labor policies, the American Society of Railroad Superintendents' subcommittee on discipline recommended in 1897 that discipline be confined to "education, government, [and] instruction, and conveys no suggestion of punishment."[34] Nevertheless, top railroad management continued to resist pressure to relax their antiliquor regulations, even as they sought other means to induce habits of thrift and sobriety.[35] As a policy document of the Chicago, Milwaukee, and St. Paul Railroad put it, "the use of intoxicating drinks has proven a most fruitful source of trouble to railways as well as to individuals, and the company will exercise the most rigid scrutiny in reference to the habits of employees in this respect. . . . Drinking when on duty, or frequenting saloons, will not be tolerated, and preference will be given to those who do not drink at all."[36]

The work of the railroads formulating a comprehensive solution to their problem, including drink control, inspired the alternative to third-party prohibition devised by the Committee of Fifty.[37] Wrote one committee member: "It is gratifying to learn that three hundred and seventy-seven [railroad] companies prohibit the use of intoxicating liquors on the roads under their control. . . . It is only a few years since any road first placed restrictions upon the men employed with reference to intoxicants . . . and these roads are the most influential ones, employing a very large proportion of all railway employees in this country."[38] Yet another indication of the new approach to drink control was the widespread passage of special labor legislation in the states and territories during the last years of the nineteenth and the early years of the twentieth century, imposing drink restrictions on a variety of occupations.[39]

In the long run, the success of welfare programs that incorporated drink reform measures depended upon the ability of large employers to stabilize the labor force and thus create conditions which were supposed of themselves to compel compliance. But this program was liable to become self-defeating because its basic aim was to increase levels of labor productivity, the increment of which could aggravate the cost of labor by increasing mobility as wages rose irregularly. This development tended to give labor as a class greater autonomy in relation to the economic power of employers, which undermined the entire project of labor reform. Furthermore, the success of welfare programs depended upon the capacity of capitalist productive units to generate sufficient surplus of capital to pay for reform.[40] Since either approach was contingent upon actually raising employee efficiency and thereby lowering costs, welfare itself was involved in the same dilemma. In the first decade of the new century these problems matured and became institutionalized in the nation's economic system. The inherent need to prevent drinking as a means of stabilizing the labor force became explicit, and was presented to the public as a solution basic to the nation's labor problems.

Railroads were not the only industrial organizations to move to eradicate the drinking habits of employees in the latter years of the nineteenth century. The Commissioner of Labor's study of the "Economic Aspects of the Liquor Problem" revealed that more than 5,300 of its 7,000 respondents did inquire into the drinking habits of prospective employees.[41] In addition some 3,500 establishments in agriculture, manufacturing, mining, trade and transportation proscribed the use of intoxicants by employees to some degree.[42] The reasons for restricting the use of liquor revealed a common concern for inefficient work and irregularity of attendance which liquor drinking was alleged to induce.[43]

Employer concern for the irregularity, inefficiency, and instability associated with employee drinking was also brought out in testimony before the U. S. Industrial Commission. C. R. Mary, the superintendent of the Raub Coal Company in Luzerne, Pennsylvania, told the commissioners that "it is generally pretty hard to get [our workers] to work the next day or two after payday . . . we have not been able to operate the mines—call it drunkenness or sickness, they were not there—presumably it was drunkenness."[44] D. C. Beamon of the Colorado Fuel and Iron Company told the commission that his company made only monthly paydays, and then paid in scrip, to mitigate the impact of the saloon. "It is within the knowledge of all," he said, "and cannot be denied that 'payday' at coal mines and in some other occupations means 1, 2, or 3 days of idleness and often that many days of dissipation." Beamon believed that "if the state legislature would prohibit sales [of intoxicants] at or near the mines, it would do more to promote the general welfare of the mines than any other law that could be enacted."[45]

On the other hand, the commission heard testimony giving qualified support to antisaloonist assumptions. For example, a large investor in mining and smelting reinforced the notion that alternative institutions could serve to mitigate and eventually eradicate the saloon. A. Hanauer of Salt Lake City believed that the labor conditions in the mining industry had gradually improved because miners were no longer spending so much of their earnings on whiskey or gambling. Libraries and other places of recreation and enjoyment had replaced the saloon, he testified, and the education of workers' children with those of bankers and lawyers had been beneficial as well. Hanauer testified that the mining companies themselves contributed to the support of schools, both through taxes and direct contributions. Hanauer was less optimistic than Beamon, however, about the efficacy of removing "grogshops" from the vicinity of the mines. If the saloons were anywhere within traveling distance, he was sure the miners would eventually get there.[46]

Hanauer's position was supported by Gower Thomas, a mine inspector for the State of Utah who formerly had been a contractor for the Gross Creek Coal Company. Thomas testified to a general improvement in the Utah miners' condition over the past twenty years. Home owning and marriage, he thought, were especially important in restricting the use of liquor, as these encouraged saving money, orderly conduct, and better citizenship. Like Hanauer, Thomas also credited the schooling of miners' children with those of merchants, bankers, and industrialists with having a favorable effect on the attitudes and habits of workers.[47]

This and similar testimony led the Commission to acknowledge that intemperance was "one of the greatest curses of the working people," and was aggravated by "poor pay, long hours, and unsanitary and uncomfortable conditions." The Commission referred to the testimony of a Boston settlement worker "that the drinking habit results largely from the weakening influence to which the poorer classes are subjected while they are children," but failed to comment about a common concern expressed by mine operators during the turbulent transition of American society—the problem of law and order.[48] Idaho had closed the saloons in the Coeur d'Alenes during the great strikes of 1898 because "men who have had any experience in the affairs of the work know that crimes of this character [i.e., strikes] are frequently hatched in the saloons." It was in the saloons, he testified, that the "criminal element" in the unions operated.[49]

Nevertheless, the Industrial Commission's report revealed a developed industrial consensus, which held that the liquor problem's solution hinged upon the formation of a liquor free environment for the working class, comprehending every aspect of its existence. The investigations of Wright's Labor Bureau also established the seriousness employers believed the effects of liquor had on the productivity of labor. It was almost universally held that men who drank were irregular and inefficient workers and constituted the principal cause of industrial accidents.[50] This assessment of the nature and importance of the liquor problem led America's industrialists to develop strict disciplinary rules governing the drinking of their employees. A more potent solution lay in creating a liquor free physical and social environment to increase labor productivity that would use all instruments of property to resolve the problem.

The effort of large industrial firms to curb employee drinking was not the result of their gaining greater mastery over their economic environment; rather, as in the case of the railroads, it was because they found it difficult to survive. The efficiency of production that was generally attributed to the large corporations did not, in fact, exist.[51] Many of the largest industrial combinations found survival most difficult, and it was these that generally sought to establish the most restrictive measures over the environments of their employees. Afer 1900 these measures became institutionalized in the spread of industrial welfare programs and safety campaigns. Here national leadership was supplied by the largest corporations.[52]

In 1904 the National Civic Federation, whose raison d'etre was to smooth the political waters for the nation's industrial giants, established a welfare department. It was headed by H. H. Vreeland, president of the New York City Railway Company; Cyrus H. McCormick, a partner in the flagging International Harvester Corporation; John H. Patterson, head of the National Cash Register Company; and Edward A. Filene, a Boston department store tycoon.[53] The purpose of the new department, to which only employers could belong, was to publicize the "moral obligation to give consideration to the general welfare of their employees."[54] Exactly what was the general welfare was made explicit during the federation's conference proceedings. The head of the Plymouth Cordage Company's welfare department stressed the need of employers to supervise unobtrusively all the activities of their employees so as to upgrade the quality of the labor supply.

The Plymouth Cordage Company had been one of the respondents to the Labor Bureau's investigation of the liquor problem, and reported that it prohibited the use of intoxicants by its employees whether on or off duty.[55] The company began its welfare program in 1899, because "after all, one's environment has a great deal to do with one's character," as W. E. C. Nizro explained to his audience that his company had instituted its sanitary program in its mills so that "the employees took home with them the lessons we were endeavoring to teach."[56]

Employee leisure time activities were of great concern to the company, which built a library and a combined luncheon and social hall to provide a focus for its welfare work. The program developed those industrial and domestic skills that management believed most useful. The cooking school, for instance, stressed financial economy and the importance of good nutrition "to build up the tissues of the body and brain."[57] Finally, the company's welfare department sponsored uncomplicated but time-consuming recreational activities.

Louis Krumbhaar of the Solvay Process Company had one difficulty that Plymouth Cordage did not have. Located in a large eastern city, his welfare program had little effect on the leisure activities of his 2,400 employees. Of the many efforts to institute an effective program, "the most satisfactory one of all [was] that of taking the children of our workingmen and training them."[58] But Krumbhaar's program contained an additional antidrinking lever that would be exploited by employers trying to curtail this working-class habit: a system of accident and sickness benefits. The Solvay benefit program was the one that would eventually characterize American industry in the Progressive years, and the company used it as a substitute for dismissal for drinking. "Any member whose disability is occasioned by the use of intoxicating liquors waives his rights to benefits, and one who . . . becomes intoxicated while on the sick list, is liable to suspension from the society."[59]

Such examples of the efforts of industrial corporations to eliminate drinking and upgrade the quality of the labor supply can be duplicated indefinitely. H. H. Vreeland spoke enthusiastically at the conference of the progress welfare work had made since the days of his employment as a brakeman: "There was absolutely no place for me in the evening when it was warm except the saloon and pool room," he recounted, but the introduction of the YMCA by the railroads had altered that situation.[60] Vreeland and his colleagues were looking toward the future, however, and the direction their efforts took was mute testimony to the failure of welfare to stabilize the labor situation and curtail drinking. At the first Welfare conference the YMCA's representative received considerable criticism for his agency's failure "to reach the men." Nevertheless, company officials acknowledged the "Y's" partial success with "our clerks and foremen and higher grade[s] of mechanics." Yet failure with ordinary workers remained uppermost in their minds.[61] The consensus developed at the conference was that, heretofore, welfare efforts had centered too much on employees themselves. Industrial conditions required that now "all our efforts should be bent to getting the best work out of our employees, and we believed that this can best be promoted by enlisting not only the personal interest of the individual employee, but the interest of his family as well."[62]

The conditions that had first developed in the railroads' operations were now beginning to characterize the economy in general, and the working force was feared to be more and more unsuited to its task. In the iron and steel industry, for example, labor costs had risen steadily since 1900. Between 1901 and 1910 the hourly wages of unskilled labor increased by more than 17 percent.[63] Moreover, the burden of this increase was borne by the industry's large producers.[64] In 1902 U.S. Steel Corporation reported earnings of more than five million dollars. It paid 21.2 percent of its gross income in wages and salaries, and another 51.1 percent was consumed by other manufacturing and operating expenses. The corporation's labor costs climbed to a high of 26.1 percent in 1911, as opposed to only 52.8 percent for other operating costs in the same year. The ten-year average for the period was 74.9 percent of total income paid out for operations. In the same years the surplus of undivided profits fluctuated erratically, but excepting the three-year period of 1905–1908 never rose above 6 percent, and after 1908 began a decline. In 1911 it was merely seven-tenths of one percent of gross income.[65]

A Commerce Department report showed that the operating expenses of one of the nation's largest independent producers were even higher than those of the Steel Corporation for the period 1906–11. But Republic Steel corporation, which specialized in finished steel products, could better afford higher wage costs because, as the report noted, U. S. Steel "has large investments in ore and coal lands which are yet unused and . . . in many of its plants it has a more elaborate mechanical equipment."[66] The net effect of this pattern was to drive wages up, particularly in those districts where the competition for labor was widespread.[67] Since the iron and steel industry had no control over the demand for its products, production was highly irregular, and periods of extreme activity alternated with those of inactivity. In 1909 the industry's labor force had the largest employment fluctuation of all major manufacturing industries. In 1910, only 37 percent of the iron and steel industry's labor force worked forty-eight or more weeks of the year.[68]

The industry's irregularity of employment had consequences similar to those the railroads were experiencing. The quality of available labor declined unpredictably. Between 1890 and 1900 the industry's proportion of native-born, English-speaking workers did not appreciably change. But from 1900 to 1908, the percentage for foreign-born rose from about 36 percent to almost 48 percent.[69] Moreover, the number of men available to operate the steel mills declined between 1907 and 1911. In 1907 the industry had available approximately 38,000 men per month to produce an average of 1.829 tons per man. By 1911, the figure had fallen below 35,000 men who were, nevertheless, required to maintain the same production rate.[70] The Commerce Department noted the importance of this fact in its analysis of the industry's production efficiency: "Besides the fluctuations due to industrial conditions, there is also much unsteady employment due to the fact that many of the men do not retain any one position for a very long period." Workers "go from plant to plant and take whatever work they can secure wherever it is offered."[71] Company records of "one of the large steel plants" substantiated the Commissioner of Labor's judgment. These records showed that between 1905 and 1910 the number of employees temporarily leaving work fluctuated according to market conditions. But the number of men who left work permanently increased in years of high production when the labor demand was great. As a consequence, the industry was required to carry a larger payroll than its production requirements would have necessitated had it had a steady pool of labor.[72]

The iron and steel industry responded to these conditions in much the same way the railroads had. The steel industry sought to combat increased competition for markets by mergers and capital expansion. Both efforts failed. Between 1899 and 1904, the peak years of the industry's mergers, the number of operating blast furnaces was reduced by only 14.7 percent, but over the next five years the number increased by 8.9 percent. During the same time, the merger movement effected a reduction of only 6.7 percent in the number of steel works and rolling mills, and between 1904 and 1909 the number of these operations increased by 7.5 percent. Capital investment, even allowing for the considerable watering of stock that the merger movement occasioned, was enormous; between 1904 and 1909 the amount invested in blast furnace operations increased by 106 percent, and the investment in steel works and rolling mills climbed from $700 million to more than $1 billion, an increase of 43 percent.[73]

The expansion of the industry's capital facilities did not achieve the economies of scale that were expected. Wages continued to rise as the number of men needed for expanded operations declined.[74] The net effect of this immense expansion was to create an industry that increased the production of steel 118 percent between 1899 and 1909. But in 1899 it required a capital investment of only $430 million to produce a product worth about $600 million. By 1909 it took a capital investment of more than double that amount to produce a product worth only about one-third more, thus confiming Carroll Wright's Iron Law.[75]

Both mergers and capital expansion failed to solve the industry's economic problems and had, in fact, complicated its labor problems. The industry, particularly with its increased lower grades of workers, found that it too had a considerable "floating element," inexperienced, unsettled, and extremely susceptible to accidents, which further impeded efficiency. By 1910 the industry's accident toll reached a rate of 245.2 accidents for every 1,000 full-time employees, almost five of which resulted in permanent disability or death.[76]

Faced with a declining efficiency of capital, diminishing shares of the market, and persistent labor shortages, the iron and steel industry's component companies moved to stabilize their work force in ways least costly to themselves. In 1906 George W. Perkins, chairman of the finance committee of U. S. Steel, introduced a comprehensive welfare and accident benefit program similar to those adopted by the railroads. Perkins had introduced an identical plan in 1904 at the International Harvester Company, which became the first major industrial firm to ignore the common law of liability and pay accident benefits on a voluntary basis.[77] U.S. Steel's program became the basis for that adopted by the industry at large and, by 1913, for the general safety movement which was nationalized by the National Council for Industrial Safety.

Perkins's accident benefit and prevention programs were designed to increase the productivity of the individual worker by reducing accidents and distributing their costs to workers and consumers. To do this, the corporation assumed that the principal cause of industrial accidents was the careless and irresponsible worker.[78] In order to develop a sense of personal responsibility for industrial accidents, each worker was compelled to contribute to an accident-benefit fund: "Thus every employee becomes financially interested in guarding against accidents and in seeing that his fellow workmen are equally careful."[79] The program also included intensive "safety first" propaganda stressing the need for workers to be alert to accidents and to foresee potentially dangerous developments. Eventually this propaganda was directed toward workers' families.

To reinforce the sanction of personal responsibility, the program denied benefits for injuries or deaths that were caused "directly or indirectly, wholly or in part by the intoxication, or partial intoxication of the employees."[81] The corporation also tried to deal with the problem of labor mobility by adopting a disability and death benefit program to cover injury and death sustained by off-duty employees. As in its provisions for work-related accidents, however, the company stipulated that "no benefits are paid when the disability is due to intoxication or the use of alcoholic liquors or to unlawful or immoral acts."[82]

What was true for the iron and steel industry also held true for the nation's manufacturers generally. Corporate expansion and the entry of additional firms into the market aggravated the new order's general labor problem. In 1910 the National Association of Manufacturers passed a resolution that affirmed that the prevention of industrial accidents was intrinsically more important "than equitable compensation to injured workers."[83] In the report of its investigation of European accident programs, the association's committee asserted that industrial accidents were part of the cost of production, and as such ought to be assumed by society, but that "serious misconduct jeopardizing the life or limb of others or self-inflicted injury diminished compensation or denies it."[84] Although the report did not say so directly, its unspoken assumption was that alcoholic beverages were themselves a sign of serious misconduct. The committee report concluded that the basic problem of industrial accidents was to find a solution which would "enable the great industries of the country to be carried on without an excessive share of the losses occasioned by industrial accidents being thrown either on the employer or the employed."[85]

Like the merger and capital expansion movements that preceded it, the initial industrial drive to stabilize and improve the labor force by inculcating habits of sobriety and regularity eventually came to naught. The industrial community would be compelled eventually to seek a national political solution to the liquor problem. The failure of local initiatives derived from the maldistribution of labor that characterized America's maturing industrial society—a society that did not always result in the formation of those large urban areas that the strategy of antisaloonism supposed and on which its tactics depended.

Maldistributed labor became more evident after 1907, when both industrial welfare progams and antisaloon political efforts merged as property's response to the nation's labor problems. In that year, Congress established the Immigration Commission to study the impact of immigrants on "the people, the industries, and the institutions of the United States."[86]

The commission's reports, forty-two volumes covering every aspect of industrialization, repeatedly attested to the failure of antisaloon welfare programs. In assessing the impact of immigration on American industry, the commission acknowledged that basic industry and "all minor divisions of manufacturing and mining" were dependent upon a labor force that it described as "moving readily from place to place according to changes in working conditions or fluctuations in the demand for labor. . . . The transitory characteristic which has developed . . . is best illustrated by the racial movements from the larger industrial centers into railroad construction, seasonal and other temporary work, and by the development of a floating immigrant labor supply."[87] The commission further observed that industrialization had helped create entire industrial communities, varying in size from ten to twenty thousand inhabitants, each of which resembled "an alien colony . . . on American soil . . . living according to their own standards and largely under their own systems of control, and practically isolated from all direct contact with American life and institutions."[88]

An earlier private study of anthracite coal communities buttressed the commission's findings. Coal operators were not able to enforce nodrinking injunctions against their workers, and the expansion of operations invariably led to more saloons in these communities. The report confirmed a steady increase in the number of liquor licenses granted in the major Pennsylvania coal districts between 1890 and 1903.[89] While the report acknowledged that most miners were not drunks, it expressed the traditional temperance concern for consequences of drinking that went beyond drunkenness: "Unless something [more] is done . . . the number of saloons will increase with advanced wages, and by the laws of heredity the rising generation will be more deeply involved in this curse than their parents, and their economic worth and social value will depreciate." It was for the "prosperity of industry and the well being of our society," the author warned, that "practical" measures should be taken against the saloon whose principal evil was its capacity to make men "lose sight of those immutable laws upon which society rests."[90]

The immigration commission's study of iron ore mining in the Mesabi and Vermilion ranges of Minnesota showed that there was not a sufficient supply of reliable labor when favorable weather conditions created a heavy demand for iron. This situation compelled companies to use "careless and reckless" laborers and to "countenanc[e] intoxication in the labor gangs." The commission surveyed fifteen towns in the Mesabi and Vermilion ranges and discovered 256 saloons operated by individuals representing eighteen different ethnic groups. Most of the saloon owners were American, followed by the Finns – whose reputation for hard drinking the report linked to their socialist politics.[91]

Similar problems compelled steel producers in areas like Morgantown, West Virginia, Sharon, Pennsylvania, and Youngstown, Ohio, to hire immigrants. Their employers described them as less reliable and more difficult to direct than native American laborers. Their attitudes made them unsuitable for promotion, if only because they did not plan to remain in America and therefore did not learn English.[92] Their drinking "constitutes the most serious moral problem of the community," the commission reported. All ethnic groups drank, according to the investigators, but Croats and Serbs were particularly notorious for prolonged drinking bouts on Sundays and holidays.[93]

The commission's study of the iron and steel industry made abundantly clear that neither mergers nor mechanization had altered the industry's dependence upon market demand for profitable operations and had, indeed, increased its dependence upon its labor supply. The expansion of capital investment and competition in the industry had not altered this reality but only produced a larger and more fragile labor supply, freed from industrial controls.[94] With regard to drinking, the commission reported: "The employers state that these [drinking] sprees incapacitate [laborers] for work on Mondays, and when the labor supply is sufficient to warrant it such laborers are promptly dismissed. Although they immediately appear at other plants or establishments, under different names, ages, and addresses and obtain work."[95] Workers were free to drink as they pleased in such a labor market, regardless of the immediate demand for hands.

These conditions persisted throughout the opening years of the twentieth century in all major industrial and manufacturing enterprises. Railroad construction companies found themselves in constant competition with seasonal demands for agricultural and other labor. They reported that beer or a "good substitute" had to be supplied because "foreigners will not stay in a camp where they cannot get beer."[96] The commission reported similar conditions in lumbering, canning and packing, and "other seasonal demands for labor" which had created and made "necessary a large body of laborers who are practically permanently employed"—even though they had no single source of employment.[97]

It was this pattern of industrialization that eventually bankrupted antisaloonism as a prohibition strategy. To men like Charles Zorn, the president of the Canton Malleable Iron Company, and other leaders of American industry, the message was clear enough. In 1916 Zorn told the *Manufacturers' Record* that "when times get normal and we can get plenty of help, we always favor the man that does not drink. We feel that drinking is a menace. . . . This is our sentiment, but, of course, when help is scarce . . . we are compelled to put up with more than we do in normal times."[98] J. S. Stillman of the Empire Steel and Iron Company in Catasauqua, Pennsylvania, echoed Zorn's complaint. Stillman observed that "it has become more difficult all the time to surround the employment of men with restrictions of any kind, particularly as may affect their leisure hours, and I believe that the average employer would hesitate to apply more stringent rules." Such employers repeatedly testified to the failure of local temperance organizations to which they contributed, and to the inability of their welfare programs to curb drinking and eliminate the influence of the saloon on their workers' lifestyles.[99]

This pattern of industrial organization and the concomitant failure of corporate measures to stabilize working-class mobility and eliminate drinking by antisaloonist measures was brought out in the testimony of industrialists before the U.S. Industrial Commission. They testified that their elaborate system of labor control had broken down under the stress of the industrial system itself. William S. Wollner, the Northwestern and Pacific Railroad's chief construction engineer, testified that the seasonal nature of railroad construction compelled the railroads to rely upon "floaters" who, he said, moved from job to job, working when and where they chose. Constant labor turnover, he said, was the major problem of all the railroads in the west. The problem was exacerbated because the season for railroad construction coincided with that of heavy agricultural production. Wollner described the efforts of the railroads to maintain labor standards by improving camp conditions—efforts that were of no avail in stabilizing labor or improving its efficiency.[100]

The criterion by which Wollner judged the failure of the railroad's welfare programs was employee drinking. "The men we get in our railroad construction camps are all drinkers—all heavy drinkers," he said. Drinking was the "common condition" among natives and foreigners alike. Wollner explained that this situation was not confined to the railroads; it existed to a "large extent" in all lumber camps and coal mining operations. In view of these conditions he believed that "organized society . . . including corporations" had an obligation to "elevate the aspirations and ideals" of workers.[101]

The labor problem of the railroads was not limited to their own lack of resources to compete with other producers. Contracting firms to which they assigned much of their work experienced identical problems. John G. Tyler, whose company, the Utah Construction Company, did year-round grading work for western railroads, testified that a high turnover of labor plagued his operations. It took a labor pool of some 8,000 men for one month's work requiring 2,000 men. Tyler said that, whether or not laborers used the company's social facilities, any company interested in the efficiency of its workers had to take steps to improve sanitation and hygiene. His company furnished housing and maintained hospitals in its camps, but the drinking habits of its workers were beyond control: "Drinking is done largely in towns when they are out of work." Liquor legislation in the various states was not effective, Tyler maintained; he had never been in a dry county where whiskey was unavailable.[102] The California Commission of Immigration and Housing confirmed Tyler's testimony and added that the high labor turnover stemmed from the floating laborers' dislike of "long hours of toilsome and monotonous work and [their] desire to drown the curse of it in liquor."[103]

Another large employer of construction labor, Frederick S. Edinger, the first vice-president and general manager of the Shattuck-Edinger Company, corroborated the testimony of Wollner and Tyler. His company also assumed responsibility for welfare work, but the high rate of labor turnover and predominance of heavy-drinking workers made it doubtful that improved conditions could achieve their ends. Edinger admitted that his firm was very reluctant to employ native-born Americans, because those who applied for this class of job were most likely to be the heaviest drinkers and most dissolute in their personal habits. Consequently their level of efficiency was below that of foreigners, who usually had reason to work longer and save more than the Americans.[104] The testimony of these men was a mute but obvious indictment of the general failure of welfare measures to improve the labor supply along the lines defined in the 1890s.

Despite the Brown system and assorted welfare efforts, the railroads continued to experience an increase in the "floating element," whose habits of intemperance and irregularity were thought to do so much to impede productive output. Nevertheless, their policy remained one of implementing programs to upgrade labor standards. In 1913 *Railway Age Gazette* predicted railroaders would have to devote even "[more] attention . . . to the intelligent supervision of labor" in the industry's track-labor department, where the problem of labor turnover was greatest.[105]

The *Railway Age Gazette*'s comment was prompted by an article by A. Kip, the mechanical superintendent of the Minneapolis, St. Paul and Sault Ste. Marie Railroad. He stressed the need of management to devise a comprehensive educational and social environment for workers. Such a program, he argued, would inspire loyalty to the employer as well as improve the quality of work. Kip called for the expansion of the railroads' YMCA programs as an alternative to the saloon and for a more rigid application of Rule G, which banned the use of intoxicants by railroad employees. The railroads would also have to do more to establish community or clubhouse alternatives to the saloon.[106]

By 1914 the railroads' problems had become so acute that J. Carstensen, a vice-president of the New York Central, termed the antisaloon work of the railroad branch of the YMCA "a necessary factor in railroad operations."[107] At the same time, H. W. Dewar praised the YMCA facilities as "better than a bar room," acknowledging that employee drinking had had a disruptive effect on the operations of the Canadian Pacific.[108] In their efforts to induce the habits of sobriety and temperance among their employees, the railroads encouraged and sponsored the vague skills of men like Billy Sunday but were forced to admit that he and the safety-first movement had little effect on unskilled and transient employees.[109]

A partial explanation of this failure was offered at a symposium held by the *Railway Age Gazette* in 1911. In a comparison of Poles and Slavs as track laborers, W. E. Dovin, a supervisor on the Pittsburgh and Lake Erie Railroad, argued that both nationalities were less responsive to discipline than Italians. Without strict discipline and supervision "they will lay off after pay days and holidays and frequently after a Sunday of drink and dissipation." These national or racial characteristics, it was widely believed, could only be overcome by constant and relentless supervision, and supervisors like Dovin and T. C. Crea of the Bessemer and Lake Erie found their task complicated by the tendency of these men to get angry when drinking and to change jobs frequently.[110]

The evidence offered to the Industrial Commission that the prerogatives of ownership were no longer functioning because of national competition for the labor supply came from George W. Perkins of the U.S. Steel Corporation and International Harvester Company. Perkins testified that U.S. Steel and the Harvester Company had felt "a very real and keen responsibility" for labor standards, and had given them "exhaustive study." In 1913 alone U.S. Steel had spent some seven million dollars "for improving conditions of working men." But while recognizing this responsibility, Perkins admitted that the size of these companies placed their daily operations beyond the scope of executive-owner control, and the most that could be done was to formulate a general labor policy. Included in this policy was the decision "to provide, wherever possible, suitable facilities to enable workmen to enjoy as much leisure and recreation as the economic conditions of the industry will permit." Here again neither U.S. Steel nor Harvester were able to establish predictable conditions, Perkins testified, with the result that when the Steel Corporation shifted to a six-day week in 1913, some 4,000 laborers quit to go and work seven-day shifts elsewhere.[111] Perkins maintained that the basic cause of industrial instability was competition, fostered by the "antiquated" economics of the federal government, which was blind to the fact that these giant corporations were the natural result of technological change and not business practices.[112]

Other industrial giants like Daniel Guggenheim were also committed to antisaloon welfare. Guggenheim's American Smelting Company hired former U.S. Commissioner of Labor Charles P. Neill to direct the work of its welfare department because "we would get a higher efficiency."[113] Notwithstanding these efforts, Guggenheim called for federal assistance in the work of improving labor conditions.[114] His confidence in the federal government derived, no doubt, from the diligence with which it had supervised the interests of corporate capital in Alaska, where the administrations of Theodore Roosevelt, William Howard Taft, and Woodrow Wilson were vigilant in suppressing the political aspirations of "the saloon element," whose basic component was an "extremely shifting" population of workers.[115]

While industrialists Perkins and Guggenheim were urging the use of the national government to aid their efforts to establish effective labor standards, the Industrial Commission heard similar ideas from smaller producers whose labor problem was substantially the same. California fruit grower George H. Hecke, for example, urged the adoption of statewide employment bureaus "to connect the man and the job." Hecke's proposal was directed toward the establishment of a system which "would be a great aid to the migratory worker and undoubtedly would result in men of that class realizing more fully their duty to themselves and to the State." Another advantage of state controlled employment bureaus would be their power to bring "the man who is able-bodied, but who will not work . . . under the direct control of the state."[116]

Carleton Parker, the executive secretary of California's Commission of Immigration and Housing, testified that the "greatest danger today that the State of California faces is the fundamental and almost necessary irregular quality of the demand for labor in the agricultural districts of this state." According to Parker, "42 percent of these accidental individuals investigated expressed extremely radical political and economic opinions." Only 30 percent indicated an intention to find steady work and settle down: "practically the remaining 70 percent gave their occupation as floating laborers; had no ambition [and] no prospect of getting a steady job."[117] Parker omitted two important points from his testimony that had appeared in his commission's report to Governor Hiram W. Johnson: "the floating laborer is necessary to production in California . . . [and] intemperance [is] one of the greatest" causes of the floating labor phenomenon: fully 77 percent of these workers drank. Parker's report, along with his testimony, revealed the concern of the state for the dilemma of employers like George Hecke. They needed to control those unwilling to cooperate in a system of capitalist production and were eager to turn to the state to obtain labor stability. Employers had discovered the unwillingness to work located chiefly in the hard-drinking, transient "hobo" element described by E. Clemens Horst, whose New Jersey corporation operated in the Far West.[118]

This type of worker and the social unrest associated with him was not confined to a particular industry. According to Edward W. Olsen, Oregon's commissioner of labor, the state was "seething with intermittent employment." Olsen did exclude the lumber industry as more stable and exceptional.[119] Yet according to one employer, even the skilled workers in his lumber company were "composed largely of young men and mostly of unmarried men," a "high strung and reckless" bunch, with tendencies to work only intermittently and "throw their money away" on drinking and gambling. When asked by a commissioner about the relationship of liquor to transient employment, the owner of the Page Lumber Company expressed a common if uninformed opinion: "I do not think the liquor habit is the cause of [transient employment]. I think men get to roving and then get into these liquor habits."[120]

Perhaps no testimony so vividly portrayed the collapse of employer social control as did that concerning the savage strike waged by the United Mine Workers Union in Colorado, principally against John D. Rockefeller's Colorado Fuel and Iron Company. The political impact of the strike on the Industrial Commission was enormous and reached a pinnacle of sorts when the commission's chairman, Frank Walsh, cross-examined the younger Rockefeller and caught him in a web of evasions, lies, and half-truths, exposing in the process a systematic effort to manipulate public opinion.[121] Walsh's outrage at Rockefeller's dissembling stemmed as much from his assumption that the responsibility of ownership to establish creditable labor standards entailed the capacity to do so as it did from his evident sympathy for the underdog in industrial warfare.[122] Nevertheless, Walsh's premise was incorrect—as evidence submitted to the commission clearly revealed.

When the Rockefellers took control of Colorado Fuel and Iron they discovered that "the company [was] notorious in many sections for their support of the liquor interests." The new owners set out to eliminate the influence of the saloon. Lamont M. Bowers, the board chairman, testified, "we have fought the saloons with all the power we possess," including the establishment of a department of sociology.[123] In 1913 Reverend Eugene S. Gaddis, a Methodist Episcopalian minister who had been doing missionary work among the company's miners, was appointed superintendent of welfare work.[124] Gaddis soon came into conflict with Bowers and Jesse F. Welborn, the firm's figurehead president, about the relation of sociological work to production policy. As a result, Gaddis appeared before the Industrial Commission as a bitter opponent of Rockefeller, whom he charged with culpable ignorance of his company's labor policies.[125]

Although Gaddis raised a wide range of charges, the heart of his complaint was that the company only superficially opposed the saloons because the superintendent maintained "that a drunken spree is really a good thing, for the miner will work harder to make up the loss of time."[126] Gaddis acknowledged that Bowers had ended the "unholy alliance" of company and saloon, but went on to charge that as of 1913 there were still twenty-eight saloons in and around four camp villages within four miles of each other.[127] He also charged that local officials violated the state's liquor laws by selling on Sunday and to minors. In Gaddis's view the company's complicity derived from its rental of buildings to saloonkeepers. Finally, he charged: "The one strongest inciting factor that precipitated the bloody struggle of last year was the camp saloon. Here men met and, irrationally inflamed, they planned deeds that no sober or well-balanced mind could entertain."[128]

To support his contention that CF&I was only superficially committed to saloon suppression via welfare programs, Gaddis prepared an exhibit of company correspondence, which purported to show the extent of the saloons' dominance of industrial life.[129] But more important than revealing the extent of the saloon operations, this evidence clearly established that Colorado Fuel and Iron's basic welfare policy was an anti-saloon one, in which not merely Gaddis was concerned but the entire executive organization of the company as well. In November 1913, Bowers wrote Woodrow Wilson to defend the company's labor practices, which he described as directed toward "improving the condition of our employees in the way of housing, schools, churches, Sunday schools and in closing and lessening the saloons." He told Wilson that the company had spent some $2.7 million between 1907 and 1913 to accomplish these goals.[130] Gaddis charged that this policy was not being executed because of conflicting interests of various company officials.

Gaddis's charge, however, was considerably wide of the mark. In 1908 Bowers had directed a company investigation of the status of the saloons on or about the firm's property. This investigation was conducted by the company's fuel department head, E. H. Weitzel, who discovered that of eighty-two saloons operating in and around the company's twenty-five camps, twelve operated on company-owned land, and, of these, eight in buildings owned by the saloonkeepers. At two of these locations saloon operators owned undeveloped land that could be made available for saloons should the company terminate its leases. In Weitzel's estimation: "They would no doubt be pleased to receive a notice to quit if they knew no one was to occupy the building on company land, as they could then keep an open house at all times and conduct gambling, which our present restrictions prevent." He recommended caution in removing the two saloons because such action "might work a serious injury to the company." Weitzel and Bowers were not unaware that in the camps where the company had control over saloon property these were the only saloons operating, but "at the other camps there are from 1 to 11."[131]

Hence, while it was clear that company policy was antisaloon, it was equally clear that there were limits placed on its power to implement that policy. A major limitation was the fact that local officials in the camps and villages were either sympathetic to the saloons or in some cases connected with the saloon's operations. The most notorious illustration of this connection was that of saloon proprietor and county sheriff, Jeff Farr.[132] Another was a saloon owner at Delaqua, which was not a CF&I camp but an incorporated town: there the saloonkeeper was the justice of the peace.[133] This type of arrangement created enforcement problems beyond the means of company executives.

The company's attack on the saloons via welfare was also hindered because the saloon owners became involved in many of the programs that were intended to destroy them. Gaddis, for example, had sought to extend the company's influence into local education by seeking the dismissal of elected school commissioners whom he accused of promoting the saloons, precipitating the conflict between him and Bowers.[134] Bowers accused Gaddis of anti-Catholicism, since the school officials in question were Irish Catholics. Bowers also recognized that since the men were state officials, the company had no power over them.

Even if Bowers had such power it is highly unlikely that he would have exercised it because he did not wish to repeat Colorado Fuel and Iron Company's earlier involvement in what he took to be corrupt local political arrangements. In addition, the bulk of his employees and many of his mine superintendents were Catholics. Any precipitous interference in their educational programs would undoubtedly have produced the unrest that the company was never in a position to tolerate. Bowers, of course, appreciated this fact to an extent that the Protestant clergyman did not. The result was that Bowers dismissed Gaddis and issued a vitriolic denunciation of "schemes of political, social and religious demagogues."[135] But this was not a denunciation of antisaloonism, which had been the purpose of the firm's welfare department since its inception. It was, nevertheless, an implicit indictment of welfare as it was usually conceived and executed. What clearly emerged from the experience was the inability of employer measures alone to root out the social institution of drinking.

After the dismissal of Gaddis, the task of keeping a check on the saloons' operations passed to the company's surgeon general, R. W. Corwin, who, in the summer of 1914, issued a circular letter inquiring into the state of camp welfare programs. Corwin requested detailed information about saloons, schools, recreational facilities, church and educational programs, and sanitation and housing.[136] His reports further revealed the failure of welfare to erode the saloon's position. In the opinion of the camp physician at Segundo, the camp area supported too many saloons despite a well-developed program of education and recreation, as well as "fairly good" sanitation and housing. "Baseball in Segundo," he observed laconically, "is not much of a game; no desirable grounds to play on, and the saloons interfere with the efficiency of the players."[137] The physician at the Ideal camp reported that the company had never operated a saloon, but "there was a saloon established adjacent to the company property line."[138] At the Calcite camp there were no saloons, but the company superintendent permitted workers "a reasonable amount" of beer in bottles or kegs.[139] In short, saloons thrived in the midst of industrial welfare programs.

Besides its concern for regular and efficient workers, the company had further reason to keep the saloon in check: independent saloons provided a basis for independent politics. This fact governed the decision of "both military and civil officials" during CF&I's labor troubles "to place whiskey out of reach. . . . The ban was first placed upon whiskey; the delivery of arms was looked upon as a secondary matter."[140] In fact, Bowers's testimony before the Commission makes it clear that the political potential of the workers' saloons was a major concern to the company.[141]

By 1914, the strategy of antisaloonism was bankrupt, and the structure of industrial feudalism supposed to undergird it had failed to materialize, despite the concerted efforts of American industrialists and manufacturers. Industrial America had become characterized by a mass of rootless workers, free to travel about the country in search of work. This proletariat was marked by its disposition for hard drinking and a seeming potential for political hostility to the established order. Moreover, it was largely independent of employer social controls which had been devised to eradicate the undesirable qualities of intemperance, irregularity, and political discontent. Neither accident prevention and welfare programs, nor an unremitting war on the saloon had eradicated proletarian habits and attitudes of antipathy both to work and more efficient production.

By 1915 American industry found itself more dependent upon the working class than ever before, and less able to control it as it desired to. In this respect, the Industrial Commission itself, by characterizing industrial conditions as feudalistic and by assailing the failure of absentee owners to exercise their proper responsibility, helped pave the way for an ultimately conservative solution of American capitalism's labor problems.[142] Industry's solution to its labor problem, in light of the failure of its efforts at social controls, was national prohibition. The coming order had been well prepared.

As early as 1903, tribute had been paid to the direct intervention of industrial corporations into the political order to achieve political temperance reform. The announcement in 1903 by the Rockefeller-controlled Lake Shore and Michigan Southern Railroad that it would expand its repair shop in Collinwood, Ohio, provided the town voted dry, and a similar announcement to the citizens of Leipsic, Ohio, by the Ohio Stove Company had been hailed in the pages of the *North American Review* as signs of the ultimate harmony of business interests and moral reform.[143] By 1914 the number of industrial firms and employers associations to have declared political war in one way or another on employee drinking and the saloon was mushrooming; the list included the American Foundrymen's Association, the National Erectors' Association, and individual firms like the American Car Foundry Company, American Sheet and Tin Plate, the Pittsburgh Steel Company, and James J. Hill's Great Northern Railroad.[144] But the most important industrial antialcoholic resolution to date would be taken by the recently organized National Council for Industrial Safety.

The National Safety Council, as it was called after 1914, was the result of efforts of the steel industry to impose its safety program on the nation's entire industrial process. Termed the "child of the Association of Iron and Steel Electrical Engineers" by its first president, Robert W. Campbell, general attorney of the Illinois Steel Company, the new safety organization was supposed to spread the steel industry's gospel of Organization, Cooperation, Education—Everywhere.[145] The council's controlling assumption was articulated by Arthur Williams, president of the steel industry's American Museum of Safety: "We know that only a third of industrial accidents can be prevented by apparatus. The remaining two thirds must be warded off through education."[146] Initially the problem of "lessening the excessive use of alcohol" was assigned to the council's Department of Industrial Hygiene as a technical problem along with ventilation, lighting, and heating.[147]

The council's assumption that drinking had to be eliminated as a necessary precondition to the success of the "safety first" campaign dominated its 1914 conference on Educating the Workman, chaired by Lew R. Palmer, the former safety director of the Jones and Laughlin Steel Company.[148] During that discussion Dr. Lucian W. Chaney of the U. S. Department of Labor stressed the need for American industry to develop a more sophisticated standard of safety engineering and to demand the manufacturing of safer industrial equipment and machinery. At the conclusion of Chaney's remarks, Carl M. Hansen, the secretary of the Workmen's Compensation Bureau of New York, took the floor to insist that such an emphasis as Dr. Chaney's would affect only 25 percent of industrial accidents. It was the other 75 percent which concerned Hansen: "Is it not quite as important to prevent an accident which is the admitted result of depleted mental acitvity of the workman himself due to the excessive use of liquor or drugs?" Hansen went on to insist that the use of liquor was of such importance that New York's compensation bureau was considering raising the insurance rates of any manufacturing plant that operated with a saloon within a thousand yards of its doors. It was a matter only of dollars and cents, he said, and added: "I am not particularly interested in *how* we obtain results . . . what vitally concerns all of us is the actual securing of such results; and I don't believe we shall get worthwhile results unless we place our mark of disapproval on the liquor question immediately."[149]

Neither did the Safety Council concern itself with means but only with ends. Dr. A. M. Harvey, the physician and surgeon of the Crane Company of Chicago, endorsed Hansen's position: "The abolition of alcohol from the industrial and business world would mean a marked gain in health and efficiency on the part of the workmen in general.[150] J. M. Eaton of the Cadillac Motor Car Company proposed that the council adopt a resolution declaring industry's support for the abolition of alcoholic drinks. He was supported by chairman Palmer, who informed his audience that he had already forwarded an antidrink resolution to the Council's president, R. W. Campbell.[151] Nevertheless, Palmer's group insisted upon passing an antidrink resolution on its own.

A. T. Marcy, the assistant to the president of the Commonwealth Steel Company, offered a formal proposal that "recognized that the drinking of alcoholic stimulants is productive of a heavy percentage of accidents and of disease affecting the safety and efficiency of working men," and resolved that employers were "in favor of eliminating the use of intoxicants among the employees of the members of the National Safety Council."[152] The following day, Campbell presented the resolution in an amended form, broadening its purpose to include "eliminating the use of intoxicants in the industries of the nation." This amendment passed without objection, and as of October 15, 1914, the National Safety Council was committed to prohibition for the nation's working class.[153]

Yet even before 1914, American industrialists were prepared to enter politics, directly or indirectly, to gain temperance objectives. In 1908 the Anti-Saloon League of America was able to establish a department of industrial relations headed by dime store tycoon S. S. Kresge to gather financial contributions for its work.[154] Before 1914 this pattern of intervention was irregular and sporadic, but it was clearly visible, and popular propagandists were kept busy reporting to the public the progress of the industrial temperance drive. Learned societies like the American Academy of Political and Social Science sponsored symposiums on the subject of the political control of drinking, where they listened to papers like that of A. R. Heath on "The Business Test of Prohibition," designed to remove any moral and political qualms about the propriety of coercing the unwilling by demonstrating that the question of drinking was actually one for the accounting department.[155]

Another fruitful source of industrial and political propaganda for prohibition was growing scientific evidence that alcohol was a behavior altering drug. The Committee of Fifty initiated this work, principally to reduce the force of third-party arguments that alcoholic drinks were poisonous. The Carnegie Institute of Washington carried on the committee's efforts. Besides Henry Lee Higginson and Elihu Root, the original board of trustees included Committee of Fifty members William E. Dodge, Jr., Seth Low, John Shaw Billings, and Labor Commissioner Carroll D. Wright. In 1913 the Institute brought physiologists Raymond Dodge and Francis

G. Benedict together to study the psychological effects of alcohol on human subjects. When Walter R. Miles replaced Dodge in 1914, the laboratory was involved in five separate investigations.[156]

The Institute in 1915 published the Dodge and Benedict research as the *Psychological Effects of Alcohol*.[157] The study's conclusions were important not so much for their intrinsic value as for the impact they had on the management of America's industrial organization in a climate of disintegrating social control. Among their findings Dodge and Benedict reported:

> There can be little doubt that even in small experimental doses along with and as part of the general depression *we have clear indications of a paralysis of inhibitory or controlling factors*. . . . It seems probable too that we have herewith come upon the grounds for a wide variety of effects which are commonly observed in the social uses of alcohol, when circumstances give the reinforcement and alcohol reduces the inhibitions.[158]

This conclusion provided the basis for propaganda of the sort that Eugene Lyman Fiske and others connected with the industrial safety movement provided. It was formulated in the argot of science and conveyed to a class-conscious social order whose productive process was inherently unstable. It reinforced the ideological antiliquor remedies for that disorder that had been worked out over the course of some two decades by America's corporate and industrial leadership.[159] By supposing that it was possible to place industrial workers in a liquor-free environment, industrial concerns expected thereby to increase their productive output and foster social and political harmony. Mitigating working-class discontent, which was also the welfare programs' goal, was as much desired as a more rational distribution of that class and regular production. This objective was made unmistakably clear by William Menkel, who described the saloon as the "principal contender" for railway labor. The object of welfare, he wrote, was "to stamp out that spirit of discontent that has caused so many costly strikes."[160]

Industry's concern about its inability to suppress drinking reflected the political and social failure of antisaloon welfare programs whose aims, even if genuinely desirable, could not be attained within the structure of antisaloonist programs. In an address George Pope gave to the Syracuse Safety Convention, he stressed the urgent need for safety conscious industrialists to devise "the best method of inculcating the spirit of caution, that indispensable psychological safeguard to every form of mechanical safeguard," if American industry were to enter a new era. "Never in our political and industrial history was the necessity for united and conservative action more imperative than now. The new era means common purpose and united impulses for all engaged in our varied industries."[161] Working-class drinking was viewed as inimical to common purpose and to united impulse, and by 1914 it had become obvious that the corporate world's anticipated solutions to the problem had failed.

It was in a political climate reflecting increased employer sophistication and diminished social controls that American industrialists and manufacturers moved to suppress drinking. Corporate industry's campaign for national prohibition was the only successful drive for such legislation ever mounted. It represented the recognition by corporate property and its nonpartisan antisaloonist satellites that twenty years of cooperative antiliquor effort to establish "prohibition in fact," as the National Municipal League's Cornelius Kidder put it, had failed. It marked the reaffirmation of the central tenet of the temperance crusade: that labor was indeed a form of national capital that the state was required to protect.[162] Hence the antisaloon coalition of corporate capital and lesser forms of property interest moved to place the capstone on the social order they had established over the preceding twenty years: the Eighteenth Amendment.

Part IV

The Reemergence of Prohibition, 1914–1919

9

The Anti-Saloon League of America and the Resurgence of National Prohibition, 1900–1917

The Anti-Saloon League of America, founded in 1895, functioned as a vehicle by which the antiliquor coalition of corporate wealth and nonpartisan middle classes attempted to implement the legislative goals dictated by antisaloon strategy. Despite the attention it has received, the League was but one such agency, and whatever hegemony it attained over others within the coalition was as much shadow as substance. The League itself was never in a position to dictate the course of antisaloon politics; the larger exigencies of America's economic order ultimately set that agenda. Nevertheless the League is not without importance for understanding the nature of the nation's antiliquor odyssey.[1]

Notwithstanding the Anti-Saloon League's claims to the contrary, it had no mass following among the electorate—even that part of the public most sympathetic to the antiliquor cause. In 1914, for example, the year immediately following the launching of its national prohibition campaign, the national headquarters received only 28,000 pledges of financial support.[2] In part, the League's difficulties stemmed from a lack of confidence in or even distrust of its national leaders. One critic characterized them as an "imposition" upon the movement, while one of its own officials complained that the League was largely a "salary raising institution."[3]

On the other hand, the League's posture as the churches united against the saloon was weakened by the activities of the major antiliquor denominations whose work was carried on under the leadership of such respected clergymen as Daniel A. Poling, Charles Scanlon, and Methodist Bishop Clarence True Wilson.[4] The League's importance, then, lies not so much in what it did, but in what it was. Throughout its travail the League faithfully reflected all the antisaloon suppositions articulated by the Committee of Fifty. Its adherence to omnipartisanship effectively neutralized liquor as a political issue for the major parties, and garnered for it the financial support of all segments of the business community, enabling it to obtain a virtual monopoly over antisaloon propaganda.

Business support of political antisaloonism was pervasive. Moreover, businessmen of every rank and degree subscribed to the League's work. For every John D. Rockefeller, Sr. and George W. Perkins there were dozens of individuals like the Follansbee brothers of Pittsburgh who owned and operated steel mills in Follansbee, West Virginia, who, it was said, were prepared to put up to $5000 to bring prohibition to that state. Even the bulk of the revenues that comprised the League's "widows' mite" derived from businessmen. For every Sarah C. Fox of Adiz, Ohio, described as a "Maiden lady" there were men such as Lewis Gibbs, the "senior member of the Gibbs Manufacturing Co." and John Blankenbuhler, "president of the Zanesville Ice Co. and Pure Milk Co." who contributed their own mites.[5] Hence the League is better understood as the political voice of business than as that of nativist and reactionary American Protestants—middle class, progressive, or otherwise.

The League's ideological ties to the antiprohibition party bloc of the temperance movement were established at its founding meeting in Washington. The National Temperance Society, William Earl Dodge's instrument for propagandizing the middle classes and channeling their political activism into nonpartisanship, and the Non-Partisan Women's Christian Temperance Union were prominently represented. The founding conference named as president Hiram Price, a Davenport banker who brought antebellum Iowa railroads and prohibition.[6] In keeping with this heritage the League's founders endorsed the venerable scheme of the National Temperance Society to establish an independent government commission to investigate the liquor traffic.[7]

Such actions, however, were mere gestures toward the past; future leadership was drawn from the Ohio Anti-Saloon League, which had received support from the state's business community, including Mark Hanna and John D. Rockefeller, Sr.[8] Although the Ohio League supplied the model for the national organization, it did not conceive the idea for such an agency. That was the product of conversations between two clergymen long associated with the temperance work of enterprising business men: Archbishop John Ireland of Minnesota, who collaborated with the Pillsbury family to restrict the saloons in Minneapolis–St. Paul, and Reverend A. J. Kynett, whose Davenport, Iowa, church had once served as the locus of Hiram Price's work.[9]

With the League's establishment as a national organization, the course of antisaloon reform appeared well set. Far from being a reaction against capitalist industrialization, the League's brand of antisaloonism was designed to be, and operated as, a cooperative effort to facilitate its development at all political levels.

Howard H. Russell, the driving force in the Ohio league's activities, illustrates the inertial procapitalist momentum the League developed. An attorney, Russell took up antisaloonism while attending Oberlin College in the 1880s. Rejecting third-party politics, Ohio's antisaloonist par excellence went to work for the giant Armour packing house firm in Chicago where he wedded his antidrink enthusiasm to the corporation's organizational design to bring forth a "syndicalist" model of reform to advance "omnipartisan" antisaloon politics.

In fact, Russell's omnipartisan syndicalist organization had been anticipated by John R. Commons, the labor historian, whose publication, *The Temperance Herald,* was "backed by well known professors and local merchants." Thus it was Commons who sought to establish a "temperance trust," just as it was Ellen Forster, backed by John D. Rockefeller, Sr., who introduced the idea of nonpartisanship into Ohio's antiliquor politics. It was left to Russell, then, to bring these ideas together. Throughout his career, Russell tirelessly and ceaselessly devoted himself to maintaining the League's ties to corporate America.[10]

Yet because the Anti-Saloon League's tactics depended so heavily upon the experience of eastern urban capitalists and intelligentsia, who erroneously supposed that increasing concentrations of capital would stabilize the labor market, and that the city would emerge quickly as the archetypal industrial social organism of the future, they eventually failed to staunch the flow of liquor to the working classes. But throughout these years the League's leadership struggled to maintain unity and a cooperative approach to the liquor problem.

Despite such efforts, which were acknowledged by businessmen as "the most rational of the efforts being made to deal with the saloon evil," the League could and did come into conflict with its major supporters. Starr J. Murphy, for example, warned the Rockefellers that aspects of the League's "law enforcement" work, smacking of vigilantism, were potentially dangerous.[11] But the material superiority of its sponsors, along with its conception of itself, worked to keep the League's leadership in line, if to some extent in disarray.

A most illuminating illustration of the operative limits of the antiliquor coalition is provided by the so-called Herrick affair. It is generally recognized that the Ohio Anti-Saloon League's opposition in 1905 to the re-election of Governor Myron T. Herrick was instrumental in bringing about his defeat. This accomplishment helped to raise the Ohio League to preeminence in the antiliquor movement.[12] The League's attack on Herrick, who endorsed the League's local option tactics, but rejected some of its particulars, coincided with the review of the last of the quarterly financial reports and political summaries that it regularly prepared for its financial sponsors.[13] When word of the attack on Herrick reached Rockefeller's headquarters at 26 Broadway, Rockefeller decided to reduce his subsidy to the League in a way that would not cripple its operations but would signal his displeasure—and bring the League's leaders to New York seeking explanations. Howard H. Russell and Purley D. Baker met with Starr J. Murphy, the tycoon's adviser, and heard that their ad hoc political decisions were not free from scrutinizing and could not be implemented with impunity.[14]

The implications of the Herrick incident are important and clarify much about the mutual relation of the League to its business support. The League learned that even its seemingly innocuous omnipartisan agitation was closely monitored, and if not scrupulously conducted could result in the League's being reduced to impotence by withdrawal of funds. On the other hand, it was equally clear that the League's "cat's paw" function was not entirely under control, and that its leaders, even if operating within a theoretically neutral context, could upset delicate political arrangements that were important independently of the liquor issue and of which they were largely ignorant. Nevertheless, the outcome was not a standoff. Ultimately the League's reliance upon big contributions placed its policymakers in a dependent relation to its supporters.

Rockefeller's reduction of aid to the Ohio League was never restored to the 1904 level of support. This meant that more and more of its leaders' time had to be devoted to the time-consuming and relatively unproductive task of local fund raising. These limitations, then, constituted a sufficient hedge upon the enthusiasms of Russell, Wheeler, et al to satisfy Rockefeller and other big contributors such as S. S. Kresge and William F. Cochran. Finally, Rockefeller's action signaled directly to his aides and indirectly to the politically attuned that he was also willing to risk losing the Herricks of this world in order to advance liquor control.[15]

But such constraints bore only upon the Anti-Saloon League's tactical freedom. The antiliquor coalition's strategic objectives of establishing de facto prohibition for the sake of a more productive working class, and of channeling middle-class temperance sentiment into antisaloonist tactics, suffered no similar limitation. If anything they became more explicit as antisaloonism foundered. It was for these ends that the League's leaders and adherents received the support and praise of prominent national political figures like J. Frank Hanley of Indiana, who praised omnipartisanism and defined a political role for Protestant denominations the League's leaders readily accepted. Men involved in this sort of work, he declared, "have never yet created a liability against the state or ever will."[16]

Howard H. Russell and the League's leadership easily accommodated their religious convictions to the dictates of antisaloonism, and accepted a supporting political role for the churches. In responding to Hanley, Russell, perhaps chastened by Rockefeller's recent cut in the Ohio League's appropriation, did not hesitate to see the state's need for "virile and unselfish patriotism" as the raison d'être for antisaloon work, and to find in Theodore Roosevelt, a son of "one of the good houses of a generation ago," the apotheosis of antisaloon morality.[17]

The Reverend Charles L. Bane, another Anti-Saloon League officer, took the occasion of the 1907 national meeting to spell out yet more clearly the church's role in improving the productive arrangements of industrial society, and praised the increasingly evident antiliquor work of business, especially that of railroad corporations and life insurance companies. Bane proclaimed a new "general doctrine [of] the churches' call to social service" and celebrated with bombastic rhetoric the churches' triumph over their own theological and dogmatic imperatives. "Temperance and Evangelism," he announced, were the "marching orders" for the churches "of our God-fearing, liberty-loving Republic."[18]

But since antisaloonism's purpose was not only to redirect middle class temperance enthusiasms, but also to increase labor productivity, the criterion of its success was business prosperity. The antisaloon formula worked, according to C. W. Trickett, the assistant attorney general for

Wyandotte County, Kansas, who recounted Kansas City's successful antisaloon campaign. Trickett claimed that increased bank deposits, higher real estate values, and a construction boom that had out-stripped the available lumber supply all resulted from closing the saloons. He also attributed greater business activity to an increment in industrial efficiency, reporting that "the packing companies [and] other large institutions" had informed him that this higher output had enabled them to raise wages, which presumably explained the area's economic prosperity.[19]

As if the immediate, direct, and material link between antisaloonism on the one hand, and middle class prosperity and capital's need for increased production on the other, had not already been made sufficiently clear, Howard Russell, the League's leader and go-between for its absentee sponsors, elaborated upon it further. The inculcation of the antisaloonist creed of civic responsibility and the need for industrial cooperation would combat anticapitalist sentiment, as it was expressed in liquor drinking and subsequent absenteeism. To this end, Russell urged workers to forgo using the Sabbath to discuss their grievances and meet during the week for this purpose. In addition, he demanded that unions mix their demands for shorter hours and higher wages with "better service and fewer beers on the part of some of their members." Should this occur, he concluded, then workers' "families would be happier and the community would be more peaceful."[20]

By 1908 however, it was becoming more and more evident that antisaloonism was not an unqualified success. Self-criticism, nevertheless, did not transcend the ideological limits of that doctrine. League spokesmen called for a redoubled effort within the operating assumptions of antisaloonism. The nature of the problem required a concerted effort to broaden the national League's constituency and a more systematic effort to reach the industrial labor force with the reasonableness of antiliquor objectives.

In 1908, Purley Baker replaced Howard Russell as the League's national superintendent, and publicly criticized the antisaloonists' failure to build a rural constituency. The "yeomen" of America, he proclaimed, were the antisaloonists' natural allies in the struggle against the saloon, and "need only to be reached to be won." After urging the League to build this constituency, Baker addressed himself to the problem of the industrial laborer. Whereas Russell, the year before, had been imperious and even hostile in his remarks, Baker took a decidedly conciliatory tone. He characterized "organized labor [as] a holy crusade," and argued that while the crusade was frequently "bunglingly conducted and sometimes at war with its best friends" (i.e. antisaloonists), nevertheless its truculence was understandable. Baker maintained that the errors attributable to the labor movement derived from its "refusing to give due recognition to the source of all righteousness." Antiliquor men could not permit this great movement to remain captive of the liquor interests, for this would mean that the nation's workers, "our natural friends," would ultimately "turn . . . against us and themselves as well." Baker concluded by insisting that the antisaloonism of the churches involved no improper union of church and state. Antisaloon work was merely "the church supporting and preserving the state by developing for her a morally ballasted citizenship."[21]

The thrust and intent of Baker's remarks should dispel finally any notion that the Anti-Saloon League and its constituent elements were guided by an archaic vision of earlier and more certain times, or that its insecurities were not ultimately rooted in the socioeconomic realities of corporate capital's structural problems and reinforced by its ideological doctrines. In the League's conception, as expressed by Baker and Russell, morality entailed a compliant labor force working according to the exigencies of business enterprise. Without this sine qua non the promise of industrialization, which the League equated with business prosperity, could not be achieved. Wayne B. Wheeler, the so-called Dry Boss of Ohio, echoed Baker when he declared that it was "a good business investment to vote out the saloons" because in a liquor-free environment labor would earn more and be more efficient.[22]

The League sought to develop this analysis and convey it both to its constituency and to the industrial labor force. In 1908, the League established its Industrial Relations Department under the direction of dime store tycoon S. S. Kresge. At the same time, Baker, Russell, and other League officials set out to obtain financing in order to acquire publication facilities to meet the needs of the new propaganda drive. By 1909, sufficient funds had been secured from Ohio bankers and manufacturers Foster Copeland, Samual Dunlap, Ernest R. Root, William L. Miller, and the like to purchase the land and erect the plant for the League's press in Westerville, Ohio, a bedroom suburb of Cleveland.[23]

The centralized publication facility at Westerville enabled the League to print all the state editions of *The American Issue* under one roof and nationalize its party line, advising antisaloonists that "the saloon curtails production and demands heavy tribute from capital and labor."[24] According to *The American Issue*'s editor, L. F. Dustman, this point was the "most important" aspect of the liquor problem. At a workshop for superintendents and workers held in Chicago in late 1909, Dustman urged League staff people to stress its paramount importance, and to give the widest publicity to "instances of the business and industrial world joining hands in the fight on [sic] the saloon." Dustman exhorted the workers conference to "blazon forth the truth" that "corporations [should] adopt rules for the safety and sobriety of their men and the protection of their patrons." He assured them that *The American Issue* would "press the fighting along economic lines," since the saloon, as he saw it, "is a pirate on the commercial sea, dangerous to every legitimate business craft."[25]

But even as the Anti-Saloon League clarified its strategic objectives and obtained greater cooperation for antisaloon strategy, signs of its intrinsic weakness continued to appear. George B. Couger, the League's superintendent in Oklahoma, reported that enforcement of statewide prohibition was left to local law and order groups, and liquor was as available in the oil and mining regions of the state as it was in large cities.[26] As early as November 1909, at the League's workshop conference, a central tenet of antisaloonism was criticized as irrelevant. Myron E. Adams of Detroit maintained that substitutes for the saloon simply did not reach the industrial worker. Adams accepted the Committee of Fifty's axiom that the saloons appealed to workers' higher social faculties, as well as to their baser instincts, but contended that even the social settlement houses, which he described as "the most splendid expression of the social spirit of our day," were abject failures. They attracted young children and women, he said, but not the men. Nor was the problem confined to the cities. In parts of Michigan where local prohibition was in force the saloon crowds still congregated, "but in places little better than the old saloon."[27]

The inherent miscalculation in antisaloonism's political and social objective was its inapplicability to a national labor pool that came and went according to seasonal market demands. The League's leadership tried to meet this difficulty within the context of its inherited ideology by seeking to obtain from Congress punitive legislation that would deprive alcoholic beverages of the status afforded to other commodities in interstate commerce. Beginning in 1902 with the introduction of the Hepburn bill, the League's Washington office either sponsored or endorsed a succession of measures designed to deprive commerce in alcoholic beverages this protection. Yet despite proportionately greater financial support from the Rockefellers for its national legislative objectives than for its state activities, political failure in Washington remained the order of the day.[28]

The inability of the League's Washington office to achieve any measure of genuine success between 1902 and 1914 was not due merely to political ineptitude.[29] Rather, it stemmed from a genuine confusion about where to direct the political arm of antisaloonism. This confusion arose out of the antisaloonist assumption that the liquor problem was an issue for the smallest manageable geopolitical unit involved, an assumption that dated back to the earliest days of the temperance movement. Failure coupled with confusion led to misunderstandings with those who believed that Washington was not the place for the League to show a particularly high profile. For example, when the League sided with southerners and westerners in opposition to House Speaker Joseph Cannon, Frederick T. Gates urged Rockefeller to cut off all aid for the League's Washington operation. Gates argued that the liquor problem was a local issue or, at most, a state problem. In any case, the myopia of Russell, Baker, and the rest of the Washington cadre had caused them to "lose perspective and balance generally." Gates did not oppose continued support for the League's operations in Ohio and New York, but insisted that "this question . . . has no place in national politics—certainly no such place as those who are running it are seeking to make of it when they undertake to defeat such men as Speaker Cannon."[30]

Gates was overridden, and the Rockefellers continued to contribute to the League's national legislative effort. But the real problem was interpreting and communicating the mutual commitment to antisaloonism's political goals.[31] At the League's 1911 national meeting, Baker vented his own confusion and frustration with a slashing attack on both the business world and churches for failing to support the League's Washington leaders in their endeavors, and thus preventing the ultimate success of antisaloonism's goal of de facto prohibition. The antiliquor movement, he asserted, was impeded by indifference and a lack of cooperation. The latter led to needless and wasteful duplication of effort. Moreover, aggressive church temperance organizations threatened the success of the antisaloon drive by acting within "too much of an ecclesiastical setting." This sort of fragmented effort, he argued, was as much a threat to the state as were the liquor-soaked masses whose principal defect, he warned, was a willingness to use the political instruments of initiative, referendum, and recall to establish socialism or worse.[32]

But Baker did not repudiate antisaloonism. He called for yet more cooperation, and urged the enfranchisement of women to help vote out the saloon.[33] Still less did he repudiate antisaloonism's strategic objective of creating an industrial environment conducive to greater productive output on demand. He called for more propaganda among industrial workers and urged that "interested men of means" provide it. Emphasizing Baker's and the League's concerns, John B. Lennon, treasurer of the American Federation of Labor and a member of the Illinois Anti-Saloon League, called for a united front against drink and inclusion of organized labor into the League's new coalition: "We must show the working man how this [liquor] business stands . . . against the shorter working day; how it jeopardizes the continuity of their [sic] employment . . . and how it attacks . . . industrially, all the things that are essential to their [sic] wellbeing."[34]

The delegates expressed their own convictions and hopes for industrial labor by passing a resolution "not[ing] with special satisfaction . . . the valuable services rendered our cause by members of Organized Labor" and recommending that the League's state affiliates and local branches "secure as far as possible, the cooperation of this class of our citizens in the effort which the League is making."[35] But organized labor was not the problem confronting the antiliquor coaltion's drive: it was the unorganized industrial working class that eluded both the League and the AFL.

Nevertheless, the League and its business cohorts undertook a major campaign to propagandize the industrial work force. In May 1912 Baker's and Lennon's rhetoric found concrete expression when the League's publishing house established a bureau of safety and efficiency. The bureau directed antiliquor propaganda toward "laymen . . . with special reference to the industrial class." In January 1913 the bureau organized an Anti-Alcohol Congress in Columbus, Ohio, cooperating with the National Safety Council's American Museum of Safety. The convention attracted businessmen from across the country, who endorsed a plan to distribute antiliquor propaganda to workers in their pay envelopes. The nation's leading businessmen, including the assistant to the president of Carnegie Steel, also "materially assisted the department in a financial way." The first set of propaganda leaflets, prepared under the direction of the welfare executives of the American Iron and Steel Institute and U.S. Steel Corporation, reached more than 50,000 workers in 104 manufacturing plants across the country. So "essential to the success of the temperance reform" was this work considered, that the national League urged its state affiliates to adopt similar operations.[36]

In October 1913 the League expanded upon this work by participating in the formation of the Council of One Hundred, headed by Daniel Poling and Frances Cora Stoddard. The council's purpose was to spread the antiliquor gospel of industrial efficiency on a nationwide basis by pointing up the "relation between alcohol and industrial problems."[37]

The League's Washington office moved in a similar direction guided by William F. Cochran, a Baltimore millionaire and member of the executive committee of the League's board of directors. Cochran's fortune was based in textile manufacturing and real estate, but he was given to describing himself as a "socialist and representing 75 percent of the working men," even though his mills had yet to adopt the eight-hour day.[38] Cochran proposed that the League establish a separate welfare department, away from its Westerville headquarters, and install as its head Charles Stelzle, a free-lance prohibitionist labor reformer then on Cochran's payroll. Cochran's idea was approved, but those involved in setting up the work began to have misgivings.

The occasion for doubt was a labor-temperance campaign then being conducted in Ohio. Cochran learned that those in charge of the campaign did not want Stelzle's material because "his connection with the League was too close . . . owing to the prejudice obtaining in the mind of labor to the League." This opinion was buttressed by a similar expression by "that wealthy man from Ohio, who is on the Headquarters Committee."[39] Stelzle himself agreed with this assessment, and Cochran wrote Ernest Cherrington, accepting his alternative by which the League would "do everything possible in an indirect way to help make Mr. Stelzle's work a success."[40] Eventually Stelzle's prepaid services to the antiliquor movement were obtained at Cochran's behest by the Federal Council of Churches in America. The Council's administrative committee, which included Gifford Pinchot and Walter Rauschenbusch, invited Stelzle to head up its social service work.[44] Thus were business approaches to temperance spread through the organized antisaloon agencies into antiliquor church groups. Yet even such conspicuously discrete cooperation among antisaloonist institutions could not rejuvenate a program whose basic suppositions were so out of harmony with industrial reality.

The reemergence of state and national prohibition sentiment was not engineered by any single reform group. It was engendered, rather, by a growing appreciation of the extent and nature of the industrial liquor problem on the part of the basic elements within the antisaloon coalition. This appreciation revived the conviction that nonpartisan agitation for any less restrictive legislation would eventually prove futile. The discrete patterns of agitation for state and national prohibition varied according to a multitude of local or regional preconditions and perceptions of the need for state control. These efforts were not always successful, but always involved combinations of corporate capital, local middle class, and one or more professional reform agencies. Politicians, corresponding to their own perceptions and needs, supported, opposed, or evaded the issue. The role of corporate capital was more or less overt, according to similar perceptions.

State and national prohibition had never been beyond the tactical capacities of the antisaloon movement. These political goals had suffered, however, from their long association with third-party prohibitionism, and because antisaloonism emphasized local prohibition within the context of industrial and social antiliquor work. Nevertheless, in states and regions where industrial labor shortages were most acute, statewide prohibition drives were mounted first, even during the high tide of the Anti-Saloon League's popularity. Such states generally lacked the sort of metropolitan base on which the Anti-Saloon League could build a reasonably strong organization. Alabama, Mississippi, and North Carolina in the South, and Arizona, Colorado, Oregon, and Washington in the West, had no metropolitan areas comparable to Cleveland, Columbus, Baltimore, Washington, and New York—where the League was relatively well organized.[42] Moreover, these areas did not possess the quasi-political instruments of social control that constituted a basic postulate of antisaloonism, designed to reach systematically into the daily life of the industrial work force.

Reverend H. M. DuBoise of Atlanta made the case for state-wide prohibition in such areas: "The South is traditionally an agricultural region, and all agricultural regions are dependent upon the character of their labor."[43] DuBoise could just as well have added that agricultural regions undergoing industrialization were peculiarly vulnerable to the vagaries of agricultural labor. Reverend Adna W. Leonard of Seattle was well aware of this fact when he argued that the proper development of the Pacific Northwest's mines, forests, and fisheries would depend upon the "teeming millions of [immigrant] souls" who would be brought into the region. The character of this foreign population had been and would continue to be overwhelmingly agricultural.[44]

But if agricultural areas provided the most acute illustrations of the problem of the character of the industrial labor force, others had the same problem. Even in Ohio, where antisaloonism was heavily entrenched, and the League itself well organized and well supported, a strong drive for state and national prohibition was mounted. More significant for our purposes was the nature of this Ohio movement.

The demand for state and national prohibition did not develop in Ohio under the auspices of the state's Anti-Saloon League. Much less was it pressed upon local politicians by an aroused electorate. Rather it was formulated and articulated as a political issue by the small cadres of industrialists who dominated the leadership of the state's Progressive party. Included in this group were Arthur Lovett Garford, the party's candidate for governor in 1912 and for U. S. Senator in 1914, James R. Garfield, who had headed Theodore Roosevelt's Bureau of Corporations, and the less politically prominent—but equally powerful—H. H. Timkin and Walter F. Brown.

The conversion of these men to prohibition cannot be attributed to any of the current explanations of the drive for a dry utopia. Garford's religious and humane convictions, for example, were limited to the simple decency of providing the thirsty with the proverbial cup of water, and he was the sort of man who expected the clergy to guide the ignorant and in turn be guided by men like himself.[45] All of them enjoyed social prestige and exercised the social and political responsibilities that accompanied it. It was a basic tenet of these men that American society had entered a new age requiring a general political readjustment to permit the business and industrial enterprise that had created it to continue to progress and prosper.[46]

In developing their strategy to insert a plank calling for state and national prohibition into the Ohio Progressive party's 1914 platform, the group decided that Garford, as the Senate candidate, should handle national issues and so carry the burden of arguing for prohibition. In addition, Garford was instructed by his strategists to avoid talking to the party regulars about "human welfare and human uplift, and that sort of thing." Instead he was to emphasize that "the liquor question" was national in scope and that the Progressive party was the first party of any real importance to advocate a national solution for it. In doing this, Garford was advised "to put yourself in the [political] picture as a hard-headed cool-nerved successful business man . . . who sees and knows that the Progressive party by virtue of the experience of its leaders and the tenets of its faith is better fitted to handle business questions for the good of business than any other party in existence." In other words, the liquor question was a business question, and national prohibition was a business answer to it.[47]

By entering the political picture as a successful businessman, Garford became a spokesman for political capitalism, calling upon the national state to establish policies which would help assure the continuation of the United States as a "commercial nation." Among these policies was national prohibition, for which the ordinary machinery of national politics seemed as unavailing as ever and which antisaloonism could not achieve. In this regard it may be inferred from the strategy of the Ohio Progressives that antisaloon measures, where successful, had compounded the liquor problem by creating what were presumed to be competitive disadvantages for businessmen who were unable to achieve some form of local prohibition. Two related issues, for example, those of woman suffrage and child labor, were dealt with during the Progressives' 1914 Ohio campaign as national, rather than as state issues, because to do otherwise would "raise barriers that no manufacturer can overcome." By dealing with these problems nationally, however, the Ohio Progressives argued that "the manufacturers of every state [would gain] an equal chance with his [sic] competitors in all parts of the country." So too with national prohibition, which offered a common standard of labor efficiency in place of an uneven one that tended to inhibit capital investment and development throughout the nation.[48]

Garford and his Progressive colleagues had always been antiliquor, and Garford himself was among those businessmen who had helped the Anti-Saloon League acquire its own publishing facilities in 1909.[49] But as late as the 1912 campaign, they fully supported conventional antisaloonist assumptions and objectives. As such, they advocated a number of changes in the Ohio constitution to divorce the brewing industry from ownership of retail saloon outlets, limit the total number of saloons to one per five hundred of population, require annual renewals of retail saloon licenses, and permit local licensing authorities to be elected. In keeping with such tactics, these measures were supposed to remove the saloons from politics, while subjecting those that remained to political harrassment from hostile local authorities—themselves vulnerable to antisaloonist pressure. Although the 1912 Ohio Progressives clearly regarded the "liquor trust" as distinct from "the whole category of special interests [because] it does not serve some useful purpose," they put forward no suggestion of prohibition.[50]

What, then, led Garford and his business colleagues to decide to make state and national prohibition a Progressive issue in 1914, candidly recognizing it would cost them the state's wet voters at the outset?[51] Aside from the countervailing hope of attracting all the state's dry voters—by no means a certainty—the answer lies essentially in the nature of the business conditions affecting them.[52]

Until 1913 Garford's principal manufacturing enterprise had been the Cleveland Automatic Machine Company (CAM), and to a lesser extent the Garford Motor Car Company. Both corporations brought him into contact with other Ohio industrialists who were concerned about the chronic shortage of labor and its depressing effect on business activity. As late as April 1914, and in the midst of campaigning, Garford was receiving reports from J. P. Brophy, his CAM manager, about the effect of the shortage of labor on some of his major customers in Illinois and other midwestern states, despite a nationwide unemployment rate of 8 percent and the greatest influx of immigrants since 1907. All of the International Harvester Company's plants were reporting "short-handed," as were concerns like the Western Electric Company and Sheffield Car Company of Three Rivers.[53]

After 1912, Garford's labor problem had become the problem of his political associates. In that year Garford sold his automobile concern to the Studebaker Company, and shortly thereafter formed the Garford Engineering Company in Elyria, Ohio. The new company manufactured aluminum alloys used in making structural steel. Garford's major partners in this venture, which by 1915 was expanding into the manufacture of fine grey iron castings, were Walter F. Brown, H. H. Timkin, and George W. Perkins. The shortage of labor in Elyria was endemic. The company tried unsuccessfully to attract labor from the Cleveland area, but was unable to do so because, as Garford admitted to Brophy, only a significantly higher wage would attract them to the area and the company was bound by the area's prevailing wage level.[54] In these circumstances financial success depended upon a major improvement in the productivity of the available industrial labor supply. Eventually Garford Engineering's partners became involved in the mining of molybdenite in Arizona—another state dependent upon migrant industrial labor—and the manufacture of molybdenum for U.S. Steel.[55]

In this matrix of expanding capital investment into areas marked by chronic labor difficulties, political capital's concern for the "human element" in the industrial equation, and therefore with the liquor problem, matured from antisaloonism into national prohibition. As George W. Perkins, the epitome of Progressivism, explained it to his business colleague and political ally, Medill McCormick: "A whole lot of us went into this Progressive movement several years ago. . . . My point of view was gained from years and years of experience in difficult kinds of business, all of a pretty big, far reaching nature and all having to do with men rather than materials." Perkins had applied his peculiar concepts of modern ethics and modern economics to the labor problems of U.S. Steel and International Harvester, and then went into politics "as a man who had put in years of work and thought in a practical way on the very problems that were being taken up." Specifically, Perkins "went into the Progressive movement" to politicize the industrial welfare labor policies of the Steel Corporation and International Harvester, which were antiliquor policies.[56]

The need to politicize such policies derived mainly from private capital's inability to implement them fully in the circumstances of a competitive economy harried by a persistent shortage of itinerant labor. Between 1913 and 1917 industrial welfare schemes like those of the Harvester Co., which combined profit sharing with YMCA antiliquor programs, failed to hold industrial workers for such concerns or to minimize wage and hour increases by raising output.[57]

It was to further these ends politically that the Progressive service commission of the Progressive party's National Committee met in September 1913 with William Cochran of the Anti-Saloon League, in an effort to obtain the services of the ubiquitous Charles Stelzle.[58] The same purpose underlay Garford's 1914 campaign to elevate the liquor question to the status of a national political issue. The success of this and similar efforts "astonished" Perkins, who enthusiastically reported the movement's headway to Theodore Roosevelt.[59]

As defined by Garford and the Ohio Progressives in 1914, the liquor question was national in scope because it was national in the magnitude of its consequences. National prohibition was urgently needed for "the conservation of human resources," a notion that covered an entire spectrum of labor issues from minimum wages to "involuntary unemployment." Garford denounced Republicans and Democrats alike for failing to provide the means to deal with this and other "large business questions of a business nation in a business like way."[60]

In so posing the problem, Garford and the Progressives merely enlarged upon the social ideas they had developed in the course of their ordinary business affairs. Nothing new of significance was added to their conception of industrial society as one essentially confined to employer-employee relations dominated by business enterprise. As the scope of the latter expanded, and capital's inability to stabilize the social order out of its own resources became more and more evident, the attractive features of antisaloonism diminished and the attraction of national prohibition became more compelling.

While campaigning for governor in Ohio as a Progressive in 1912, Garford set forth his ideas concerning "Industrialism and its Relationship to the Community at Large." These ideas established the limits of his progressive social vision.[61] By 1914 his own business enterprise and that of his associates led him to apply them nationally rather than merely to Cleveland, and to opt for national prohibition to replace metropolitan antisaloonism. Garford assumed that the industrial process itself created and sustained the community's wealth, and, hence, the community's political obligation was to furnish the conditions that would permit this relationship to prosper. These included moral and social agencies "filled with the children of industrial workers of the city, . . . [because] an industrial city must stand or fall at the hands of those now growing in mind and body." After all, he pointed out, Cleveland's annual industrial payroll turned the wheels of local retail commerce, built up the city's great financial institutions, and "kept the real estate ball rolling."[62]

Garford's Progressive social vision also assumed that "the industrial worker and industrial employer are interdependent." From this it followed, however mysteriously, that leadership in guiding the community fell upon "h[im] who draws his workers from it," since all too frequently it was easier for the worker to obtain another job than for his interdependent counterpart to obtain another worker, or to move his factory or store where labor was in abundant supply. In asserting this natural right to leadership for capital, Garford instructed his audience about the purpose of welfare.

The success of any industrial enterprise entailed two components, "the material element and the human element." The community's purpose in undertaking welfare activity in conjunction with capital was "getting the best work out of a man or force of men that it is possible to get, and to do this . . . we must analyze the human mind and body carefully and see in what way it [sic] can be brought up to the highest state of productive ability."[63] This was the purpose of welfare as it was the objective of antisaloonism. By 1914 the national state was seen as the valid analogue to Cleveland and national prohibition as the proper analogue to localized antisaloonism.

This weltanschauung was not solely the apprehension of Progressives like Garford and Perkins. It belonged as well to absentee owners like Judge Elbert H. Gary and the John D. Rockefellers, who preferred a discrete political role to hustling for votes. Certainly the structural problems they confonted were as acute as any that faced Ohio's progressive industrialists. In Rockefeller's case, the violence of the Colorado Fuel and Iron Company's strike of 1913–14 exposed the bankruptcy of antisaloonist welfare and brought together that state's capitalist and middle-class political alliance for statewide prohibition. For the Rockefellers it was as unprecedented a departure from antisaloonist policy as Garford's and Perkins's had been.

Colorado, like most industrializing states, was plagued by labor problems ultimately rooted in the preindustrial social characteristics of the bulk of its industrial workers and exacerbated by fluctuating seasonal and market demands for labor. These conditions produced a chronic shortage of labor that made possible the infiltration of the industrial rank and file by union organizers and political radicals. At the same time companies were compelled to advance wages to hold their workers and defuse union agitation. Similarly, these conditions rendered ineffectual most of the efforts companies had made to establish industrial welfare programs or to root out the saloon and drinking.[64]

The Colorado Fuel and Iron Company knew these frustrations well. CF&I was managed by Lamont M. Bowers, whom Rockefeller had thrust upon the company's board of directors to preserve his 40 percent interest from being plundered by the western railroad interests also involved in the company's management. Bowers took a firm hand in adjusting company policy to satisfy the Rockefellers. He discovered that CF&I was thoroughly embroiled in the state's politics and set about to destroy the management infrastructure of saloonkeepers and private police that dealt with local and state political affairs.[65] In the midst of his labor troubles in 1913, Bowers refused to buy into a newspaper that would have supported his management policy, saying that the old CF&I had been too actively involved in local politics. Bowers also set out to rid CF&I of the saloon, which he held to be the keystone of the political machine developed by John G. Osgood, CF&I's former owner. Bowers and Jesse F. Welborn, CF&I's nominal president, had "devoted an enormous amount of time over the past five years" to getting rid of the saloons operating within the company's property.[66]

But if Bowers could control CF&I's management for Rockefeller, he could not alter the basic labor situation and its attendant consequences. Nor could he diminish the effects of increasing competition from the company's rivals. Despite his best efforts, the company's profits were marginal, labor agitation was persistent, wages advanced inexorably, and the work of its antisaloonist sociological department was frustrated. Gross earnings for 1913 were less than two million dollars, and, although the company was able to pay a 4 percent dividend on its preferred stock, and $700,000 of its accumulated debentures, Bowers had to report that "several millions invested for many years in common stock has never brought one cent of return."[67]

To prevent the incursion of union and other agitators Bowers had to employ detectives, and he had to meet the success of union organization elsewhere by raising his employees' wages, which, he believed, "keeps them in line and reasonably happy." In 1912 this meant wage advances totaling a quarter of a million dollars, "covering less than one half of our fiscal year." Between April 1912 and the close of fiscal 1913, CF&I's labor costs in wages alone increased by more than one-half million dollars.[68]

Bowers's antisaloon policy met with as little success as had his pay increases. But this was not for want of trying. In a report that was subsequently attacked as unfair to Colorado's mine owners, Reverend Henry A. Atkinson acknowledged the work in this area of CF&I's sociological department and its rivals; but he insisted that such work was "fragmentary and only partially successful [although] the companies, especially the Colorado Fuel and Iron Company, have been honest in their attempts to do this type of work." Its range varied from CF&I's vigorous and systematic antisaloon campaign, which sociological department head Gaddis criticized as a total failure, to the Victor-American Fuel Company's efforts to regulate drinking by retailing liquor and beer in a series of company-owned club houses.[69]

The responses of CF&I and Victor-American to the saloon liquor problem illustrate the dilemma confronting industrial owners in regulating the habits of their employees. Victor-American was CF&I's largest competitor in the state and was owned by John G. Osgood. As we have seen, CF&I sought to extirpate the saloon altogether, while Osgood, who was not a tee-totaler much less a prohibitionist, told Atkinson's investigators that he believed miners were too often tempted to drink excessively, and that, consequently, "we have always felt that by keeping a regulating hand on the saloons that we accomplish a great deal." Osgood's company did not accept scrip or provide credit for drinks, and it enforced a strict "no-treating" rule. The company's club houses, he said, offered other facilities such as reading rooms that sought "to surround a man with respectability, so that when he drank he was doing what he had a perfect right to do."[70] There was also a third approach to the liquor problem: some Colorado companies franchised saloon operations on an exclusive basis, receiving between twenty-five and forty cents a month per employee from its franchise holders.

Such circumstances negated antisaloon tactics available to the antiliquor coalition. Nevertheless, employers, whatever their personal stance toward liquor drinking, sought to restrict in some fashion or other the consumption of alcohol by their workers. In the circumstances of a competitive market and a highly mobile, drinking labor force, all employers were caught between the rock and hard place to some extent, for not to provide this commodity flirted with discontent and labor turnover, which threatened production, in the same way that providing it diminished production because of absenteeism. The crucial degree of pressure could not be calculated beforehand, but the companies that wished to extirpate liquor altogether in these circumstances were at a competitive disadvantage vis-à-vis those which made some gesture toward supplying it.

Landlords, whether absentee or resident, were not the only ones to be affected by these conditions. Local communities frequently became dependent upon liquor dealers whose franchise operations provided both the revenue and time for activity in local politics. The relationship between owner and liquor dealer practically insured mutual favoritism in this area, against which the towns had little recourse since the actual liquor business was carried out in large measure on private property in which mining camps were a law unto themselves. In its totality, the situation revealed the bankruptcy of metropolitan antisaloonism.[71]

In CF&I's social crisis of working-class revolt, company-owned saloons became the focal point of public attention and concern, cutting through the mugwump veneer of good government and civic regeneration. The federal grand jury sitting at Pueblo, Colorado, said the camp saloons "produce a deplorable situation among miners . . . thereby impairing their efficiency by lessening the production and increasing the hazard in operating the mine." Their operations, moreover, were conducted beyond the reach of the state's laws and helped to create an atmosphere inimical to law. To illustrate the problem, the grand jury reported the existence of one saloon that for years flew "the red flag of anarchy [sic]" to which was affixed an open knife. "This saloon," the jury concluded, "is a rendezvous for anarchists, and many crimes are chargeable to its influence."[72]

The situation in Colorado in 1914 was ripe for the antiliquor coalition of absentee capital and resident middle class to move for state prohibition. So a mining state that had only two years before rejected a similar proposition, moved to implement it. When Howard Russell approached the Rockefellers for financial suppport of the Colorado drive, they had never before supported such a move, nor had they provided financial assistance to the Anti-Saloon League of Colorado. But the inadequacy of their capital alone to make CF&I a profitable venture by establishing an effective antiliquor welfare program to increase labor productivity compelled a reassessment of their policies.

Starr Murphy, one of Rockefeller's specialists in social welfare, asked Bowers to evaluate the probable effects of statewide prohibition for CF&I. Bowers took the position that it would probably benefit the company more than it would Colorado. Because of the remoteness of the camps from the towns and cities, Bowers believed that enforcement would be relatively easy in the mining districts. Bowers told Murphy that CF&I's difficulties were with camp saloons maintained by rival companies on their own property. Even these, because they were widely scattered, were preferable to those in the towns and cities, where, he maintained, only the worst class of miner would go. So, based upon Bowers's belief about what was good for CF&I, the Rockefellers abandoned traditional antisaloonism and contributed substantially to the Colorado prohibition drive. In relaying this decision to Russell, Murphy wrote candidly of the Rockefellers' motives:

> We have always entertained great doubts as to whether State-wide prohibition was the best way to handle the evils of intemperance. We have, however, sought advice in other quarters with regard to the situation in the mining districts of Colorado, and are advised that the enforcement of a prohibitory law in such territory would be much more successful than in the cities, and with such a law conditions in mining districts would be greatly improved.

Russell's reply to the Rockefellers' ten thousand dollar anonymous contribution was equally candid about middle-class expectations regarding prohibition. Prohibition, he wrote, was "vitally connected" with the "mainten[ance] of the peace and order of the state against anarchy and red revolution."[73] Three months later the Rockefellers contributed five thousand dollars to Arthur Garford's prohibition campaign in Ohio.[74]

The candor, if not cynicism, of these spokemen for the antisaloon coalition should put to rest the supposition that successful antidrink politics in America is not based upon class distinctions or class-conscious pursuit of material interests. It should equally dispel comfortable assertions that the thrust of reform in these years was toward an abstract, albeit moralistic, ideal of human welfare and well being. Such ideas, as well as those of social betterment and human uplift, were functionally related to the exigencies of industrialization carried on at the direction of business enterprise. Both elements of the antisaloonist constituency made this distinction. Howard Russell told the senior Rockefeller that prohibition had brought "a revolution in economic affairs" to Colorado and that he would be pleased by the "improved condition sobriety brings to industry" in the state. The basis upon which Reverend W. S. Richardson recommended an additional six thousand dollar contribution for the prohibition coalition in Colorado to Starr Murphy was that prohibition "means a business advantage to [Rockefeller]. . . . [the] better moral conditions in every way in city and county, the better business conditions." Prohibition, according to Richardson, meant that "all good work is easier to do."[75] Antisaloonism was abandoned peremptorily by the antiliquor coalition as soon as it became evident that the social control it sought was beyond the resources of local society to meet without enlisting the power of the state.

When the Anti-Saloon League of America held its national meeting in 1915, two of the featured speakers were Colorado Governor George A. Carlson and Eugene N. Foss, former governor of Massachusetts and president of a large manufacturing company. Carlson explained why his state had adopted antisaloonism. Both men spoke of the need to establish a uniform industrial labor force.

Foss declared that national economic prosperity "depends in very large part on the intelligence and sobriety of the worker." He charged that the regulatory strategy of antisaloonism had caused the "cracking [of] this foundation of our prosperity." Foss concluded that "local control of the liquor traffic is impossible in a social and industrial structure built as compactly together as the United States [and] the crying need everywhere is for uniformity of legislation; and the only possible hope of uniformity in suppressing liquor is through constitutional amendment."[76] For his part, Carlson, the political representative of Colorado's mine owners, recorded the details of liquor's baneful effects upon the state's business prosperity, and focused on the camp saloon that had remained immune to fifteen years of antisaloonist agitation. Although by 1914 antisaloonist politics had dried up 103 Colorado towns and 92 percent of the state's jurisdictions, it had been unable to achieve similar success in the mining regions. Drinking, the governor charged, took away the mine workers' margin of profit, and in so doing was responsible for creating industrial unrest as well as business depression, which in turn threatened the state. Colorado responded by implementing prohibition because when the saloons were closed by military edict during the CF&I strike, "it was soon noticed that more coal was produced by the same number of men. . . . Accidents decreased and for the first time it was brought home that the man with a clear eye and rested brain is the best safety device that can be brought into the mine."[77]

The implementation of Colorado's discovery for the entire nation became a realistic possibility in December 1914, after the House of Representatives gave a four-vote majority to the so-called Hobson resolution to submit a constitutional amendment banning the commercial production, distribution, and sale of alcoholic beverages in the states. The Hobson resolution was intended to be the symbolic climax of an elaborately staged Anti-Saloon League show of popular support, and not a genuine test of dry sentiment in the lower house. But the political rivalry of Alabama politicians Richmond P. Hobson and Oscar W. Underwood forced a show of strength for which neither proponents nor their opposition was prepared. This unexpected victory caught the political agents of the antiliquor coalition in a state of disarray that was not resolved even as the movement to submit a constitutional amendment gathered momentum.[78]

Eventually a ragged united front of antisaloonist organizations was established to present a facade of unity that cloaked a wide range of individual differences that, while involving personal ambition in some cases, more often than not reflected a genuine inability to assess the national political scene and its implications for prohibition.[79] The National Prohibition Amendment Commission, as these groups styled themselves, did work out a bare bones strategy of seeking to demonstrate to the Congress that the business community of the nation urgently felt the economic need for national prohibition, which itself was now viewed as the only appropriate remedy to the alcohol problem—a fact that would be attested to by leading national public figures.[80] In addition, the Hobson resolution offered the Congress the opportunity to slough off responsibility for prohibition onto the states. But on the question of tactics there was confusion and dissention. When victory came with the ease that it did, and by the margin that it did, Anti-Saloon League prohibitionists were astonished.[81]

A central figure in this maneuvering was Richmond Pierson Hobson, the Alabama congressman whose regulation and submission strategy precipitated the frantic efforts to coordinate the diffuse antidrink prohibition elements that sought to extend political capitalism into the area of moral reform. As with Garford, Perkins, and other prohibitionist Progressives, Hobson's prohibitionism cannot be attributed to conventional ideals of humanitarianism, status honor, religious evangelicalism, or rural antipathy for industrialization. Rather, Hobson was a spokesman for the new industrial order and capitalist economic development.

Hobson was a native of Alabama who, following a southern tradition, sought a career in the military and established himself as a political force in his native state through marriage to the daughter of an influential Wall Street banker. By 1906 he had parlayed these assets into a congressional seat, from which he beat the war drums of the New South. Hobson consistently sought the full economic and political integration of the South into the burgeoning industrial economy of the nation, and to this end favored "securing all legitimate aid from the federal government" and the eradication of the liquor traffic.[82] Hobson was a vigorous supporter of a battleship navy as a means of securing for "our cotton products and other commodities . . . a fair chance in the markets of the world."[83] After the election of Woodrow Wilson, Hobson worked to secure the appointment of railroad magnate James J. Hill as secretary of agriculture because Hobson believed "our country is still in the process of Empire-Building, particularly the South, and . . . [Hill] has few equals as an Empire-Builder."[84]

Hobson favored disfranchising blacks and others whose politics and work habits were, by his malign but respectable definition, proof of their inferiority.[85] Disfranchisement, however appropriate for the South, was inapplicable elsewhere, and so Hobson's main concern became to eradicate liquor drinking, which he charged provided the masses with "a specific for degeneracy [that] automatically tends to tear down the top part of the brain, the seat of character and center of patriotism."[86] Hobson contended that science itself demonstrated that beverage alcohol affected principally "the cortex cerebrum . . . where resides the center of inhibition, or will power, causing partial paralysis, which liberates lower activities otherwise held in control." The "lower activities" of the industrial labor force, Hobson told his House colleagues when presenting his resolution, were principally responsible for the conflict between capital and labor, and thus were the major threat to national success in the struggle for industrial supremacy.[87]

Underlying the pseudoscientific argot of "alcohol . . . a protaplasmic poison . . . and the specific cause of degeneracy" was a coherent weltanschauung that pinned the success of capitalist industrialization upon uniting the supposed productive capacity of labor with the presumed genius of business enterprise. The observable impediments to that unification were labor strikes and political discontent, both seen as part of a political and social environment dominated by liquor, or "the liquor traffic." Hobson tied productive efficiency to patriotism, and argued that the survival of free institutions, including business enterprise, was menaced by "a lowered patriotism and virility" produced by alcoholic beverages. In liberating the inhibitions of industrial labor, the liquor traffic disqualified itself as a legitimate business enterprise because its commodity produced "antisocial forces . . . taking the form of industrial hate, class hate, national hate, race hate, breeding respectively industrial strife, lawlessness, anarchy, destructive revolution and war."[88] In the struggle between legitimate business enterprise and the liquor traffic, Hobson concluded that it was only natural that the traffic would utilize the worst of its progeny: "the Reds in America."[89]

Given his ideological orientation, Hobson sought advice from business and worked indefatigably to organize it for prohibition, particularly after his defeat in Alabama's 1914 senatorial primary forced him into the Anti-Saloon League's lecture circuit. In addition, he sought to capitalize on his talent as a political reformer after the fashion of an entrepreneur, a tactic that created difficulties for the advocates of prohibitionism in their hours of trial. When, in mid-1916, the question of his remuneration from the prohibition movement came to a head, Hobson threatened the loosely knit united front of reform groups with forming an independent businessmen's organization for national prohibition, a move which by that time was not feasible since business had long since joined the front.[90]

The problem that actually confronted the professional reformers was not to obtain business support for national prohibition so much as it was to obtain its backing for a political campaign conducted under the reformers' auspices. Here the Anti-Saloon League's long identification with antisaloonism and local prohibition worked against it, as did its less than enviable record of political endeavor in the nation's capital. Hobson's own father-in-law, for example, who for fifty years had been connected with the financing of the steel industry, was convinced that the Anti-Saloon League was simply too parochial and petty to accomplish its task, which he believed should be undertaken directly by the country's industrial leaders.[91] Henry Ford agreed.[92]

Skepticism about the capacity of the League and its allies to direct a successful national political campaign was not confined solely to businessmen. Reformers at the state and local level also expressed doubts. Shortly after the Hobson resolution obtained its unexpected majority, W. G. Nyce, who ran the Intercounty No License Federation of Pennsylvania, wrote Hobson to express his own reservations about the League's leadership, and to urge, "as being immediately essential to victory," the organization of the national business community for prohibition. Nyce cited from his own experience the personal interest of such Pennsylvania industrialists as Charles L. Huston, the autocratic ruler of Coatesville and the Lukens Steel Company, Sylvester S. Marvin, head of the National Biscuit Company, and "perhaps a dozen others in Philadelphia" who had themselves considered an independent organization of businessmen but whose enterprises absorbed too much of their time and energy.[93]

However dubious some may have been concerning the League's capabilities, important members of the national business community provided the League with guidance throughout the submission campaign. Fillmore Condit, who built the giant Union Oil Company of California, was chairman of the League's executive committee. Foster Copeland, head of Cleveland's City National Bank, served as treasurer. S. S. Kresge supervised fund raising, while other less prominent, but important businessmen like William S. Witham, treasurer of Bankers Trust Company of Atlanta, served in the field.[94]

Beginning in 1914 and continuing through the passage of the Eighteenth Amendment legislation, Howard Russell "was engaged almost continuously in holding luncheon-meetings for manufacturers, business and professional men in cities." Russell's basic objective was to secure funds to promote the submission campaign by discussing "methods to promote safety, efficiency, and preparedness by increased sobriety." Russell's meetings in each of the more than 100 cities he visited had been planned by cadres of local "industrial leaders." They were the "key to the success of the drive," he said, and by September 1916 the campaign had netted $91,065.[95]

Spurred by the realization that the 1920 reapportioned Congress would probably return forty to fifty representatives hostile to prohibition, the League's executive committee authorized Russell to devote his time to raising a special $100,000 "emergency fund" over and above what he had already garnered from the League's business constituents. To launch their special fund raising effort, the League's officers convened a luncheon meeting in Atlantic City on July 5, 1916, the day before its annual convention opened. The League invited "about two hundred well known businessmen who are interested in the [prohibition] proposition" to attend and subscribe. Foster Copeland handled the arrangements and S. S. Kresge oversaw the collection of contributions that resulted from the formation of a Manufacture and Business Committee.[96] The nation's businessmen responded with alacrity to the emergency appeal. In the year following the Atlantic City meeting, $81,500 in cash was raised, and business money continued to pour in for the ratification campaign. Even the skeptical, such as Rockefeller's advisors, recognized that the crisis had to be met with the leaders at hand, and recommended additional financial support.[97]

Nineteen sixteen presented the coalition of antiliquor forces with a bewildering array of political problems. Within the Anti-Saloon League there was unanimity that if submission did not come in the next two years, it would likely never come.[98] At first the League pursued an erratic course endeavoring to obtain a prosubmission plank in the platforms of the two parties.[99] Yet even here contradictory orders issued from the League's leaders.[100] Eventually neither party took any action on the submission proposal. The fears registered by Ernest Cherrington, however, did not materialize. The League struck a bargain with the congressional leadership whereby the League, "deferring as far as possible" to the wishes of its congressional friends, agreed not to press the matter until Congress reconvened after the election. For their part, the League's friends engineered the indefinite postponement of consideration of the submission bill so as to insure greater latitude in bringing it up.[101] In the meantime, the Washington office rode herd on the enthusiasms of their affiliates to assure no indiscrete actions would snarl the elaborate staging of the submission ritual.[102]

The task of organizing a substantial show of public support for constitutional prohibition was undertaken for the League by Yale University's Irving Fisher, who was possessed of a boundless faith in capitalism and a pseudoscientific explanation of social disorder that carried him into eugenics as well as prohibition. Fisher recognized that partisan political activity on behalf of prohibition could not be openly indulged in by the churches. What was called for was a broadly based show of support independent of any existing reform group. Such a group could then come forward in a spirit of disinterestedness to vouch for the urgent importance of national prohibition and obtain congressional support of submission to the states.[103] In writing to Hobson of his plans for a meeting of reform leaders to organize the publicity campaign, Fisher told him that "[it] will bring into the antialcohol movement new forces from the side of science, religion, and business, which have only recently declared themselves."[104]

Fisher had no trouble selling his scheme to the "influential men" he thought could deliver the endorsement for national prohibition. David Starr Jordan, chancellor of Stanford University, agreed to serve as honorary president. Wisconsin's progressive sociologist, E. A. Ross, accepted a vice presidency, as did William F. Slocum of Colorado College, an original member of the Committee of Fifty. The Rockefeller Institute for Medical Research contributed Jacques Loeb. Samuel McCune Lindsay of Columbia University also agreed to serve. So also did William Allen White, and former Governor of Minnesota Samuel R. Van Sant. Capital's interests were represented by William F. Cochran of Baltimore and Eugene F. Foss.[105]

Fisher's Committee of Sixty, as it styled itself, set out to obtain one thousand signatures of "manufacturers, bankers, railway presidents, university leaders, scientists, physicians, labor leaders, editors, and men in public life." In January 1917 Foss wrote to Harry P. Judson, president of the University of Chicago, and assured him that "this demonstration will have a weighty influence" in securing national prohibition.[106] Among those who declared for prohibition were Judge Elbert H. Gary, chairman of U.S. Steel, V. Everit Macy, president of the National Civic Federation, John D. Rockefeller, Sr., John S. and Charles S. Pillsbury, L. A. Osborne, vice president of the Westinghouse Machine Company, S. S. Kresge, Frederick Frelinghuysen, president of Mutual Benefit Life Insurance Company, Foster Copeland, president of the City National Bank of Columbus and national treasurer of the Anti-Saloon League, and Frank G. Vanderlip and Samuel McRoberts, both of the National City Bank of New York.

Fisher's committee obtained the signatures of numerous Progressive social reformers as well. Florence Kelley of the National Consumers' League, Judge Ben B. Lindsey, Walter Rauschenbush, Ray Stannard Baker, Robert A. Woods of Boston's South End House, Lawrence F. Abbott, publisher of the reform journal, *The Outlook,* all declared for national prohibition. So too did numerous academics like Harvard's Frank W. Tausig, William Z. Ripley, John Graham Brooks, and Pennsylvania's Simon N. Patten.[107]

In its larger outline Fisher's memorialists were identical to those whose work on the Committee of Fifty had produced antisaloonism. But, in the main, the signatories were active in business enterprise. Men like J. A. Jeffrey of Columbus, Ohio, whose company manufactured mining machinery, Jesse Welborn, CF&I's president, F. C. Kupp, president of both a shipbuilding and lumber company, E. C. Speer of the Cheney-Bigelow Wire Works in Springfield, Massachusetts, James N. Jarvie, a New York investment capitalist, watch manufacturer Charles H. Ingersoll, and George A. Farrall, vice president and general manager of the Johnston Harvester Company of Batavia, New York, constituted the base of Fisher's memorialists.

The failure of Fisher's committee to commit either one of the major parties to a formal declaration for national prohibition is as unremarkable as it was unnecessary to the eventual success of prohibition. It did, however, rekindle in some minds the thought that an organization made up exclusively of businessmen should be established to insure the eventual success of the movement. But as Cherrington pointed out to Hobson shortly after the November 1916 elections, prohibition's recent successes were almost entirely "due to the fact that we had finally interested business men of large interests and large calibre in this movement and they gave liberally to see this thing through." Never had the Anti-Saloon League received so much money for its national program as it had in the preceding twelve months, and, Cherrington argued, following Rockefeller's assumptions concerning funding, that the League's enforced poverty had been a spur to constant agitation for more general business support. It had paid off, Cherrington believed, and thus "the prospects for national prohibition were never so bright as they are today."[108]

Cherrington believed that business supported the League's prohibition drive out of the conviction that his organization was a tried and proven success. In fact, the Anti-Saloon League had always been the political creature of the financial masters who established and sanctioned the parameters of its activities according to their own sense of political wisdom and expediency. Thus, at the same time that Cherrington was congratulating himself on the League's ability to command "the cooperation of hard headed business men with fat pocketbooks," John D. Rockefeller was objecting to Starr J. Murphy's recommendation that he match S. S. Kresge's contribution of $10,000 to the League's special Eighteenth Amendment fund on the grounds that he had already given $18,000 that year to the League's national and state operations. It was Murphy's evaluation of the situation, and not the League's successful methods, that secured the additional $10,000 for the submission campaign. Murphy, who usually regarded the League's leaders as a liability, told Rockefeller that if the League's work in "Washington meant an impairment of the work in individual states it would be of questionable wisdom"; hence any support for national prohibition would have to come from those able to finance it "without impairing their support to the state agencies." It was on this basis that the national efforts of the Anti-Saloon League's united front achieved Rockefeller's support.[109]

In the last analysis, however, what made Rockefeller and others spend money for prohibition was their belief in its ability to end the instability of the nation's industrial labor force as a menace to business prosperity, a challenge industrial society could not resolve within the confines of state or local political units. This belief, and the resort to prohibition, was based upon the failure of the social order to achieve stability within the context of antisaloonism. When antisaloonism's failure was perceived as national in scope, a national class of businessmen emerged to present Congress with a demand for a comprehensive solution to the liquor problem."[110] The movement's middle-class reformers knew this as well as did Arthur Garford. When Congress voted overwhelmingly to submit the Eighteenth Amendment to the states, William D. Anderson, head of the New York Anti-Saloon League, wrote to John D. Rockefeller: "In light of what your money made possible . . . we trust that you will feel repaid for your investment."[111] Even as it exaggerated the importance of Rockefeller's money, Anderson's characterization aptly described the relation of social reform to business enterprise.

10

Denouement: Drink Reform and the American Experience

The prohibition movement was never an eccentric aberration in a period of liberal, humanitarian reform. Nor was it primarily an expression of middle-class hostility to industrial concentration and expansion. Indeed, most reformers and wealthy capitalists believed the transformation of American society into a productive order based upon capital concentration and a truly stable, reliable working class, required the creation of a liquor free social environment. Organizations as disparate as the American Playground Association and the National Conference of Charities and Corrections, the National Municipal League, and the Railroad YMCA, all supported prohibition. The nation's burgeoning industrial enterprises also devoted themselves to anti-saloonist prohibition with welfare and safety education programs. Notwithstanding this enormous social effort, the working class—at least the significant portion of it located in the basic industries of mining, agriculture, lumbering, transportation, and steel production—found itself free of the elaborate social controls devised to stabilize it.

Such conditions led George W. Perkins—with the contempt men of his sort have always displayed for those who made them wealthy—to describe industrial America as "a lunatic asylum" and to come to view national prohibition as the solution for corporate capital and its middle-class allies to a problem arising from the basic structure of national economic life.[1] At the forty-sixth annual convention of the National Conference of Social Work held in Atlantic City in June 1919, Raymond Caulkins, who had prepared the Committee of Fifty's program of saloon alternatives more than twenty years before, explained to a generation of reformers what had happened since then, and in doing so revealed the connection between their efforts and national prohibition.

> The experience of these years has shown that no appreciable progress in the provision of saloon substitutes was possible as long as the saloon remained in any form what-so-ever. The hope . . . of the Committee of Fifty that the saloon might gradually be shorn of its social features, while in the meantime these were provided by the community, by private philanthropy or commercial enterprise, was proved to be without foundation. . . . It has been proved beyond peradventure that the problem of providing the needed social opportunity furnished by the saloon can be successfully undertaken only when the saloon itself has ceased to exist.[2]

At the same conference another reformer, Robert A. Woods, affirmed the need and value of national prohibition, giving voice to the expectations of industrial capital and its reforming allies.

> It will give enormous stimulus to all forms of sound, productive labor organization. The liquor business has been in many ways like a kind of sabotage to . . . the bearings that have to do with making organized labor strong, resourceful and responsible. National Prohibition is going to reinforce all that is good in it as a force for a more equitable social order.[3]

Industrial capital required national prohibition as a solution to a major problem inherent in economic expansion: the problem of transient and undisciplined workers who, in the context of political society, were believed to be inimical to general political order. Moreover, the discontent usually attributed to the demand for temperance reform after 1900 was based upon a commitment to industrialization and to a political order that assumed a permanent class structure of property owners and workers.

Working-class unrest, often manifested by the simple expedient of walking off the job to look for work elsewhere, did not remotely threaten such a social order but in the context of market competition, capitalists had much to fear from labor irregularity. Such concerns matured into class consciousness during the antisaloon years of 1900–17. National prohibition was resorted to in the face of the failure of antisaloon regulations, local reform, and less strict and comprehensive measures to achieve the objectives the corporate community expected of them. It was viewed as a prerequisite for the successful continuation of antisaloonist reform of the social habits and attitudes of the working class that had been elaborated by the Sociological Group and its successor, the Committee of Fifty to Investigate the Drink Problem.[4] As such, prohibition sought to make national political control of the working class the capstone of the emerging edifice of corporate America, an edifice that would rest upon the political power of the national government to accomplish what its builders' social power could not.

After 1900, the nonpartisan middle class fully subscribed to the view of reality that had been developed within the corporate community, and supported reform measures that corporate leaders thought were needed to control the leisure activities of their workers. Satisfying business's desires had always been at the heart of the antiliquor movement and an important political objective as capital moved to reshape nineteenth-century American society. Corporate America sought "prohibition in fact" and not merely a legislative fiat to that effect. Wayne B. Wheeler boasted to an appalled Lincoln Steffens that the Anti-Saloon League's cynical political opportunism was aimed first at the American working class. Most Progressive Era reformers accepted, often eagerly, suppression of working-class saloons that all concerned recognized were among its major social and political institutions.[5]

This aspect of progressive social reform viewed the working class as business had always viewed it: as a form of capital to be preserved and improved, according to the needs of enterprise. This view and these needs were aptly summarized by Woodrow Wilson when he asserted that "we must hearten and quicken the spirit and efficiency of labor throughout our whole industrial system . . . by making the conditions that surround labor what they ought to be."[6]

For Wilson and others this strategy included stringent antiliquor measures. When financier Henry Lee Higginson wrote to the president of his concern that prohibition could exacerbate the class animosity it was supposed to suppress, he declared, nevertheless, that he did "not want any beer, wine, or liquor and shall be glad to see them all wiped off the face of the earth." The tepid defender of democracy replied: "I realized how entirely I concurred with you in the judgment you expressed." Two years later, in 1919, Wilson's antiliquor convictions won out over his reticence. In January of that year he informed his cabinet that wartime conservation needs no longer required the suppression of brewing. He asked his colleagues "whether from a temperance point of view and from a legal point of view" he should continue the ban on brewing. The cabinet, with William B. Wilson, secretary of labor, dissenting, recommended continuation of the ban and Wilson acceded.[7]

American historians have long recognized that capitalist industrialization has a tendency toward social domination. They have been skeptical of capital's ability to develop sufficient internal restraints to mitigate this tendency and so generally have regarded reform movements as efforts to check its inherent tendency toward domination. Social reform movements, in particular, have been described as the work of cultural, religious, or humanitarian groups to preserve or restore social values threatened by capitalist hegemony.

But the history of the antiliquor movement poses fundamental questions about the relation of social reform to industrialization under capitalist auspices. Indeed, it raises questions about the origin and nature of the social problems reformers set out to resolve.[8] The definitions of the liquor problem in America originated in America's capitalist class. That class first perceived customary drinking as an obstacle to the orderly transformation of society, and to achieve that transformation, it sought first to remove drink from the interstices of the workday and to inculcate a social habit of abstemiousness entailing the acceptance of the unending need to produce for profit. Then reformers shifted the focus of attention to the saloon, which had superseded older drinking customs. Thus, in the case of the temperance movement, the reform impulse derived from the felt needs of an aggressive, expansionist social class that also dominated the process reform is supposed to check or mitigate. Moreover, it was capital's promise that increased productivity and wealth would result from this reform that was seized upon by the small property holders and entrepreneurial reformers who, flocking to the Sons of Temperance and similar institutions, transformed temperance into a quasi popular political movement. Whatever were its historical fortunes and rhetoric, temperance reform offered the fantasy of reducing cheaply the social and political costs of production for profit.

The antiliquor movement's history suggests that, rather than challenging or countering capitalist hegemony, historically, social reform movements sought to provide a bulwark for it. For while it is probably true that industrialization exacerbated the evils of excessive drinking, and that genuinely humane efforts were made to alleviate them, it is equally true that the liquor question itself was the ideological creation of America's dominant social class seeking to expand its hegemony over the lives of the country's propertyless masses. Without capital's need for profit there would have been no liquor question or temperance movement as they came to be in America.

Epilogue: The Era of Constitutional Prohibition

The infatuation of America's capitalists with constitutional prohibition proved short-lived indeed. Even as the amendment's ratification campaign reached its climax, a few skeptical businessmen were organizing the Association Against the Prohibition Amendment (AAPA).[1] Over the course of the ensuing decade they were joined by numbers of their fraternity, grown doubtful of their handiwork. The development of capitalist disenchantment with the "noble experiment" sheds additional light on the motives, aims, and objectives of this country's preeminent social class with respect to the use of the state as an instrument of social control.

Historians considering the eventual rejection of prohibition have isolated several factors that contributed to the antiprohibition animus that enveloped the country in the nineteen twenties. Among these was a popular and growing suspicion that national prohibition did not and could not "work." Accompanying this suspicion was a perception that law and order generally were breaking down. Others have suggested, somewhat cynically, that the wealthy, finding odious the burden of personal income taxes, looked to a revived liquor traffic to lighten their load. More recently, David Kyvig has illuminated conservative anxieties about the relationship of federal to state and local power.[2]

As much as each of these considerations sheds light on the rejection of national prohibition, they fail to reach the heart of the matter. In so failing, moreover, they ignore salient facts that help us understand better the country's experience with national prohibition. Among such is the rapid (not to say stunning) eclipse of the Anti-Saloon League, the WCTU, and a host of prohibitionist organizations sponsored by the churches. Another such is the reassertion of a vigorous antisaloonist capitalism that not only led the drive for repeal, but also established a program for an antiliquor regime to succeed the failed experiment. The eclipse of the former and concomitant rise of the latter ought to lay to rest forever notions that modern America is a middle-class democracy of contenders for status honor and other such fanciful explanations of moral reform movements. For, while such middle-class organizations were undoubtedly necessary in the passage of the Eighteenth Amendment, they were not decisive. Power to propose and dispose lay elsewhere, and it is there that we should also look to understand repeal.

Constitutional prohibition presented America's capitalists with both a promise and a challenge. The promise was that of an orderly industrial class, submissive to capitalist social organization and discipline, and culturally attuned to both the production and consumer needs of the industrial order. In short, national prohibition promised, as it had from the days of Justin Edwards's "Well Conducted Farm," a contented and domesticated worker.[3] That is, one who not only accepted the discipline of the work place, but that of middle-class domestic life as well. What prohibition promised in the latter respect was workers satisfied to subordinate their values of comradeship, conviviality, and political solidarity to those of the emerging consumer society: acquisition of automobiles, radios, washing machines, and vacuum cleaners; cultivation of the nuclear family and development of hobbies and pastimes to attain mythic levels of individual fulfillment that industrial capitalism now promised.

Prohibition's challenge, on the other hand, was to avoid aggravating social class tensions about which banker Henry Lee Higginson had warned Woodrow Wilson.[4] As had conservative temperance men who opposed Massachusetts' Fifteen Gallon Law in 1838, Higginson viewed national prohibition as a threat to social harmony because it amounted to class legislation. However, since the saloon, itself, was so widely and deeply perceived to be the root of such tensions, prohibition's challenge was in

1917–19 not so clear as its promise was inviting. Nevertheless, conservative corporate interests were as alert to oversee the Eighteenth Amendment as they had been to pass it.

The Association Against the Prohibition Amendment emerged in the 1920s as American capital's instrument for monitoring prohibition, and subsequently fashioned its antisaloon sentiments into a political voice that led to the demand for repeal. Established in 1918 by William H. Stayton, a leading figure in the U.S. maritime industry, AAPA alerted antisaloonist capital to political problems accompanying the prohibition regime, organized its sentiment for either modification or repeal, and worked out antisaloonist alternatives to prohibition.

From its inception, AAPA functioned as a voice of corporate American business. Irrespective of relatively "modest" or "comfortable" origins, AAPA's dominant leaders were or had become men of enormous wealth and power upon the advent of national prohibition.[5] The origins, for example, of the Association's founder, Stayton, were not so modest as to preclude appointment to the U. S. Naval Academy and a subsequent professional career that sent him to law school and into corporate maritime law. Even John J. Raskob's immigrant parents had been able to provide him with both high school and business school education that gained him contacts in the business world of Canada. These brought him as a young man to the acquaintance of Pierre S. DuPont, for whom he went to work with what proved to be astonishing results. Before age forty, Raskob had become a millionaire.[6] Thus, with respect to AAPA, we are not speaking of drug store owners, green grocers, hardware merchants, and the like. We are speaking of Charles Francis Adams, who described himself "modestly" as a banker living in Portland, Oregon. We are speaking of Frederick W. Allen, a partner in Lee Higginson and Company; W. G. Besler, chairman of New Jersey Central Railroad; James G. Blaine, president of Marine Midland Trust of New York; W. E. Boeing of Seattle, chairman of United Aircraft and Transportation, whose company, today, dominates America's aircraft industry; Edward S. Butler of New Orleans, a "Cotton Exporter"; Robert S. Cassatt (the artist Mary Cassatt's uncle), banker and railroad magnet; Joseph Sill Clark and Joseph Dillworth, respectively, a Philadelphia lawyer and Pittsburgh banker whose sons, Joseph, Jr. and Richardson, would lead the political rebirth of Philadelphia in the 1950s; Stanley Field, a "director" of Marshall Field and Company of Chicago; Edward S. Harkness, a "philanthropist" and director of the New York Central and Southern Pacific railroads.[7]

Such men as these observed the course of national prohibition and directed AAPA's response to it. In the course of time the association moved beyond its self-imposed corporate boundaries to enlist popular support for the concerns it had developed. In 1928, nearly a decade following passage of the Volstead Act, the Association reorganized itself, surplanting Stayton with a corporate executive committee, headed by Pierre S. duPont, and an enlarged board of directors selected from "the leading industrialists, bankers, lawyers, scientists and business executives from twenty-nine states of the Union."[8] The association also undertook to attract more members, capitalizing (as it were) on popular discontent with a prohibitionist regime. Between 1928 and 1932 its membership rolls increased from 12,000 to 432,000, an increase of some 360 percent.[9]

In accommodating its new members, who were unburdened by membership fees or other financial requirements, AAPA's corporate directorate neither surrendered nor modified its political goal, but managed to project a political message that preyed upon latent fears of America's middle classes, while it also proffered acceptance and a measure of dignity to the industrial work force. In so doing, antisaloonist capitalists structured an organization subservient to their will, yet peculiarly American in its composition.

To understand this accomplishment, we should first establish firmly what was AAPA's ultimate political goal. It was not repeal. Rather, it was the preservation of capitalists' ability to intervene directly through the state into any such aspects of the nation's social life that appeared threatening to corporate business. Few, if any, of AAPA's corporate directors articulated this objective better than did James J. Wadsworth and Pierre S. DuPont.

Wadsworth, a long-term congressman and senator from New York, was modestly described in AAPA literature as a "farmer" living in New York. But Wadsworth was no mere farmer. He regularly purchased with his unearned income large herds of Texas beef stock to be fattened for eastern beef markets, and he was a real estate and banking power in his upstate county. The self-made men of his New England family had been agents for such Revolutionary War land speculators as Robert Morris, Aaron Burr, and DeWitt Clinton, and had accumulated large tracts of real estate as their commissions. Marriage joined the Wadsworths in the early nineteenth century to the Philadelphia merchant banking family of Mary Craig Wharton. Wadsworth and his family were in every sense New York "patricians," who married happily with mercantile and industrial capitalists.[10]

Wadsworth vigorously opposed the saloon and advocated state control of the liquor traffic. He did not oppose—indeed endorsed—a constitutionally sanctioned role for the federal government in its interdiction.

"It would have been infinitely better," he wrote a political colleague in 1926, "had we [Congress], recognizing the liquor traffic and the saloon as a national problem, adopted a simple constitutional amendment conferring power upon the Congress to legislate freely upon the liquor traffic."[11] What Wadsworth was seeking was what might be called a power of flexible response and intervention on the part of the state into the nation's social life. Wadsworth sought an active system of liquor control that would preclude the saloon, but permit individuals restricted access to alcoholic beverages. In fact Wadsworth was a proponent of a state liquor monopoly, which would control access to alcoholic beverages, but itself be subject to local political control.[12]

For Wadsworth and the AAPA the promise of the Eighteenth Amendment had been achieved with the destruction of the saloon, which, they never tired of reminding their audiences, had been their purpose all along. As Wadsworth put it in a 1925 Saratoga Springs address, once "men came to realize that heavy drinking incapacitated the individual for effective labor. . . . the saloon was recognized as the plague spot and there came a grim determination among the people that the saloon must go."[13] Insofar as it had achieved that objective, Wadsworth opined, national prohibition deserved "to be known in history as one of the great reform measures."[14]

For his part Pierre DuPont echoed Wadsworth. In a 1929 radio address DuPont provided his audience with a "Business Man's View of Prohibition." DuPont doubted that national prohibition would have succeeded "had there been no saloons with their accompanying evils." As did Wadsworth, DuPont objected to the rigidity of the Eighteenth Amendment and the subsequent tieing of the state's hands: "In recent years we have discovered a fault in the inflexibility of the XVIIIth [sic] Amendment. Had Congress been authorized to direct and control the liquor traffic, the subject would have been approached in the manner and to the degree dictated from time to time. . . . Today we have no such option."[15]

The corporate antisaloonists who controlled the Association Against the Prohibition Amendment railed against restrictions the Eighteenth Amendment had forced upon them and their implications for future social controls as a means of cajoling the middle class out of their utopian dream of a Dry America. In a 1926 Labor Day speech, Wadsworth warned that the working man would not "submit" to controls that would cost him "his liberty and his self-respect." If such were imposed, he continued, individual working men "will join with others similarly threatened to set up a power capable of successful resistance."[16] By 1929, AAPA had refined

Wadsworth's implied threat into an image of the average working man that harmonized with corporate antisaloonism's view of the middle classes, and heaped scorn upon prohibitionists acting as protectors of labor.[17]

In his widely circulated "Radio Talk" Pierre DuPont addressed the middle class's concerns about the working class under a prohibitionist regime. He reminded his listeners that "working men, so-called, and their families constitute pretty nearly ninety percent of the people of the United States."[18] It was time now, he argued, that "our 'workingmen' . . . decide whether or not their self-appointed guardians have acted wisely" with respect to national prohibition.[19]

Here DuPont proffered stick and carrot. The middle classes must resign themselves to a working class that must be accorded a voice in the polity, lest, as Wadsworth suggested, they take matters into their own hands. Corporate capital's recognition of the need to hear labor's voice in matters of public policy was in the last analysis self-serving, but, nevertheless, a gain for workers and a muted concept of industrial democracy. The AAPA's conservative realists recognized that Anti-Saloon League and WCTU drink phobia underlay the middle class's utopian vision of a "Dry America," and they moved decisively to surplant it with antisaloonist regimes that afforded corporate businessmen their accustomed control over the state's prerogatives in such matters.

In the long run, then, the heart of the matter involved the control of drinking by state enforcement in order to suppress the saloon. To achieve the former the authority of the latter had to be maintained, for it is the state as the enforcer of law that shields, as well sustains, operative power relations. Upon this dilemma national prohibition had, in the eyes of AAPA's leaders, foundered. As expressed by Wadsworth, control of drinking "is primarily a question of Government and not of drink."[20] Once America's capitalists realized they could not have both, they moved decisively to remove the thorn of national prohibition from the side of the state.

Two episodes—one occurring at the beginning of the decade and the other at its end—further serve to illustrate capitalistic concern for preserving respect for the illusion of a neutral state, and thus its capacity for intervening in the social life of its subjects.

The Eighteenth Amendment was unique in that it gave the states concomitant power to enforce it. All any state need do was pass its own version of the federal government's enforcement act (Volstead Act), marshal its police forces, and wail away at law breakers. Immediately the apparatchiks of the Anti-Saloon League sought to control federal and state enforcement mechanisms.[21] Just as quickly the disapprobation of antisaloonist capitalists made itself felt—nowhere more so than in New York.

There the League's sachem, William H. Anderson, ran afoul of the Rockefellers and their *eminènce gris* of social policy, Raymond Fosdick. Anderson's persistent efforts to obtain for the League a role in selecting state enforcement officials brought an open rift in 1921 with the Rockefellers, who, it should be recalled, had endorsed national prohibition primarily as a means of supporting antisaloon efforts at the state level. Anderson's efforts to outflank the Rockefellers' insistence that the League confine its activities to educating the public to accept prohibition eventually led to his personal downfall, and the New York League never recovered from the loss of Rockefeller support, which became final in 1926.[22]

Men such as the Rockefellers, Fosdick, and New York's Senator James W. Wadsworth, Jr., believed that an enforcement role for the League could only undermine the authority of the state, based as it is on a supposition of neutrality. By the end of the decade their opposition to the ambitions of Anderson, Wayne B. Wheeler (Ohio's self-anointed "Dry Boss"), and their ilk spent ruination for the League. Even so staunch a constitutional prohibitionist as S. S. Kresge abandoned the League in 1930, confessing his own belief that his contributions had been "wasted"—a waste, he averred, confirmed by the unwillingness of men like he to sustain any longer the League's work.[23]

Toward the decade's close capitalist concern for the state's authority and continued control of drinking had congealed sufficiently to compel the Hoover administration to establish the National Commission on Law Observance and Enforcement (NCLOE). Although it had a broad mandate to scrutinize problems of law and enforcement, examination of the Volstead Act was the commission's de facto priority.[24]

Hoover's choice to head the commission, Wall Street lawyer George W. Wickersham, had been William Howard Taft's attorney general. The choice of Wickersham is significant for two reasons. First, Wickersham had once drawn the Anti-Saloon League's fire for his handling of the old Webb-Keynon interstate liquor traffic bill. On the other hand, he had been a resourceful practitioner of antisaloon law enforcement while attorney general. Thus, having once been a subject of League criticism and at the same time a staunch supporter of state-enforced antisaloon measures, Wickersham represented fully the emerging consensus of antisaloon capitalism, as expressed by the AAPA, that a neutral state was the best agent to control drinking.[25] Moreover, Wickersham's antisaloon activities had been prompted by his concern that the "saloon element" created problems for the Guggenheim family's mining interests along the Copper River Northwest Railroad's construction sites, particularly with respect to its presumed impact on the native labor force.[26] As chairman and chief spokesman for the commission, Wickersham insured a report uninfluenced by extremist prohibition organizations.

In preparing its report, Wickersham's commission initially planned to interview the Anti-Saloon League, associations opposing prohibition, and representatives of the American Federation of Labor.[27] With the approval of Raymond Fosdick, it hired an official of the Rockefeller's Bureau of Social Hygiene, Leonard Harrison.[28] Within months, however, the commission changed course, and Harrison resigned. Following a confidential discussion with Treasury Secretary Andrew Mellon, the commission embarked on an extensive debate concerning the propriety of offering a forum to "partisans" of prohibition.[30] Eventually, the commission chose not to interview representatives of the Anti-Saloon League, WCTU, or any of myriad other pro-Eighteenth Amendment groups, deferring that task to the Senate Judiciary Committee. The commission did, however, expend much of its time and energies investigating prohibition's impact on the working classes.

The commission conducted a far-ranging inquiry into the impact of prohibition on the attitudes of workers and their families. It selected a self-described tee-totaler, James J. Forrester, to conduct field interviews with workers in eastern and midwestern industrial states, and invited representative labor leaders to Washington to express their views.[31]

What they learned could only have disquieted the commissioners. Forrester's reports revealed, without exception, that, far from the prohibitionists' ideal of the contented and domesticated worker, the regime had produced a working class smoldering with "strong and bitter resentment." Forrester's concluding report established that many workers believed that the prohibition amendment was never intended "to be applied to any but the working man. . . . they complain," he added, "that the wealthy . . . can get all the liquor they want," and so, flouted the law with impunity. Furthermore, Forrester reported, the workers he interviewed (frequently in their homes) freely admitted they also broke the law with ease, but remained deeply resentful that they could not obtain "properly made" beer and wine for their household tables. Finally, expressing a personally difficult judgment, the commission's teetotaling investigator conceded that workers had not prospered—"*ever*"—under the prohibition regime. Yet while confessing prohibition's failure to produce the contented and prosperous worker, Forrester's report held out hope to his more sophisticated employers that America's workers were not so disaffected that no measures of liquor control would be acceptable and therefore unworkable. In fact, Forrester concluded, his investigations showed workers, as much as they insisted upon change, to be opposed to a return to the saloon era; they were thus amenable to a role for the state in the control of liquor.[32]

In an act of political acuity, widely misunderstood at the time, the Wickersham commission did not recommend an "unconditional repeal" of the Eighteenth Amendment. To have done so would have placed the state's enforcement apparatus in an untenable position and opened the doors to changes that might not be subject to control. Instead the commission established prerequisites for repeal while, at the same time, the reports of individual commissioners argued inter alia for repeal.[33]

In effect the Wickersham commission's work served the felt needs of America's antisaloonist capitalist elite as had that of the Committee of Fifty some forty years earlier. It provided "objective facts" upon which a liquor control regime could be established and furnished a rationale for change. "The facts," as the commission had put them, AAPA's Pierre du Pont commented, "could not have been put in better words for our purposes."[34]

These two episodes, the earlier involving a great capitalist family and a political zealot and the other an investigation by the state itself, well superintended by an antisaloon capitalist, reveal the commitment of America's antisaloonist capitalists to using the state as an instrument to control behavior beyond the work place where the immediate prerogatives of property could not reach.

In abandoning prohibition it was never the intention of capital's antisaloonists to abandon control of the liquor traffic. Rather it was to preserve the authority of the state so as to continue to exercise that control by "averting a nationwide disregard for law, with all the attendant abuses that follow in its train."[35] While such was the case, Edward M. House argued to the inner circles of the Democratic party, it nevertheless remained "essential to the general welfare that our citizens do not drink to excess, and the State should put out a restraining hand in order to bring this about."[36] Upon this position there was general conviction in the upper reaches of American society, a conviction that had been forged in the 1830s by entrepreneurial and industrial capitalists such as Neil Dow and William Earl Dodge, and carried into the twentieth century by their successors. It remained unchallenged throughout the debate over prohibition, and has provided the basis for subsequent liquor control legislation.

Perhaps more important, just as the movement of antisaloon capitalists for repeal reveals their concern to preserve the image of the neutral state, it also unveils their greater desire to control better the social circumstances in which drinking occurs than to control drinking itself. The drive for national prohibition, it should be remembered, had been born in the failure of corporate capital's efforts to suppress the working-class saloon, efforts which, themselves, originated in the work of the Committee of Fifty. To a considerable extent national prohibition destroyed that institution, and so may be regarded as a success.[37] Having accomplished that objective, however, its costs had to be repaired even at the further expense of disillusioning middle-class zealots made drunk by their dreams of a dry utopia.

Even with respect to the destruction of the working-class saloon, however, caution must be exercised in judging the role of national prohibition. It must be remembered that the saloon of antisaloonist capitalists was largely an ideological construct wherein workers gathered, drank alcoholic beverages, read Marx and Engels, and, thus inflamed, ignored their families and set out to destroy the "foundations of social order" (nee capitalism). As Perry Duis has shown, both the saloon as an institution and the customs of public drinking were undergoing significant changes throughout the years 1880–1920. Much of this change did result from antisaloon onslaughts, and national prohibition was one such, the capstone of a century-old effort. Nevertheless, it was but one of many pressures—industrial, social, and organizational—that were making a fiction of what had always been, at best, a stereotype. In any event, when antisaloon capitalists like James W. Wadsworth, Jr. realized that even the stereotype had vanished, but that in its place new institutions and customs had to be superintended, the handwriting for national prohibition came upon the wall.

Today the scope of what is considered inimical to capitalist social discipline extends beyond alcoholic beverages themselves. Ironically, however, the "noble experiment" that failed is applied with vigor in these latter areas, while the question why such commodities are in such demand goes largely unasked, much less answered.[38]

Notes

Preface

1. Gutman's and Rumbarger's scholarly concerns derived to some extent from their differing class and cultural backgrounds. Gutman was nurtured in a New York working-class environment, enriched by traditions of Jewish radicalism. Rumbarger was from Philadelphia's Main Line; his family's heritage was firmly capitalist, infused with a streak of Irish Catholic rebelliousness.

Many of Gutman's essays are in *Work, Culture and Society in Industrializing America* (New York, 1977). E. P. Thompson wrote the classic study, *The Making of the English Working Class* (New York: 1963).

2. Joseph R. Gusfield, *Symbolic Crusade: Status Politics and the American Temperance Movement* (Urbana, Illinois, 1963, second edition 1986). The quoted phrase is from the new Epilogue in the second edition in which Gusfield re-evaluates his arguments and ideas. Richard Hofstadter, *The Age of Reform: From Bryan to F.D.R.* (New York, 1955) pp. 289–90.

3. See especially: James Timberlake, *Prohibition and the Progressive Movement, 1900–1920* (Cambridge, 1963); Ian Tyrell, *Sobering Up: From Temperance to Prohibition in Antebellum America, 1800–1860*) (Westport, Conn., 1979); Jack

Blocker, *Retreat from Reform: The Prohibition Movement in the United States, 1890–1913* (Westport, Conn., 1976); Norman Clark, *Deliver Us From Evil: An Interpretation of American Prohibition* (New York, 1976); Paul Johnson, *A Shopkeeper's Millennium: Society and Revivals in Rochester, New York 1815–1837* (New York, 1978). Jack Blocker (ed.) *Alcohol Reform and Society: The Liquor Issue in Social Context* (Westport, Conn., 1979).

4. Gusfield, *Symbolic Crusade* p. 2. In *Deliver Us From Evil,* Norman Clark developed some of these themes emphasizing the way temperance spoke to fears and fantasies about the middle-class family and what Clark called the "bourgeois interior" of American culture. I have also discussed this in some of my own work, especially: "The Discovery of Addiction: Changing Conceptions of Habitual Drunkenness in America," *Journal of Studies on Alcohol* 39 (January 1978): 143–74; "Temperance and Women in America" in O. Kalant (ed.) *Alcohol and Drug Problems in Women,* Vol. 5 of Research Advances in Alcohol and Drug Problems, (New York, 1981) pp. 25–67; "The Alcohol Problem in America: From Temperance to Alcoholism," *British Journal of Addiction* 79 (1984): 109–19.

5. Tyrell, *Sobering Up;* also see Tyrell's fine chapter in *Alcohol Reform and Society*; Johnson, *A Shopkeeper's Millennium,* p. 80; Roy Rosenzweig, *Eight Hours For What We Will: Workers and Leisure in an Industrial City, 1870–1920.* (Cambridge, 1983); Blocker, *Retreat from Reform.* Several other interesting recent studies are: Perry Duis, *The Saloon: Public Drinking in Chicago and Boston: 1880–1920.* (Urbana, Illinois, 1983); W. J. Rorabaugh, *The Alcoholic Republic: An American Tradition* (New York, 1979); and Barbara Epstein, *The Politics of Domesticity: Women, Evangelism and Temperance in Nineteenth Century America* (Middletown, 1981). This work constitutes some of the best of the new historical research and writing on temperance and drinking in America. John Allen Krout's book is *The Origins of Prohibition* (New York, 1925).

6. In my own writing I have borrowed from and built upon Rumbarger—especially his path-breaking work on the Committee of Fifty. Following Rumbarger, my research focused on the economic and political elite's involvement in developing policy alternatives to prohibition in both the Progressive era (1900–1920), and in the prohibition era (1919–1933). The Committee of Fifty's proposals finally triumphed in 1933 with the publication and wide acceptance of the report sponsored by John D. Rockefeller Jr. and authored by Raymond Fosdick, Rockefeller's trusted advisor. The general policies and laws the Rockefeller lawyers and public administrators drew up were eventually adopted by most state governments. See: H. G. Levine, "The Committee of Fifty and the Origins of Alcohol Control," *Journal of Drug Issues* (Winter, 1983): 95–116; and H. G. Levine, "The Birth of American Alcohol Control: Prohibition, The Power Elite, and the Problem of Lawlessness," *Contemporary Drug Problems* (Spring, 1985): 63–115.

7. For example, Jed Dannenbaum "The Social History of Alcohol" in

The Alcohol and Drug Surveyor 19, (April, 1984): 7–11. The new sympathy with temperance arguments is also sometimes apparent around the edges of some current writing about temperance that perhaps unwittingly employs the vocabulary and concepts of Alcoholics Anonymous.

8. W. J. Rorabaugh, *The Alcoholic Republic* pp. 232–233.

9. March 22, 1989: I was about to mail this to publisher when *New York Times* columnist Russell Baker proved, once again, that good journalists often beat out scholars in revealing what perhaps should have been obvious in the first place. "The blue noses are on the march in this country," writes Baker. And then, for those who may not know, he identifies what have been the economic underpinnings of American campaigns for moral wholesomeness.

> Historically, temperance and health movements have been powered by industrialists with a money stake in uplift. A society on a sound moral and physical regimen provides employers with a profitably malleable labor force.
>
> Periodic efforts to make Americans amenable to factory discipline date from the early 19th century and usually travel under cover provided by the forces of moral and physical uplift. Before about 1830, in the supposedly idyllic age of the early American craftsman, Americans were famous for getting drunk often and whenever they pleased.
>
> Since this manifestation of independent spirit would have crippled the Industrial Revolution unless tempered, capitalism and uplift have cooperated ever since to tame the impulse (p.A27).

Introduction

1. Richard Hofstadter, *The Age of Reform: From Bryan to F.D.R.* (New York, 1955), pp. 288–93.

2. Joseph Gusfield, *Symbolic Crusade: Status Politics and the American Temperance Movement* (Urbana, 1963); see also Louis Hartz, *The Liberal Tradition in America* (New York, 1966); and Richard Hofstadter, "Preface" for the Hebrew edition of *The American Political Tradition and the Men Who Made It,* 25th anniversary ed. (New York, 1973), especially pp. xxiii–xxiv.

3. Gusfield, *Symbolic Crusade*, pp. 1–7.

4. Ibid.

5. Ibid., pp. 1–2.

6. Andrew Sinclair, *Prohibition, The Era of Excess* (New York, 1964);

James Timberlake, *Prohibition and the Progressive Movement 1900–1920* (Cambridge, Mass., 1963); Norman Clark, *Deliver Us from Evil: An Interpretation of American Prohibition* (New York, 1976); Jack S. Blocker, *Retreat from Reform: The Prohibition Movement in the United States, 1893–1913* (Westport, Conn., 1976). See also Geoffrey Blodgett, "The Impulse to Deny: Two Views of the Prohibition Movement," *Reviews in American History* 5 (September 1977): 374–78.

Despite its murky argument, *Retreat from Reform* does a good job illuminating tensions besetting the Prohibition Party in the 1890s. The indebtedness of all these works to Peter Odegard's classic study, *Pressure Politics: The Story of the Anti-Saloon League* (New York, 1928), should be acknowledged. Odegard's depiction of the Anti-Saloon League as a Machiavellian organization of American churches has riveted the attention of historians ever since. The most recent elaboration of this theme is Austin Kerr, *Organized for Prohibition: A New History of the Anti-Saloon League* (New Haven and London, 1985). Kerr attempts to utilize the works of Robert Wiebe and Alfred DuPont Chandler to argue that the League's adoption of modern business organizational and administrative practices led to its successfully orchestrating the adoption of the Eighteenth Amendment. For a supporting view of the League as deus ex machina, see Virginius Dabney, *Dry Messiah: The Life of Bishop Cannon* (New York, 1949). James J. Cannon, Jr., was an unpleasant and deceitful person who did not hesitate to make capital from his League activities. In the long run, however, Cannon and the League were small potatoes.

7. It seems appropriate here to inform my readers of those works that have led me, however inadvertently, onto this course: Thomas C. Cochran and William Miller, *The Age of Enterprise: A Social History of Industrial America* (New York, 1942); Matthew Josephson, *The Politicos, 1865–1896* (New York, 1938); *The Robber Barons, The Great American Capitalists, 1861–1901* (New York, 1934); Gabriel Kolko, *The Triumph of Conservatism: A Reinterpretation of American History, 1900–1916* (New York, 1963); Karl Mannheim, *Ideology and Utopia: An Introduction to the Sociology of Knowledge* (New York, 1936); Barrington Moore, *Political Power and Social Theory* (Cambridge, 1958), *The Social Origins of Dictatorship and Democracy: Lord and Peasant in the Making of the Modern World* (Boston, 1966), and *Injustice: The Social Bases of Obedience and Revolt* (New York, 1978); Franz Neumann, *The Democratic and Authoritarian State: Essays in Political and Legal Theory,* ed. Herbert Marcuse (New York, 1957); Karl Polanyi, *The Great Transformation: The Political and Economic Origins of Our Time* (Boston, 1957); Thorstein Veblen, *Absentee Ownership: The Case of America* (Boston, 1923), and *The Theory of Business Enterprise* (New York, 1904). These works led me to read those of Tom Bottomore, Herbert Gutman, Christopher Hill, Eric Hobsbawm, and Edward P. Thompson.

8. See Paul E. Johnson, *A Shopkeeper's Millennium: Society and Revivals in Rochester, New York, 1815–1837* (New York, 1978), pp. 55–82 passim, for

the appeal of temperance to businessmen. Ian Tyrell, *Sobering Up: From Temperance to Prohibition in Antebellum America, 1800–1860* (Westport, Conn., 1979), substantiates this appeal and supplants John Allen Krout, *The Origins of Prohibition* (New York, 1925) as authoritative for the antebellum years. For an account of drinking among lumbermen in the 1840s, see G. W. Rumbarger to J. L. Rumbarger, 16 August 1921, Rumbarger Family Papers (hereafter RFP). The Rumbarger Family Papers are being collected for the Forest History Society, Durham, North Carolina.

9. *American Lumbermen, The Personal History and Public and Business Achievements of One Hundred Eminent Lumbermen of the United States*, 3d series (Chicago, 1906), pp. 348–52.

10. *The North American* (Philadelphia, Pa.), 18 February 1922; Henry J. Rumbarger, Jr. to John J. Rumbarger, 6 May 1987, RFP; *The Wood-Worker,* 22 February 1917, p. 22; *New York Lumber Trade Journal,* 15 March 1929.

11. "A Lumberman from Youth," *American Lumberman*, 24 December 1904, p. 1; *The Advocate,* Parsons (Tucker County), W. Va., 20 March 1947.

12. *The North American*, 18 February 1922, 8 March, 1929. Despite their Republican convictions, where their business interests seemed to require it, the Rumbargers maintained close association with Democrats. See H. G. Davis to J. J. Rumbarger, 18 July 1904, RFP. Davis was then the Democrats' vice-presidential nominee.

13. *American Lumberman,* 24 December 1904.

14. Blodgett, "Impulse to Deny," pp. 374–75.

15. Henry J. Rumbarger, Sr., to John J. Rumbarger, 15 May 1987, RFP.

16. U. S. Senate, Committee on the Judiciary, *Proposing an Amendment to the Constitution Prohibiting the Sale, Manufacture, and Importation of Intoxicating Liquors: Hearings before a Subcommittee of the Committee on the Judiciary of the United States on S. J. Res. 88 and S. J. Res. 50*, 63rd Cong., 2d sess., 1914, pp. 30, 48, 53.

17. Committee Papers of the Committee on the Judiciary (64th Cong.), Records of the U. S. House of Representatives, Record Group 233, File 64A–F20.3., National Archives.

18. Mark Doolittle, "Temperance, A Source of National Wealth," in Edward C. Delavan, *Temperance Essays and Selections from Different Authors* (Albany, 1865), pp. 219–29. Doolittle's essay first appeared in 1834.

19. The change of the name of DuBois, Pa., in 1877 helps, perhaps, to illustrate how fantasy overcame reason. At its establishment, the town bore, natu-

rally enough, the name Rumbarger. John DuBois, the Canadian capitalist whom Rumbarger introduced to the area, was soon taken by those who had purchased Rumbarger's town sites to be the town's greater benefactor, by virtue of his timbering operations. Eventually, the town's name became a political issue, and in 1877 the townsfolk voted to adopt for their community the name of the greater of the two capitalists. Here we see a minor but significant expression of capitalism as idolatry and thus representative of a transition from reason to fantasy.

20. See Johnson, *Shopkeeper's Millennium,* for insightful analysis of how day-to-day separation of owners from managers and workers aggravated the owners' perception of the "drink problem."

21. The best scholarly study of the early modern saloon is Perry R. Duis, *The Saloon: Public Drinking in Chicago and Boston, 1880–1920* (Urbana and Chicago, 1983). The distinctions between empirical reality and antisaloonist mythology are striking when not appalling. Despite its remarkably faithful observations and exceptionally acute analysis, however, Duis's study is limited by its focus on drinking establishments of major metropolitan areas. "Public" drinking was by no means confined to such urban institutions, which, nevertheless, bore the brunt of antisaloonism's misguided crusade. Studies of such antebellum institutions as "grog shops" and postbellum resorts as "Blind Tigers" and "camp saloons" would help provide a richer portrait of common drinking. Nevertheless, Duis furnishes us a benchmark for what should follow. Those interested in the saloon and industrializing of the American West should consult the classic film *McCabe and Mrs. Miller,* itself an unrivaled meditation on the American quest for success.

Chapter 1

1. John Allen Krout, *The Origins of Prohibition* (New York, 1925); Clifford S. Griffin, *Their Brothers Keepers: Moral Stewardship in the United States, 1800–1865* (New Brunswick, 1960).

2. John Marsh, *Temperance Recollections: Labors, Defeats, Triumphs, An Autobiography* (New York, 1866), p. 11; Krout, *Origins*, pp. 68–69.

3. Charles A. Ingraham, *The Birth at Moreau of the Temperance Reformation* (New York State Historical Association, 1905); Nathaniel B. Sylvester, *History of Saratoga County, New York* (Philadelphia, 1878); Marsh, *Temperance Recollections*, pp. 11–12; Krout, *Origins*, p. 79.

4. Marsh, *Temperance Recollections*, p. 11; Krout, *Origins*, chap. 2; Alice Felt Tyler, *Freedom's Ferment: Phases of American Social History from the Colonial Period to the Outbreak of the Civil War* (New York, 1962), pp. 314–15. Ernest Cherrington, *Evolution of Prohibition in the United States of America: A Chronological History* (Westerville, Ohio, 1920), pp. 21–22.

5. Unless otherwise noted, all material on Rush is from David Freeman Hawke, *Benjamin Rush: Revolutionary Gadfly* (New York, 1971), especially pp. 113–14, 300–306, 338, 370–71.

6. Besides the *Enquiry*, see Rush's "An Account of the Progress of Population, Agriculture, Manners and Government in Pennsylvania," and "An Account of the Manners of the German Inhabitants of Pennsylvania," cited in Hawke, *Benjamin Rush*, p. 443. According to his biographer, Rush maintained that the republic's citizens "must be taught that study and business should be [their] principal pursuits of life."

7. Sylvester, *Saratoga County*, p. 432.

8. Krout, *Origins*, p. 78; Ingraham, *Temperance Reformation*, p. 9.

9. William Hay, *The History of Temperance in Saratoga County* (n.p., n.d.), pp. 13–16.

10. Hay, *Temperance in Saratoga*, p. 15.

11. See Robert Doherty, "Social Bases for the Presbyterian Schism of 1837–1838," *Journal of Social History* 2 (1968): 69–79; and Seymour Martin Lipsett, *The First New Nation* (New York, 1963), for examples of the impact of entrepreneurial values on religion.

12. See, for example, Krout, *Origins*, p. 79, for the difficulties of Isaac B. Payne, who informed his associates that he could not abolish completely the use of liquor because his "business required a few excellent laborers, not one of whose help I could obtain without [furnishing] liquor." For an example of agricultural resistance to temperance reform, see *A Hasty Defense of the Farmers & Distillers of York County (Pa.) Against the Aspersions of Temperance Societies* (York, Pa., 1833). *An Address to the Farmers of Burlington County (N.J.)* (Burlington, N.J., 1836) is an appeal for temperance support that argued that grain could be raised profitably for other than distilling use.

13. John Dunlap, *The Philosophy of Artificial and Compulsory Drinking Usage in Great Britain and Ireland* (London, 1839), pp. 176–78. In this study Dunlap, a temperance reformer, applied the theory of analysis developed in America.

14. George McNeil, ed., *The History of the Labor Movement* (New York, 1887), pp. 333–34.

15. Helen Wild, "Galen James," *Medford Historical Record* 40 (1908): 84–88.

16. Dunlap, *Artificial and Compulsory Drinking*, p. 16.

17. Thomas Hertell, *The Causes of Intemperate Drinking* (New York, 1819).

18. Hertell, *Intemperate Drinking*, pp. 5–13. A perusal of the popular songs of the seventeenth through nineteenth centuries confirms Hertell's analysis. See, for example, Theodore Maynard, ed., *A Tankard of Ale: An Anthology of Drinking Songs* (New York, 1920).

19. Hertell, *Intemperate Drinking,* pp. 40–48.

20. Ibid.

21. Lyman Beecher, *Autobiography*, ed. Barbara M. Cross, 2 vols. (Cambridge, Mass., 1961), 1:179–84. Recently social historians Ian Tyrell and Paul Johnson have provided illuminating discussions of evangelical religion's energizing impact on temperance reform. Tyrell concentrates on antebellum Worcester, Massachusetts, and Johnson on Rochester, New York. My differences with both are slight, but important: the temperance reformation was taken up by the Protestant churches in response to social changes introduced by capitalist industrialization. But, it needs reminding, the temperance reform was well underway when the churches entered the fray; its ideological and material origins were secular and capitalist. See Ian Tyrell, *Sobering Up: From Temperance to Prohibition in Antebellum America, 1800–1860* (Westport, Conn., 1979); and Paul Johnson, *A Shopkeeper's Millennium: Society and Revivals in Rochester, New York, 1815–1837* (New York, 1978).

22. Krout, *Origins*, p. 85.

23. Lyman Beecher, "The Means of National Prosperity," in *Addresses of the Philadelphia Society for the Promotion of National Industry,* ed. Mathew Carey (Philadelphia, 1820), pp. 264. Beecher first delivered this sermon on December 2, 1819.

24. Ibid., p. 264.

25. Ibid., pp. 264–65.

26. Ibid., p. 285.

27. Ibid., p. 279.

28. Ibid., pp. 280–81.

29. Ibid., p. 283.

30. Ibid., pp. 280–83.

31. Walter Channing, *Thoughts on the Origin, Nature, Principles and Prospects of the Temperance Reform* (Boston, 1834).

32. American Temperance Society (ATS), *Fourth Report of the American Temperance Society* (Boston, 1831), p. 10.

33. ATS, *Seventh Report of the American Temperance Society* (Boston, 1834), p. 116.

34. ATS, *Seventh Report*, pp. 1–15. The Anti-Saloon League of America inherited this class-conscious analysis and strategy.

35. ATS, *Fourth Report*, p. 14.

36. Ibid., p. 7. Tyrell, *Sobering Up*, pp. 61–65, argues that leadership of the ATS by men such as Justin Edwards gave evangelicals the opportunity to become "the architects of temperance reform." This, I think, gives Edwards and his kind more than is due. In the first place, Edwards and John Marsh were operating officers, not executives, and the strategic direction of the ATS and its successors remained firmly in the hands of the capitalist directorate that Tyrell, himself, lists (p. 62). Such men as Edwards could be trusted to follow executive direction, and they could be trusted because the Protestant clergy of the elite had a material concern in preserving their constituency's leadership in politics, no matter where it went.

37. ATS, *Fourth Report*, pp. 8–9. This experiment probably was the basis for Edwards's famous propaganda tract, *The Well Conducted Farm,* which Tyrell does not discuss. Whether Edwards's essay was purely propagandistic or the result of actual observation is relatively immaterial. Certainly the goals and expectations of the reformers are clearly set forth. With respect to altered behavior—if it occurred—the issue of its cause is less clear. Repression can have many sources, not least of which is economic.

38. Ibid., pp. 107–8; Tyrell, *Sobering Up,* pp. 74–75.

39. ATS, *Sixth Report of the American Temperance Society* (New York, 1833), pp. 15–16.

40. ATS, *Fifth Report of the American Temperance Society* (Boston, 1832), p. 22.

41. Ibid., pp. 27–45.

42. See ATS, *Sixth Report*, pp. 15ff, 50–51.

43. ATS, *Fourth Report*, p. 69.

44. New York Temperance Society (NYTS), *Temperance Recorder* 2, no. 11 (7 January 1834). Both Tyrell and Johnson place considerable emphasis on the role of evangelicalism in advancing the temperance movement, and Johnson is particularly persuasive in his analysis of how the social dynamics of church membership worked to convert individuals to the cause.

45. NYTS, *Temperance Recorder* 2, no. 5 (2 July 1833).

46. NYTS, *Temperance Recorder* 2, no. 3 (7 May 1833).

47. NYTS, *Temperance Recorder* 2, no. 11 (7 January 1834).

48. ATS, *Seventh Report*, p. 113. The complete convention proceedings can be found in NYTS, *Temperance Recorder* 2, no. 4 (4 June 1833).

49. Ralph V. Harlow, *Gerrit Smith: Philanthropist and Reformer* (New York, 1939), pp. 109–12; Daniel D. Bernard, *A Discourse on the Life, Services and Character of Stephen Van Rensselaer* (Albany, 1839), pp. 30–33.

50. Most of this information is drawn from the *Dictionary of American Biography* (New York, 1927–37). The *DAB* ignores the basis of family wealth in many cases and is vague or skimpy on interfamily relations. Moreover, its conception of what constitutes a significant contribution to American national life ignores the facts of class position, superior resources, and the complications that result therefrom.

51. NYTS, *Temperance Recorder* 2, no. 4 (4 June 1833).

52. Ibid.

53. Ibid. See especially "immorality of the Traffic." The phrase "as a drink" may have been an attempt at compromise, in that it could be construed narrowly against retail sellers of whiskey and rum, and not against distillers. The reformers' first political efforts were directed against the retail trade; but, however construed, the resolution did not confront the inherent "threat to property" in its own position.

54. ATS, *Sixth Report*, p. 96.

55. Ibid., p. vii.

56. George B. Cheever, "The Temperance Reformation," *American Quarterly Observer* 1 (July 1833): 58–80. The fifth meeting of the ATS was held in May 1832, a year before the national convention. See Tyrell, *Sobering Up* (pp. 91ff), for a detailed analysis of no-license/prohibitionist agitation in industrializing Worcester, Massachusetts. Johnson, *Shopkeeper's Millennium*, generally supports Tyrell. Tyrell, surprisingly, does not discuss the formation of the United States Temperance Union. Yet, representatives from Worcester of the sort I describe were there. Similarly, Johnson makes no note of Rochester's participation; and, again, such men as I have described did represent Rochester's local temperance society. See *Temperance Recorder . . . Extra* 2, no. 4 (4 June 1833) for the names of Worcester's and Rochester's delegates.

57. "Reports of the American Temperance Society, and of the New York Temperance Society," *North American Review* 36, no. 78 (1833): 188–204.

58. NYTS, *Temperance Recorder* 2, no. 11 (7 January 1834).

59. Ibid.

60. Ibid.

61. Ibid.

62. See Tyrell, *Sobering Up,* pp. 94–108, for a commentary focusing upon Worcester, Massachusetts. He observes, for example, that "the concern of entrepreneurs with the drinking practices of working men clearly extended wherever the industrial system was emerging."

63. ATS, *Fifth Report*, p. 21.

64. Marsh, *Temperance Recollections*, pp. 124–25.

65. *Letter to Governor King of N.Y.: An Appeal for Cooperation in the Temperance Reform* (Albany, 1857), pp. 13–14.

Chapter 2

1. *The Mistakes and Failures of the Temperance Reformation* (New York, 1864). This pamphlet is a polemical attack on the leadership of the American Temperance Union, which, the author maintained, transformed the movement into an "institution" by turning its management over to "specialists . . . professional reformers . . . stipendary agitators, men who . . . gradually develop a monomania" (p. 12). In addition, he charged that the ATU represented "corporate interests and a corporate spirit, besides the reform which it espouses" (p. 13). The writer reflected the ideological perspective of the Washingtonian enthusiasm, which was primarily a working-class phenomenon, ultimately conservative in its politics but decidedly pragmatic about the evils of drinking and antiauthoritarian in its social views—two attributes that led to its subversion by propertied temperance reformers. This critic concluded his attack by charging that prohibitory legislation was "quackery" and that the reform's current leadership was bent upon repeating the errors of the past (pp. 36–40).

2. *Letter to the Mechanics of Boston Respecting the Formation of a City Temperance Society, from a Committee of the Massachusetts Society for the Suppression of Intemperance* (Boston, 1832); New York Temperance Society, *Temperance Recorder* 2, no. 3 (7 May 1833). Some employers' reports suggested the scarcity of labor prevented imposition of de facto prohibition and compelled a cooperative approach.

3. George McNeil, ed., *History of the Labor Movement* (New York, 1887), pp. 333–34.

4. Mark Doolittle, "Temperance: A Source of National Wealth," p. 220, in Edward C. Delavan, ed., *Temperance Essays and Selections from Different Authors* (Albany, 1865), pp. 218–29.

5. Doolittle, "Temperance," pp. 220, 222.

6. NYTS, *Temperance Recorder* 2, no. 11 (7 January 1834). John Allen Krout, *The Origins of Prohibition* (New York, 1925), pp. 153–59; John Marsh, *Temperance Recollections: Labors, Defeats, Triumphs, An Autobiography* (New York, 1866).

7. Marsh, *Temperance Recollections*, pp. 45–46.

8. Krout, *Origins*, pp. 157–59; Marsh, *Temperance Recollections*, pp. 45–46.

9. Krout, *Origins,* pp. 157–59, 171–73; Ian Tyrell, *Sobering Up: From Temperance to Prohibition in Antebellum America, 1800–1860* (Westport, Conn., 1979).

10. At one time or another, John and Arthur Tappan, Stephen Van Rensselaer, John Jacob Astor, Peter Remsen, John H. Cocke, and Henry Dwight contributed to the ATU. Others, like Samuel Ward, also contributed. Delavan gave unstintingly; in 1836 alone he contributed $10,000.

11. Krout, *Origins*, pp. 171–73; Neal Dow, *The Reminiscences of Neal Dow, Recollections of Eighty Years* (Portland, Me., 1898), pp. 231–35; Tyrell, *Sobering Up*, pp. 94–95, 237–39. See also Harry Gene Levine, "The Discovery of Addiction: Changing Conceptions of Habitual Drunkenness in America," *The Journal of Studies on Alcohol:* 39 (January 1978) no. 1, pp. 143–74.

12. George Faber Clark, *History of the Temperance Reform in Massachusetts, 1813–1833* (Boston, 1888), pp. 37–43. Krout, *Origins*, pp. 262–71, gives a full account.

13. George F. Clark, *Temperance Reform*, p. 37.

14. Walter Channing, *An Address on Temperance to the Massachusetts Temperance Society* (Boston, 1837), p. 33; Walter Channing, *Annual Address before the Massachusetts Temperance Society* (Boston, 1838), p. 22.

15. American Temperance Union, *Twelfth Annual Report of the American Temperance Union* (New York, 1840), p. 14.

16. Massachusetts Society for the Suppression of Intemperance, *Twenty-fifth Report of the Massachusetts Society for the Suppression of Intemperance* (Boston, 1837); Massachusetts Temperance Union, *Annual Address and Report of the Massachusetts Temperance Union* (Boston, 1839), pp. 13–14, 31–33.

17. Marsh, *Temperance Recollections*, pp. 64–65; Krout, *Origins*, pp. 271–72.

18. Albert Barns, *The Connexion of Temperance with Republican Freedom: An Oration* (n.p., 1835). See also Daniel Drake, *An Oration on the Causes, Evils, and Preventives of Intemperance* (Columbus, Ohio, 1831). Drake argued that temperance was, along with industry, intelligence, and religion, the "founda-

tion of our liberties." By adopting it, America "will then defy the revolutions which have prostrated . . . other lands; and endure from generation to generation; a proud monument of . . . national grandeur." When not promoting temperance, Drake was enthusiastically promoting railroad construction. See Daniel Drake, *Railroads from the Banks of the Ohio River to the Tidewaters of the Carolinas and Georgia* (Cincinnati, Ohio, 1835).

19. Leon Withington, *Review of the Late Temperance Movements in Massachusetts* (Boston, 1840); George F. Noyes, *On the Duties of the Influential Classes to the Temperance Reform* (Boston, 1846).

20. William G. Hawkins, *Life of John H. W. Hawkins* (Boston, 1863), p. 62.

21. B. Y. D. C. Burdick, *The Old Landlord Reformed, Evolution of Washingtonianism or Society Mirror* (Owego, New York, 1843), is an authoritative statement of Washingtonianism "containing the true principles adopted at the Washingtonian State Convention held in Utica." Burdick was a reformed tavern proprietor. See also Tyrell, *Sobering Up*, pp. 159–90 and passim, for an enlightening discussion of Washingtonianism.

22. E. L. Cleveland, *A Discourse on the Existing State of Morals in the City of New Haven* (New Haven, Conn., 1850).

23. Burdick, *Washingtonianism*, pp. 3–5.

24. Hawkins, *Life of Hawkins,* pp. 65–66.

25. Marsh, *Temperance Recollections*, pp. 76–82.

26. Ibid.

27. Hawkins, *Life of Hawkins,* pp. 44–50, 61–69. Marsh, *Temperance Recollections*, pp. 76–82; Krout, *Origins,* pp. 182–207; George F. Clark, *Temperance Reform*, pp. 47–51.

28. Marsh, *Temperance Recollections*, p. 95.

29. Krout, *Origins*, pp. 200ff; Burdick, *Washingtonianism*, pp. 13–15.

30. John B. Gough, *Autobiography and Personal Recollections* (Springfield, Mass., 1870), p. 173. Tyrell, *Sobering Up*, p. 217, merely notes Gough's alliance with ATU regulars.

31. Gough, *Autobiography*, p. 192.

32. Marsh, *Temperance Recollections*, pp. 120–26; Gough, *Autobiography*, pp. 497–98.

33. Marsh, *Temperance Recollections*, pp. 126–27; Gough, *Autobiography*, pp. 192–96, 499.

34. Gough, *Autobiography*, p. 196.

35. Marsh, *Temperance Recollections*, pp. 188–97. Marsh omits the controversies that surrounded the proabolitionist Irishman and caused him to cancel his appearance in Richmond, Virginia.

36. Gough, *Autobiography*, p. 499, quotes an August 1844 issue of the *Mercantile Journal* to this effect. For differing analyses of Washingtonianism, see Krout, *Origins*, pp. 200ff; Alice Felt Tyler, *Freedom's Ferment: Phases of American Social History from the Colonial Period to the Outbreak of the Civil War* (New York, 1962), pp. 238–39; and Tyrell, *Sobering Up*, pp. 191–224.

37. Tyrell, *Sobering Up*, p. 98; Paul Johnson, *A Shopkeeper's Millennium: Society and Revivals in Rochester, New York, 1815–1837* (New York, 1987), pp. 60–82.

38. See Tyrell, *Sobering Up*, pp. 168–69, for instances of the ambiguities of social change and self-reformation.

39. Samuel Ellis, *The History of the Order of the Sons of Temperance from Its Organization on the 29th September, 1842, to the Commencement of the Year 1848* (Boston, 1848), pp. 9–11. Ellis was a high-ranking member of the Order. See also Tyrell, *Sobering Up*, pp. 203–5.

40. Ellis, *Sons of Temperance*, pp. 9, 15.

41. Sons of Temperance, *Proceedings of New York Division No. 1, from the Commencement of the Order until the Formation of the Grand Division of the State of New York* (New York, 1842).

42. Ellis, *Sons of Temperance*, pp. 29, 83; *Proceedings of New York Division No. 1,* pp. 1–12; Krout, *Origins*, pp. 202–12. This judgment is harsher than that of Tyrell, *Sobering Up*, pp. 203–205.

43. J. Henry Clark, *The Present Position and Claims of the Temperance Enterprise* (New York, 1847), pp. 8–14.

44. Ellis, *Sons of Temperance*, p. 34.

45. D. Stuart Dodge, *Memorials of William E. Dodge* (New York, 1887), p. 151.

46. Marsh, *Temperance Recollections*, pp. 230–32; Ernest Cherrington, *Evolution of Prohibition in the United States of America: A Chronological History* (Westerville, Ohio, 1920), p. 145.

47. George F. Clark, *Temperance Reform*, describes the proliferation of temperance fraternal organizations. Dogmatism, factionalism, and extraneous political issues account for the various orders of knights, sons, and templars. All

offered some program of benefits and required their members to pledge total abstinence.

48. Noyes, *Duties of the Influential Classes*, pp. 8–9.

49. F. B. Gage and F. A. Gage, *Freemen Beware of Your Liberties* (Bellows Falls, Vt., 1849); and Martin Stowell, *An Exposition of the Secret Order of the Sons of Temperance, with Facts in Relation to Secret Societies, Generally* (West Brookfield, Mass., 1848), are attempts to expose the Order as subversive of republican politics by seeking clandestinely to place "temperance men" in political office. Since the Order's members were theoretically known only to each other, the charge was plausible. In any case, it became widely known that the Order did not restrict itself to fraternal activities. Tyrell, *Sobering Up*, pp. 207–209, also furnishes valuable information on Washingtonianism and the labor movement that reinforces my contention that, as the artisan class was swept away, the temperance movement caught some while most found other ways to cope with their new circumstances.

50. American Temperance Union, *Proceedings of the Fourth National Temperance Convention*, Saratoga Springs, N. Y., 20 August 1851, p. 23.

51. Frank L. Byrne, *Prophet of Prohibition: Neal Dow and His Crusade* (Madison, Wis., 1961), p. 4. Krout, *Origins*, pp. 283–96, correctly attributes Dow's temperance concern to his business operations. For valuable sources depicting the movement as it wished to be seen by the public, see Henry S. Clubb, *The Maine Liquor Law: Its Origin, History, and Results, Including a Life of Hon. Neal Dow* (New York, 1856); and John Marsh, *The Napoleon of Temperance: Sketches of the Life and Character of the Hon. Neal Dow, Mayor of Portland, and Author of the Maine Law* (New York 1852). Dow's own *Reminiscences* remains the fullest and most accurate source available to historians, but see also Tyrell, *Sobering Up*, pp. 252–89.

52. Dow, *Reminiscences*, pp. 181ff. Dow's account matches those described for Worcester and Rochester by Tyrell and Johnson.

53. Ibid., pp. 184–91. Dow described Portland as the "fountainhead" of New England distilling. The Portland society muted the emphasis on total abstinence and developed an approach similar to the Massachusetts society, which did not adopt a pledge requiring total abstinence from distilled liquor until 1827.

54. Ibid., pp. 161–67, 193–95.

55. Ibid., pp. 153ff.

56. Ibid., pp. 168–72.

57. Ibid., pp. 200–201.

58. Byrne, *Prophet*, pp. 10–18.

59. Ibid., pp. 14–15; Dow, *Reminiscences*, pp. 205–10.

60. Byrne, *Prophet*, pp. 15ff; Dow, *Reminiscences*, pp. 211–12.

61. Dow, *Reminiscences*, pp. 229–31. Dow singled out the Portland oligarchy's control of the churches as crucial in developing consciousness with respect to the city's customary drinking usages.

62. Byrne, *Prophet*, p. 18.

63. Dow, *Reminiscences*, pp. 215–17; Byrne, *Prophet*, p. 16.

64. Dow, *Reminiscences*, pp. 217–20.

65. Ibid., p. 214.

66. Ibid., pp. 231–36, 240–48. Appleton, originally from Massachusetts, first proposed using the state to ban the liquor traffic in 1832 (p. 265); Krout, *Origins*, pp. 284–85.

67. Dow, *Reminiscences*, pp. 250ff.

68. Ibid., pp. 27–74; Krout, *Origins*, pp. 286–87; Byrne, *Prophet*, pp. 27–34.

69. Dow, *Reminiscences*, pp. 250–60. For an illuminating discussion of the removal of drink from the work place, see Johnson, *Shopkeeper's Millenium*, pp. 55–61.

70. Marsh, *Napoleon of Temperance*, and Clubb, *Maine Liquor Law*, have the full text. Dow, *Reminiscences*, has an abbreviated version. Dow's legislation also required licensing of manufacturers, an innovation that was probably welcomed by Portland's large distillers. See also Tyrell, *Sobering Up*, pp. 254–60.

71. Dow, *Reminiscences*, pp. 260ff.

72. Ibid., pp. 205–11.

73. Ibid., pp. 153, 161–68. Tyrell, *Sobering Up*, p. 275, appears to be persuaded by this temperance propaganda. It would seem, on the face of it, that between 1850 and 1900, American society rid itself of slavery and became a world power propelled, as it were, by the efforts of an army of industrial drunks.

74. See Perry Duis, *The Saloon: Public Drinking in Chicago and Boston, 1880–1920* (Urbana and Chicago, 1983) for a valuable discussion of the urban saloon in industrial America. Roy Rosenzweig, *Eight Hours for What We Will: Workers and Leisure in an Industrial City, 1870–1920* (London and New York, 1983), furnishes a provocative analysis of working-class culture in an industrial and urban setting. His treatment of workers and the saloon is outstanding and establishes itself as a benchmark for similar work.

75. Tyler, *Freedom's Ferment*, p. 348. The states were Vermont, New Hampshire, Connecticut, New York, and Delaware.

76. F. I. Heriott, "The Transfusion of Political Ideas and Institutions in Iowa," *Annals of Iowa* 6, 3d series (April 1903): 46–54; Cyrenius Cole, *Iowa through the Years* (Iowa City, 1940), pp. 162–63. Hiram Price, "Recollections of Iowa Men and Affairs," *Annals of Iowa* 1, 3d series (April 1893): 3–4.

77. B. F. Gue, "The Public Services of Hiram Price," *Annals of Iowa* 1, 3d series (January 1895): 587ff.

78. "The Pioneer Railroad of Iowa" *Iowa Historical Record* 13, no. 3 (July 1893): 125; Gue, "Hiram Price," p. 592; Henry W. Farnam, *Memoir of Henry Farnam* (n.p., n.d.), p. 52.

79. Charles F. Carter, *When Railroads Were New* (New York and London, 1952), p. 54; Robert E. Riegel, *The Story of the Western Railroads from 1852 through the Reign of the Giants* (Lincoln, Nebraska, 1964), pp. 229ff, discusses chronic labor shortages and irregular work habits affecting construction.

80. Carter, *Railroads*, pp. 54–55.

81. Farnam, *Memoir*, pp. 18–24, 65–66.

82. Price, "Recollections," pp. 7–8; Gue, "Hiram Price," p. 588.

83. Farnam, *Memoir*, pp. 45–46, 75–77.

84. Dan E. Clark, "The History of Liquor Legislation in Iowa, 1846–1861," *Iowa Journal of History* 6 (January 1908): 55–88; David S. Sparks, "The Birth of the Republican Party in Iowa, 1854-1856," *Iowa Journal of History* 54 (April 1956): 1-30; Gue, "Hiram Price," pp. 590–91.

85. For a discussion of the influx of temperance men into Republican politics, see Clifford S. Griffin, *Their Brothers' Keepers: Moral Stewardship in the United States, 1800–1865* (New Brunswick, 1960), p. 232, quoting Neal Dow, pp. 223–25, 237. Eric Foner, *Free Soil, Free Labor, Free Men: The Ideology of the Republican Party before the Civil War* (New York, 1970), pp. 237–39, 241–42, discusses temperance as an ethnic issue abandoned by Republicans searching for popular support. Tyrell, *Sobering Up*, pp. 299-301, argues cogently that ethnicity was not a significant factor in the reform's history.

86. Floyd B. Streeter, "History of Prohibition Legislation in Michigan," *Michigan History Magazine* (April 1918): 289–308; Frank L. Byrne, "Maine Law versus Lager Beer: A Dilemma of Wisconsin's Young Republican Party," *Wisconsin Magazine of History* 42 (Winter 1958–59): 115–20; John A. Krout, "The Maine Law and New York Politics," *New York History* 17 (July 1936): 262–72. See also Foner, *Free Soil*, and Griffin, *Brothers' Keepers*. For examples of how the issues

of race and women's rights factionalized temperance fraternal orders like the Sons of Temperance and Good Templars, see Byrne, *Prophet*, pp. 67–69, 78–85; and George F. Clark, *Temperance Reform*, pp. 56–66, 117–24.

87. Gue, "Hiram Price," pp. 592–94.

88. *Proceedings of the Fourth National Temperance Convention, Held at Saratoga Springs, New York, August 20, 1851*, pp. 68–69, 73–76.

89. *Proceedings of the Fifth National Temperance Convention, Held at Saratoga Springs, New York, August 21, 1851*, pp. 41–47.

90. (New York, 1853.)

91. *Appeal*, pp. 11–12.

92. *Appeal*, pp. 13–18.

93. *The Whole World's Temperance Convention Held at Metropolitan Hall, New York City, September 1–2, 1853* (New York, 1853), pp. i, 1–7.

94. *Whole World's Convention*, pp. 13, 20–21.

95. *Whole World's Convention*, p. 22.

96. *Proceedings of World's Temperance Convention Held at Metropolitan Hall in the City of New York, September 6, 1853, with all the Correspondence and Documents of the Convention*, p. 7.

97. *World's Temperance Convention,* pp. 27–28.

98. W. J. Rorabaugh, "Estimated U. S. Alcoholic Beverage Consumption, 1790–1860," *Journal of Studies on Alcohol* 37, no. 3 (March 1976): 357–64. As Rorabaugh admits, reliable data for the antebellum years are virtually nonexistent, and his figures must therefore be used with caution. See also Tyrell, *Sobering Up*, pp. 252–316, and Johnson, *Shopkeeper's Millennium*, pp. 55–133. Both Tyrell and Johnson give weight to evangelical revivalism that I discount. Nevertheless, both have grasped the essence of temperance reform as a movement of a social class caught up in and directing a historical social transformation.

Chapter 3

1. F. I. Herriot, "The Transfusion of Political Ideas and Institutions in Iowa," *Annals of Iowa* 6, 3d series (April 1903), p. 46.

2. Richard Lowitt, *A Merchant Prince of the Nineteenth Century: William E. Dodge* (New York, 1954), pp. 110–26; Carlos Martyn, *William E. Dodge: The Christian Merchant* (New York and London, 1890), p. 99ff; Phelps-Dodge &

Co. Papers, box 5, folder 14, New York Public Library; D. Stuart Dodge, *Memorials of William Earl Dodge* (New York, 1887), p. 151.

3. Martyn, *Christian Merchant*, p. iii.

4. Ibid., pp. 173–78; Dodge, *Memorials*, p. 74.

5. Martyn, *Christian Merchant*, pp. 114–15.

6. Lowitt, *Merchant Prince*, pp. 205–7; Dodge, *Memorials*, p. 77; Martyn, *Christian Merchant*, pp. 170–85.

7. Lowitt, *Merchant Prince*, pp. 211–16; Dodge, *Memorials*, p. 164.

8. Dodge, *Memorials*, pp. 91–97, 106, 135; Martyn, *Christian Merchant,* pp. 209–43; Lowitt, *Merchant Prince,* pp. 225–30, 261–63.

9. Dodge, *Memorials*, p. 127–35.

10. Ibid., pp. 133–34.

11. Ibid., pp. 57–58, 153, 267; William S. McFeeley, *Yankee Stepfather: General O. O. Howard and the Freedmen* (New York, 1968), pp. 86–87, 314.

12. Dodge, *Memorials*, pp. 156–57; *Temperance in the American Congress, addresses . . . delivered on the occasion of the first meeting of the Congressional Temperance Society, Washington, D. C.* (New York, 1867), pp. 26–31.

13. Martyn, *Christian Merchant*, pp. 84–96.

14. Ibid., pp. 136–37; William E. Dodge, *The Church and Temperance* (New York, 1880), pp. 12–13; Dodge, *Memorials*, pp. 162–63.

15. Matthew Josephson, *The Politicos, 1865–1896* (New York, 1938), pp. 39–40; Dodge, *Memorials*, pp. 122–24.

16. Dodge, *Memorials,* p. 103.

17. U. S. Congress, House, *Investigation by a Select Committee of the House of Representatives Relative to the Causes of the General Depression in Labor and Business, Etc.,* 45th Cong., 3d sess., 1878, House Miscellaneous Document no. 29, pp. 553–61.

18. Dodge, *Church and Temperance*, pp. 16–18, 22–24; Lowitt, *Merchant Prince*, p. 286.

19. Dodge, *Memorials*, p. 60.

20. Ibid., p. 382. Among those paying homage to Dodge's career were A. A. Colquitt, Abram Stevens Hewitt, John Wanamaker, and John Villiers Farwell.

21. *Proceedings of the Fifth National Temperance Convention Held at*

Saratoga Springs, New York, August 1–3, 1865 (New York, 1865), pp. 3–4 (hereafter cited as *NTC Proceedings, 1865*); August Fehlandt, *A Century of Drink Reform in the United States* (New York, 1904), p. 233.

22. Barrington Moore, "The American Civil War: The Last Capitalist Revolution," in Barrington Moore, *Social Origins of Dictatorship and Democracy: Lord and Peasant in the Making of the Modern World* (Boston, 1966), pp. 111–55.

23. *NTC Proceedings, 1865*, pp. 5–6.

24. Ibid., pp. 29–36.

25. Ibid., pp. 55–58.

26. Ibid., p. 64.

27. Ibid., pp. 74, 78–80.

28. Ibid., pp. 65–66.

29. Ibid., pp. 78–79.

30. Ibid., p. 80.

31. The basis for this analysis can be found in Franz Neumann, "Approaches to the Study of Political Power," in Herbert Marcuse, ed., *The Democratic and Authoritarian State: Essays in Political and Legal Theory* (New York, 1964), pp. 3–21, and Barrington Moore, "Notes on the Process of Acquiring Power," in *Political Power and Social Theory: Seven Studies* (New York, 1962), pp. 1–29.

32. *NTC Proceedings, 1865*, pp. 55–59.

33. Ibid., pp. 81–82.

34. Ibid., pp. 57, 65.

35. Ibid., pp. 81–82.

36. Cherrington, *Evolution of Prohibition*, pp. 163–64; Fehlandt, *Drink Reform*, pp. 224–25; Dodge, *Memorials*, p. 158; "Minutes of the Board of Managers, 14 November 1865 to 26 December 1882," Records of the National Temperance Society and Publications House, RG 54, Presbyterian Historical Society, Philadelphia, Pa. (hereafter cited as NTS Records, PHS).

37. Entry for 21 July 1868, NTS Records, PHS.

38. Ibid.

39. *Proceedings of the Sixth National Temperance Convention Held at Cleveland, Ohio, July 29–30, 1868* (New York, 1868), p. 118 (hereafter cited as

NTC Proceedings, 1868); James Black, *Brief History of Prohibition and of the Prohibition Reform Party* (New York, 1880[?]), pp. 29–30.

40. Black, *Brief History*, p. 5.

41. John Russell, "A Plea for a National Temperance Party," *NTC Proceedings, 1868*, pp. 116–19.

42. Black, *Brief History*, p. 6.

43. Ibid., p. 12; Fehlandt, *Drink Reform*, pp. 250–52; *New York Times*, 2–3 September 1869.

44. Black, *Brief History*, pp. 12–14.

45. Ibid., pp. 9–10.

46. Gerrit Smith, "Address to the People of the United States," in Black, *Brief History*, pp. 14–18; William E. Dodge, "Open and Close [sic] Organizations," in *NTC Proceedings, 1868*, pp. 103–9.

47. Black, *Brief History*, pp. 6–7, 12–13. The prominence given to prohibition at the Chicago meeting was based upon "expediency" according to resolutions adopted.

48. William E. Dodge, "Old New York," in Martyn, *Christian Merchant*, pp. 250ff.

49. *New York Times*, 6 November 1869.

50. "The War Against Alcohol," *The Nation* 8 (1 April 1869): 250–52.

51. "The Future of Prohibition," *The Nation* 9 (18 November 1869): 429–30.

52. Ibid.

53. The annual reports of the National Temperance Society and Publication House from 1884 to 1897 (19 through 32) report these individuals as the NTS's major contributors. See "Minutes," NTS Records, RG 54, PHS. Thereafter, support declined. John Wanamaker was its last president. Carnegie continued his support up to 1915. The next year the directors merged the society with the Federal Council of Churches of Christ in America. Andrew Carnegie to J. W. Cummings, 9 January 1915, in vol. 2, letterpress books of the National Temperance Society, Presbyterian Historical Society, and "Minutes," NTS Records, RG 54, PHS.

54. *Proceedings of the Fourth National Temperance Convention* (New York, 1851), pp. 19–20.

Chapter 4

1. For the complete text, see D. Leigh Colvin, *Prohibition in the United States: A History of the Prohibition Party and of the Prohibition Movement* (New York, 1926), pp. 75–81; James Black, *Brief History of Prohibition and of the Prohibition Reform Party* (New York, 1880 [?]), pp. 14–18.

2. Colvin, *Prohibition in the United States*, p. 78.

3. Wendell Phillips, "The Foundation of the Labor Movement," Platform of the Labor Reform Convention, Worcester, 4 September 1871, in Theodore C. Pease, ed., *Speeches, Lectures and Letters by Wendell Phillips,* 2 vols. (Boston, 1892), 2: 154.

4. Ibid., p 167.

5. Colvin, *Prohibition in the United States*, pp. 84–86, reprints the Massachusetts platform.

6. Ibid., p. 85.

7. *New York Times*, 16 September 1870. The *Times* ridiculed Phillips's campaign to join forces with "Labor Reformers." In 1870 the Prohibitionists ran statewide tickets in six manufacturing and industrial states: Illinois, Michigan, New Hampshire, New York, Ohio, and Massachusetts.

8. Colvin, *Prohibition in the United States*, pp. 91–93, reprints the complete text.

9. Black, *Brief History*, p. 27.

10. "Why We Do Not Believe in Prohibition," *The Nation* 12 (25 May 1871): 353–55.

11. *New York Times*, 10 May 1873.

12. *New York Times*, 29 August 1873; "Minutes," National Temperance Society, 7 January 1873.

13. *Congressional Record*, 43rd Cong., 1st sess., 1872, 2, pt. 1: 141, 1581.

14. *Congressional Record*, 1872, 2, pt. 2: 1581.

15. *Congressional Record*, 1873, 2, pt. 2; 1581–82, 1760.

16. *Congressional Record*, 1873, 2, pt. 2: 1806–09, 1828–30, 2028–29.

17. "Minute Book of the Judiciary Committee," file H.R. 43–A–F.14.11, pp. 62–63, Records of the U. S. House of Representatives, Record Group 233, National Archives; see also Records of the Senate Finance Committee (45th Cong.,

2d sess.), Record Group 46, File 45A–H7, National Archives; House Committee on the Judiciary, House Report No. 250, 43d Cong., 1st sess., 6 March 1874, 1: 1.

18. House Committee on Judiciary, House Report No. 250, 1: 1.

19. Ibid., pp. 2–4.

20. *Congressional Record*, 43d Cong., 1st sess., 1875, 3, pt. 2: 1601.

21. George L. Case, "The Prohibition Party: Its Origins, Purpose, and Growth," *Magazine of Western History* 9, no. 3 (January 1889): 243–49.

22. Kirk H. Porter and Donald Bruce Johnson, *National Party Platforms, 1840–1956* (Urbana, Ill., 1956), pp. 52–53.

23. "The Causes and Cures of Industrial Depression," *Banker's Magazine and Statistical Register* 13 (July 1878): 19–20.

24. *Banker's Magazine* 13 (September 1878): 174–75.

25. House Miscellaneous Document No. 29, *Investigation by a Select Committee of the House of Representatives Relative to the Causes of the General Depression in Labor and Business, Etc.,* 45th Cong., 3d sess., 1878, pp. 554–63 (hereafter cited as *Causes of the General Depression*).

26. Ibid., pp. 557–59.

27. Ibid., pp. 555–57.

28. Ibid., pp. 554–55.

29. Ibid., pp. 561–63.

30. Ibid., pp. 656–64.

31. House Executive Document No. 5, *Report of the Secretary of State: The State of Labor in Europe*, 46th Cong., 1st sess., 1879, p. 35 (hereafter cited as *Labor in Europe*); Chester L. Barrow, *William M. Evarts, Lawyer, Diplomat, Statesman* (Chapel Hill, 1941) pp. 183–89, 462–63; *New York Times*, 31 October 1878.

32. *Labor in Europe*, p. 35.

33. Ibid.

34. Ibid., p. 38.

35. Ibid., p. 37.

36. Ibid., p. 38.

37. Ibid., p. 37.

38. Ibid., pp. 38–39.

39. Ibid., p. 37.

40. Senate Committee on Education and Labor, *Report of the Committee of the Senate upon the Relations between Capital and Labor and Testimony taken by the Committee*, 4 vols. (Washington, 1885), 1: 41–44, 414–15, 427–31, 741–43; 3: 251–53 (hereafter cited as *Relations between Labor and Capital*); *Causes of the General Depression*, pp. 10–11.

41. Brainerd Dyer, *The Public Career of William M. Evarts* (Berkeley, 1933), pp. 234–35; House Executive Document No. 102, *Report upon the Commercial Relations of the United States*, 45th Cong., 2d sess., 1878, p. 53.

42. *Labor in Europe*, p. 39.

43. *Relations between Labor and Capital*, 2: 282; James Leiby, *Carroll D. Wright and Labor Reform: The Origins of Labor Statistics* (Cambridge, Mass., 1960) is an excellent monographic study of labor statistics.

44. *Relations between Labor and Capital,* 3: 419–20.

45. Ibid.

46. John P. St. John, "The Great Issue," *American Journal of Politics* 1 (August 1982): 411.

47. "Report of a Survey of the Different Funds Controlled by the National Temperance Society," Records of the National Temperance Society, RG 54, Presbyterian Historical Society.

48. Dodge, *Memorials*, pp. 51, 153.

Chapter 5

1. *The Statistical History of the United States from Colonial Times to the Present* (Stamford, Conn., 1965), p. 14.

2. E. L. Godkin, *Problems of Modern Democracy* (New York, 1907), p. 138; Allen Nevins, *Abram S. Hewitt, With Some Account of Peter Cooper* (New York, 1935), p. 507ff.

3. Richard T. Ely, "A Program for Labor Reform: Report to the Sociological Group by a Committee Consisting of Seth Low and Richard T. Ely," *Century Magazine* 39 (April 1890): 938–39 (hereafter cited as Ely and Low, "Report to the Sociological Group").

4. As noted above, Paul Johnson (*A Shopkeeper's Millennium: Society*

and Revivals in Rochester, New York, 1815–1837 [New York, 1978], pp. 55–82) reports the separation of leisure activities from the workplace. The rapid commercialization of these pastimes, which included drinking, became a source of consternation to temperance reformers. The urban saloon evolved quickly from the grogshop, which dispensed draughts of whiskey out of a barrel stored beneath a counter, into a complex small retail business operation, endeavoring, not always successfuly, to respond to consumer demands, alternative methods of beverage distribution, product competition among manufacturers, and other perils that beset the small operator—insufficient capital and credit.

In addition to such mundane problems, urban saloons faced continual harassment from temperance and other urban reformers. In such circumstances internal, interest-group unity was almost impossible to achieve: Distillers and brewers were often at odds and often found themselves drafted into the temperance reform as a matter of survival. Moreover, "liquor interests" politics were almost entirely reactive. See Perry Duis, *The Saloon: Public Drinking in Chicago and Boston, 1880–1920* (Urbana and Chicago, 1983), pp. 83–85, 98–99, 114–42. Also see Roy Rosenzweig, *Eight Hours for What We Will: Workers and Leisure in an Industrial City* (London and New York, 1983), especially pp. 93, 126.

5. E. L. Godkin, "Criminal Politics," *Problems of Modern Democracy,* p. 153. It is not my intention here to argue that nineteenth-century elections were conducted with probity. It does not follow, however, that those involved in sharp election practices did not or could not have legitimate political aspirations.

6. E. L. Godkin, "The Real Problems of Democracy," *Problems of Modern Democracy,* pp. 285ff; Edward C. Kirkland, *Dream and Thought in the Business Community, 1860–1900* (Chicago, 1964), pp. 117–19, 125–26.

7. *Report of the Commission to Devise a Plan for the Government of the Cities in the State of New York* (New York, 1877), pp. 1–10 (hereafter cited as *Cities in the State of New York*).

8. Ibid., p. 13.

9. E. L. Godkin, *Unforeseen Tendencies of Democracy* (Boston and New York, 1898), p. 149.

10. Godkin, "Criminal Politics," p. 123; *Cities in the State of New York,* pp. 29–30.

11. Godkin, "Criminal Politics," pp. 123–25.

12. Ibid., pp. 130–38.

13. Ibid., pp. 137–38.

14. Ibid., p. 147.

15. Ibid., pp. 151–54. Rosenzweig, *Eight Hours,* is the most useful correc-

tive for this mythology. Senator Henry Blair's 1879 investigative hearings into the causes of depression also supply much direct evidence to the contrary.

16. *The Political Prohibitionist for 1888* (n.p., n.d.), pp. 122–27; Robert D. Marcus, *The Grand Old Party: Political Structure in the Guilded Age* (New York, 1971), pp. 3–21.

17. D. Leigh Colvin, *Prohibition in the United States: A History of the Prohibition Party and of the Prohibition Movement* (New York, 1926), pp. 131–35; *Twenty-fifth Annual Report of the National Temperance Society and Publication House* (New York, 1889), p. 80; Frances E. Willard, *Glimpses of Fifty Years: The Autobiography of an American Woman* (Chicago and Philadelphia, 1889), pp. 377ff.

18. Willard, *Glimpses*, pp. 392–97.

19. Kirk H. Porter and Donald Bruce Johnson, *National Party Platforms, 1840–1956* (Urbana, 1956), p. 71; *Statistical History*, pp. 415, 713; Kirkland, *Dream and Thought*, p. 119.

20. Porter and Johnson, *National Party Platforms*, p. 70–72.

21. Colvin, *Prohibition*, p. 164.

22. *Statistical History*, p. 682.

23. Porter and Johnson, *National Party Platforms*, pp. 63–64.

24. Colvin, *Prohibition*, p. 161.

25. *The Nation* 42 (January 1886): 52; *New York Times*, 22 July 1886, p. 2.

26. *New York Times*, 26 May 1888, p. 4; *Political Prohibitionist for 1888*, p. 52; Griffin to Rockefeller, 25 January 1887, John D. Rockefeller Papers, Rockefeller Family Archives, Tarrytown, New York. In addition to bankrolling Griffin's efforts for nonpartisan antisaloon politics, Rockefeller and his colleagues, businessmen E. W. and I. W. Metcalf of Eleria, Ohio, supported Ellen Forster's campaign to reclaim the WCTU from Frances Willard's heterodoxy, and even supported Forster's husband as secretary of the National League for the Suppression of the Liquor Traffic. See Austin Kerr, *Organized for Prohibition: A New History of the Anti-Saloon League* (New Haven and London, 1985), pp. 58–61.

27. *The Nation* 42 (June 1886): 483–84, and 43 (November 1886): 407; Edwin Pierce, "The True Politics for Prohibition and Labor," *Arena* 4 (November 1891), 723–29; Fred E. Haynes, *Third Party Movements Since the Civil War* (New York, 1936), pp. 196–97; Iowa Bureau of Labor Statistics, *Second Biennial Report* (1887), pp. 204–11; Colvin, *Prohibition*, pp. 166–68; *Political Prohibitionist*, pp. 80–120.

28. Theodore L. Cuyler to John D. Rockefeller, 2 February 1886, Rockefeller Papers.

29. *Century Magazine* 39 (November 1889): 26.

30. Biographical information is from Joseph G. E. Hopkins, ed., *Concise Dictionary of American Biography* (New York, 1964).

31. *Century Magazine* 40 (September 1890): 26–31.

32. Ibid., p. 26.

33. Ibid., p. 27.

34. Ibid., pp. 27–28.

35. Ibid.

36. Ibid., pp. 28–29.

37. Ibid., pp. 29–30.

38. Samuel W. Dike, "Problems of the Family," *Century Magazine* 39 (January 1890): 385–95.

39. Ibid., p. 393.

40. Ibid., p. 386.

41. Richard T. Ely, "A Program for Labor Reform, Report to the Sociological Group by a Committee Consisting of Seth Low and Richard T. Ely," *Century Magazine* 39 (April 1890): 938–51.

42. Ibid., p. 951.

43. Ibid., p. 939.

44. Ibid., p. 945.

45. Ibid.

46. Ibid., p. 946.

47. Ibid., pp. 945–46.

48. Ibid.

49. Ibid., p. 947.

50. Ibid., p. 948.

51. Ibid., pp. 949–50.

52. Ibid., p. 942.

53. Ibid., p. 951.

54. Seth Low, "The Government of the Cities in the United States," *Century Magazine* 42 (September 1891): 730–36.

55. Low, "Government of the Cities," pp. 730–31.

56. Ely and Low, "Report to the Sociological Group," pp. 946, 938–39.

57. Ibid., p. 951.

58. Ibid., pp. 938–39.

59. U. S. Congress, Senate, S. Rept. 82 to accompany S. 182, 49th Cong., 1st sess., p. 6.

60. Ibid., pp. 8–13.

Chapter 6

1. E. L. Godkin, "Who Will Pay the Bills of Socialism," *Forum* (June 1894), reprinted in *Problems of Modern Democracy,* pp. 225–48; also Godkin, "The Nominating System," *Unforeseen Tendencies of Democracy* (Boston, 1898), pp. 48–96.

2. See, for example, Seth Low to Washington Gladden, 12 November 1894, Seth Low papers, Columbia University, box 13, for an analysis of the political role of city and good government clubs, and instruments like the Committee of Seventy. Low was more optimistic than others that this activity would produce genuine reform among the masses. E. L. Godkin, like others, was "not sanguine about the future of democracy" as he understood it. See Rollo Ogden, ed., *Life and Letters of Edwin Laurence Godkin*, 2 vols. (New York, 1907), 2: 199.

3. Farnam to Horace White, 8 December 1893, Henry W. Farnam papers, Yale University, box 374; Seth Low to R. Fulton Cutting, 26 December 1899, Low papers, box 14; and Low to Herbert L. Harding, 19 March 1890, Low papers, box 13.

4. Godkin's magazine, *The Nation*, was particularly concerned by "the increase of the liquor selling evil" and the defection of middle-class voters to third-party politics. *The Nation* 42 (January 1886): 52, and (June 1886): 462–63, 482–83.

5. D. Leigh Colvin, *Prohibition in the United States: A History of the Prohibition Party and the Prohibition Movement* (New York, 1926), pp. 187–99.

6. Colvin, *Prohibition*, p. 197; Jack S. Blocker, Jr., *Retreat from Reform: The Prohibition Movement in the United States* (Westport, Conn., 1976), pp. 39–99.

7. Colvin, *Prohibition*, p. 240. This attention to related issues may have had some influence on the election of the first Prohibitionist to Congress, Kittel Halborsen of Minnesota, who was endorsed by the state's Farmers' Alliance.

8. F. E. Haynes, *Third Party Movements Since the Civil War* (Iowa City, 1918), pp. 256–59. See Blocker, *Retreat from Reform*, chap. 3, pp. 53–58, for details of Frances Willard's efforts. The opposition to prohibition was led by Ignatius Donnelly and "Sockless" Jerry Simpson, who argued that poverty caused intemperance and not vice versa. This was also the position of Edward Bellamy, for whom Willard had great admiration. (See "An Interview with Edward Bellamy, *Our Day* 4 [November 1889]: 539–42.) The opposition based their criticism, however, on an erroneous interpretation of the Prohibitionist position. James B. Weaver, on the other hand, supported Willard's efforts.

9. Austin Kerr, *Organized for Prohibition: A New History of the Anti-Saloon League* (London and New York, 1985), pp. 43–44, 64–65.

10. "The True Politics for Prohibition and Labor" (November 1891), pp. 723–29.

11. Ibid., pp. 728–29.

12. Ibid., p. 729.

13. John P. St. John, "The Great Issue," *American Journal of Politics* 1 (January 1892): 414–18.

14. Thomas E. Watson, *The People's Party Campaign Book* (n.p., n.d.), quoted in Norman Pollick, ed., *The Populist Mind* (New York, 1967), pp. 202–3.

15. Colvin, *Prohibition*, p. 241.

16. Neal Dow, "The Temperance Movement," *Harper's Weekly* 38 (31 March 1894): 306; Colvin, *Prohibition*, p. 242.

17. Blocker, *Retreat from Reform*, pp. 79–81.

18. Colvin, *Prohibition*, pp. 246–49. All quotes are from reprinted platform text, pp. 247–49.

19. The convention had earlier voted down a free-coinage-of-silver plank by a large majority.

20. Colvin, *Prohibition*, chap. 7, is a full-dress review of the party's attitude toward the political system.

21. Roscoe C. Martin, *The People's Party in Texas: A Study in Third Party Politics* (Austin, 1933). The Prohibitionists had been identified with Texas Populism from its inception (p. 55), and eventually "the leaders of the old anti-liquor party became trusted advisors of the new third party" (pp. 81–82). See Blocker,

Retreat from Reform, pp. 22–25, for evidence of Cranfill's eccentricity. A closer source is Cranfill's *From Memory: Reminiscences, Recitals, and Gleanings from a Bustling and Busy Life* (Nashville, 1937).

22. Colvin, *Prohibition*, pp. 251–52. Among the party's broad-gauge opponents were publisher Issac K. Funk and John D. Rockefeller's associate, William T. Wardwell. Blocker, *Retreat from Reform*, pp. 110–20.

23. Francis G. Peabody and Samuel W. Dike to William E. Dodge, Carroll D. Wright, Richard Dana et al., 9 February 1893, Seth Low papers, box 21. Charles W. Eliot, "Study of American Liquor Laws," *Atlantic* 79 (February 1897): 177–87.

24. Eliot, "American Liquor Laws," p. 177.

25. John S. Billings et al., *The Liquor Problem: A Summary of Investigations Conducted by the Committee of Fifty, 1893–1903* (Boston and New York, 1905) contains a complete list of the Committee and gives its structure. Biographical information is taken from the *Dictionary of American Biography,* Allen Johnson and Dumas Malone, eds. (21 vols., 1928–44) and from *Who Was Who.*

26. The Committee also asked Marshall Field of Chicago, railroad magnate James J. Hill, Frank Thompson of the Pennsylvania Railroad, and Cornelius Vanderbilt, a longtime financial supporter of the National Temperance Society, to serve on the Committee. Francis G. Peabody to Field, Hill et al., 5 June 1893, Low papers, box 21.

27. Billings et al., *The Liquor Problem*, pp. 4–6. Houghton, Mifflin Co. of Boston was publisher to the Committee. Besides *The Liquor Problem,* the Committee's publications were: Charles W. Eliot et al., *The Liquor Problem in Its Legislative Aspects* (1897); John Koren and Frederick Wines, *Economic Aspects of the Liquor Problem* (1899); Raymond Caulkins, *Substitutes for the Saloon* (1901); W. O. Atwater et al., *The Physiological Aspects of the Liquor Problem*, 2 vols. (1903). Jacob Greene, the insurance company executive, was to have prepared a sixth publication covering the "Ethical Aspects" of the Committee's investigations, but his death prevented its completion. A brief summary of this study, however, appeared in *The Liquor Problem*, pp. 137–42. Other committee-sponsored articles appeared in *The American Journal for Medical Science* in January and April of 1896 and *Popular Science Monthly* in March 1897. See "The Committee of Fifty for the Investigation of the Drink Problem, 27 March 1897, Henry Farnam papers, box 102.

28. Henry W. Farnam, "Some Economic Aspects of the Liquor Problem," *Atlantic Monthly* 88 (May 1899): 644–53. Farnam was secretary of the Wright committee. For Walker's influence on Wright, see Scrapbook of the Department of Interior, *Records of the Bureau of Labor Statistics*, National Archives, RG 257, entry no. 10–001, NNR 1231.

29. Peabody and Dike to Dodge, Wright, Dana et al., 9 February 1893, Low papers, box 21.

30. "The Committee of Fifty for the Investigation of the Drink Problem," 27 March 1897, Farnam papers, box 102.

31. "The Committee of Fifty for the Investigation of the Drink Problem," n.d., Farnam papers, box 102.

32. Francis Peabody in Billings et al., *The Liquor Problem*, pp. 3–4.

33. Billings et al., *The Liquor Problem*, pp. 8–9.

34. Ibid., pp. 9–10.

35. Nevins, *Abram S. Hewitt, with Some Account of Peter Cooper* (New York, 1935), pp. 476–79.

36. Jacob L. Greene, "A Summary of Investigations Concerning the Ethical Aspects of the Liquor Problem," in Billings et al., *The Liquor Problem*, pp. 138–42. Of course, given their objectives and experience, the Committee's corporate members must be acknowledged as political realists of the first rank. Such political realism, so admired by pundits and other savants, however, does not always produce socially desirable outcomes.

37. Raymond Caulkins, "A Summary of Investigations Concerning Substitutes for the Saloon," in Billings et al., *The Liquor Problem*, p. 143–82. See also Raymond Caulkins, ed., *Substitutes for the Saloon* (Boston, 1901).

38. Caulkins, "Substitutes," in Billings et al., *The Liquor Problem,* pp. 145–47.

39. Ibid., p. 156. Caulkins's study presented no empirical evidence for its contention that saloons "monopolized" workers' lives. Both Perry Duis, *The Saloon: Public Drinking in Chicago and Boston 1880–1920* (Urbana and Chicago, 1983) and Roy Rosenzweig, *Eight Hours*, on the other hand, while demonstrating that the everchanging saloon played vital roles in workers' lives, convincingly demonstrate that neither its purveying of drink nor other functions controlled workers politically, socially, or economically—not to say intellectually or morally.

40. Roy Rosenzweig's discussion of the response of urban workers to temperance reform is not only pertinent but also ironic. Urban workers were not so beholden to the liquor interests as the Committee asserted, nor were they as enthralled to drink itself. For a variety of political, cultural, and economic reasons they responded to temperance reasoning and temperance demands in diverse but, nevertheless, rational fashion. Swedes, for example, were hostile to countrymen entering the liquor trade; Irish established their own total abstinence societies; native Protestants endorsed governmental regulation of the traffic; unions and frater-

nal organizations that comprised all ethnocultural groups adopted no-liquor policies to ensure members' benefits programs. See *Eight Hours for What We Will: Workers and Leisure in an Industrial City, 1870–1920,* (London and New York, 1983).

The Committee of Fifty could not have been ignorant of these facts. Yet it chose in its publications to ignore them and to present a picture of workers wholly at variance with them. The irony lies in the outcome: While the Committee's antisaloonism appeared to succeed politically, its ostensible concern for a temperate America appeared to fail—even as the nation's workers remained throughout reasonably temperate. See Rosenzweig, *Eight Hours*, pp. 102–17. Bruce Lawrie, "'Nothing on Compulsion': Life Styles of Philadelphia Artisans, 1820–1850," *Labor History* 15 (Summer 1974): 337–66, reveals how deeply this tradition of temperance in the working class extended.

41. Charles W. Eliot, "A Summary of Investigations Concerning the Legislative Aspects of the Liquor Problem," in Billings et al., *The Liquor Problem*, p. 51. Actually, this opinion was shared by prohibitionists; but where conservatives placed fault on a vague failure of "public sentiment," prohibitionists indicted national political authorities.

42. Eliot, "Legislative Aspects," in Billings et al., *The Liquor Problem*, pp. 52–53.

43. E. R. L. Gould, "The Temperance Problem: Past and Future," *Forum* 18 (November 1894): 339–51.

44. U. S. Commissioner of Labor, "The Gothenberg System of Liquor Traffic," *Fifth Special Report of the Commissioner of Labor* (Washington, D. C., 1893), especially pp. 239–42.

45. Eliot, "Legislative Aspects," in Billings et al., *The Liquor Problem*, p. 74. It can and perhaps should be argued that the Committee of Fifty wanted to prove this point and consequently tailored its methodology to achieve that purpose. Its researchers studied "communities which differ widely in character"; among the differences it supposed would be significant were the relation of native to foreign-born, and population density. It reported wide divergences of opinion concerning the causes of intemperance and the effects of liquor legislation; but as it made no effort to establish control groups, the results of its sampling are inherently suspect—a fact that reinforces the idea that the committee sought to justify its bias rather than observe reality. Again, the previously cited works of Rosenzweig, Duis, and Lawrie have exposed the fatuity of the Committee's work in these areas.

46. Eliot, "Legislative Aspects," in Billings et al., *The Liquor Problem,* p. 78.

47. Carroll D. Wright to Henry W. Farnam, 29 October 1896, Farnam papers, box 102; Charles W. Eliot, "Study of America's Liquor Laws," *Atlantic*

Monthly 79 (February 1897): 177–87. Eliot reported: "The subcommittee on economic aspects waited until it should be determined what parts of numerous desirable investigations should be undertaken by the National Bureau of Labor at Washington. The fields to be occupied by the National Bureau having been determined toward the close of 1895, the subcommittee on the economic aspects of the drink problem then began the prosecution of several interesting inquiries" (p. 177). It seems somehow superfluous but necessary to observe that such arrangements were not available to other interested parties.

48. Henry W. Farnam, "Some Economic Aspects of the Liquor Problem," *Atlantic Monthly* 88 (May 1899): 644–53.

49. Henry W. Farnam, "A Summary of Investigations Concerning the Economic Aspects of the Liquor Problem," in Billings et al., *The Liquor Problem*, pp. 79–134. For the statements on race and nationality, see pp. 114–15.

50. Farnam, "Economic Aspects," in Billings et al., *The Liquor Problem*, p. 128. See also Farnam, "Some Economic Aspects," *Atlantic Monthly* 88 (May 1899): 653.

51. Farnam, "Economic Aspects," in Billings et al., *The Liquor Problem*, p. 134.

52. "Report of the Special Subcommittee on Substitutes for the Saloon," 18 April 1900, Papers of the Scientific Temperance Federation (PSTF), Michigan Historical Collections, Ann Arbor, and Ohio Historical Society, *Temperance and Prohibition Papers*, series 9.

53. W. O. Atwater to H. P. Bowditch, 15 February 1900, PSTF.

54. "Suggestions by Prof. W. N. Rice Regarding 'Report on the Present Instruction in the Physiological Action of Alcohol,'" attached to Atwater to Bowditch, ibid.

55. "Memorandum to Accompany Dr. Billings' Suggestions for Conclusions By the [Physiological]Sub-Committee," typescript, n.d., PSTF.

56. Frances Willard, "Scientific Temperance Instruction in the Public Schools," *Arena* 12 (March 1895): 10ff.

57. Laurel G. Brown, "Scientific Temperance Federation," in Randall C. Jimmerson et al., eds., *Guide to the Microfilm Edition of Temperance and Prohibition Papers* (Ann Arbor, 1977), pp. 161–64; Mary H. Hunt, *History of the First Decade of the Department of Scientific Temperance Instruction in the Schools and Colleges* (Boston and Washington, 1891).

58. "Memorandum For Dr. Bowditch Regarding the Report on the Present Instruction in the Physiological Action of Alcohol," in Atwater to Bowditch, 15 February 1900, PSTF.

59. Justin H. Smith to H. P. Bowditch, 17 December 1891, PSTF. Smith was an officer of the publishing house Ginn and Company.

60. "Report on Some of the Physiological and Pathological Aspects of the Drink Problem," typescript, n.d., PSTF, pp. 9–10.

61. "Suggestions for Summary of Report of the Physiological Subcommittee," in Atwater to Billings, 31 March 1904, PSTF.

62. Hunt to Bowditch, 1 January 1896, PSTF.

63. Hunt to Atwater, 23 September 1895, PSTF.

64. Atwater to Hunt, 3 October 1895, PSTF.

65. Ibid.

66. Ibid.

67. (N.p., 1904); Hunt to Atwater, 7 July 1897, PSTF.

68. "Memorandum to Accompany Dr. Billings' Suggestions," PSTF.

69. Billings to Bowditch, 9 February 1900, PSTF.

70. Ibid; "Dr. Bowditch's comments on Dr. Billings' article and Prof. Atwater's suggestions," typescript, n.d., PSTF.

71. "Bowditch's Comments," PSTF.

72. Atwater to Hunt, 3 October 1895, PSTF.

73. "Memorandum to Accompany Dr. Billings' Suggestions," PSTF.

74. Jacob Greene to Committee of Fifty, 12 April 1900; Atwater to Bowditch, 13 February 1899; U. S. Congress, Senate, *Alcohol and Alcoholic Beverages*, Senate Report no. 1498, 55th Cong., 3d sess.; Atwater to Bowditch, 4 April 1899; Atwater to Bowditch, 30 March 1901; Albert H. Plumb to Bowditch, 20 January 1896; Mary H. Hunt to Bowditch, 1 January 1896; G. W. Fitz to Bowditch, 16 November and 2 December 1898; Atwater to Bowditch, 4 and 8 April 1899; Atwater to Francis Peabody, 18 December 1899, all in PSTF.

75. Circular letter from the subcommittee on ethics to the Committee of Fifty, 1 October 1898, Farnam papers; Francis Peabody, "Substitutes for the Saloon," *The Forum* 21 (March 1896): 595–606.

76. Elan E. Salisbury, "Our National Defeat," *American Journal of Politics* 2 (April 1893): 399–400.

77. *Harper's Weekly* 40 (June 1896): 638–39.

78. *Annals of the American Academy of Political and Social Science* 10

(July–December 1897): 266–67. For an illustration of the cooperation of the civil authorities of Boston with the Committee's investigation, see Peabody, "Substitutes for the Saloon," pp. 595–606.

79. *Annals of the American Academy* 10 (July–December 1897): 267. In the following issue of the *Annals*, in which he revealed his connection with the Committee as an explanation for his failure to sign his original review, Devine apologized for the "personal bias" remark and added that he himself wished to "add a tribute of appreciation to the well-deserved praise which their work has received." *Annals of the American Academy* 11 (January–June 1896): 226.

80. (Cincinnati and New York, 1904), pp. 293–94.

81. Fehlandt, *Drink Reform*, pp. 411–18.

82. *Our Day* 2 (August 1888): 74.

83. *North American Review* 148 (September 1888): 344–45.

84. Joseph Cook, "New Combinations of Temperance Forces," *Our Day* 4 (August 1889): 191–93, 284–86; 6 (October 1890): 282–86; 7 (June 1891): 470–71.

85. David Dudley Field, "The Mistake of the Strikers," *Our Day* 9 (February 1893): 221–23.

86. *Our Day* 12 (July 1893): 73–74. The WCTU's leader, Frances E. Willard, had been an editor of *Our Day* since its inception. In addition, the autocratic Mary Hunt was a member of the editorial board.

87. *Our Day* 13 (January 1894): 32–33.

88. *Our Day* 13 (July–August 1894): 376–79.

89. *Our Day* 13 (May–June 1894): 277–80.

90. *Our Day* 13 (July–August 1894): 379. *The Independent* carried Cook's article on 9 August 1894. Almont Lindsey, *The Pullman Strike: The Story of a Unique Experiment and of a Great Labor Upheaval* (Chicago and London, 1942), pp. 313–14.

91. Colvin, *Prohibition*, pp. 255–56. Colvin, the party's official historian, wrote in the full flood of victory following the passage of the Eighteenth Amendment, and consequently, gives little attention to what transpired in the years between 1892 and 1896. Blocker, *Retreat from Reform*, pp. 68–125, gives a detailed analysis of the issues and struggles underlying the "broad gauge" versus "narrow gauge" division in the party.

92. Colvin, *Prohibition*, pp. 256–57; Blocker, *Retreat from Reform*, pp. 111–15.

93. Colvin, *Prohibition*, p. 258. The conservatives nominated a wealthy Baltimore businessman, Joshua Levering, who was also a president of that city's YMCA; the populist element nominated a Nebraskan, C. E. Bently, and a Southerner, J. H. Southgate.

94. Fehlandt, *Drink Reform*, pp. 386–94. Levering received 132,009 votes in 1896 compared with Bidwell's 279,191 in 1892. The radical faction's candidates drew less than 15,000 votes, indicating that most of this group went to Bryan.

95. Colvin, *Prohibition,* p. 253. The quote is from the party's national platform of 1892.

96. Seth Low to Edward Atkinson, 15 January 1900, Low papers, box 14.

Chapter 7

1. Roy Rosenzweig, *Eight Hours for What We Will: Workers and Leisure in an Industrial City, 1870–1920* (London and New York, 1983), pp. 93–95.

2. Frank Mann Stewart, *A Half Century of Reform: A History of the National Municipal League* (Berkeley and Los Angeles, 1950). Page 200 lists all those who attended the initial conference.

3. *Handbook of the National Municipal League, 1894–1904* (Philadelphia, 1904), p. 35; Stewart, *National Municipal League*, p. 18.

4. Stewart, *National Municipal League,* p. 202.

5. Quoted in Ibid., p. 18.

6. *Handbook of the National Municipal League*, pp. 11–12.

7. Stewart, *National Municipal League*, pp. 166–67.

8. *Proceedings, National Municipal League Held at Louisville, May 1897.* Ritchie spoke on "Commercial Organizations and Municipal Government" (pp. 118–28), and MacVeagh on "The Business Man in Municipal Politics" (pp. 133–44). See also Samuel P. Hays, "The Politics of Reform in Municipal Government in the Progressive Era," *Pacific Northwest Quarterly* 55, no. 4 (October 1964): 157–69; and James Weinstein, "Organized Business and the City Commission and Manager Movements," *Journal of Southern History* 28 (1962): 166–82.

9. Ritchie, "Commercial Organizations," p. 121.

10. Ibid., pp. 121–27. The Cleveland experience was by no means unique. *Municipal Affairs* 1 (September 1897): 491–508, carried a lengthy article, "Business Men in Civic Service: The Merchant's Municipal Committee of Boston," by Rob-

ert C. Brooks, which described the activity of Boston businessmen in arranging an informal political detente with regular municipal authorities in 1896. This activity was praised as "a simple informal means of utilizing this latent civic energy without incurring the delays and miscarriages incident to legislative action, or interfering in any way with the basis of representation" (p. 491).

11. MacVeagh, "The Business Man," p. 134–44.

12. *Handbook of the National Municipal League*, p. 43–46, lists all affiliates.

13. "The Function of Business Bodies in Improving Civic Conditions," *Proceedings of the National Municipal League, Held at Pittsburgh, Nov. 1908*, p. 414.

14. Clinton Rogers Woodruff, "The National Municipal League," *The American City* 1, no. 3 (November 1909): 109–10.

15. Ibid.

16. English, "Business Bodies," pp. 415–16.

17. Leo S. Rowe, "American Ideas and Institutions in their relation to the Problem of City Government," *Proceedings, National Municipal League* (Louisville, 1897), pp. 317–28.

18. Ibid., pp. 326–27.

19. Ibid., p. 327.

20. Ibid., pp. 327–28. Rosenzweig, *Eight Hours*, pp. 171ff, argues cogently that "commercialized leisure" was by no means under the control of either city fathers or reformers. The National Municipal League's concerns bear out his argument and point toward the comprehensiveness of its programs to advance industrialization by developing instruments of social control.

21. Rowe, "American Ideas and Institutions," p. 328.

22. At the banquet concluding the Louisville conference, William B. Hornblower of New York addressed the audience on "the necessity for civic pride," calling for the middle class to rally behind urban social reform. *Proceedings, National Municipal League* (Louisville, May 1897), p. 349.

23. *Handbook of the National League*, pp. 9–10. Other national associations included American Park and Outdoor Art Association (1897), League of American Municipalities (1897), and American League for Civic Improvement (1900).

24. English, "Business Bodies," p. 416.

25. Ibid., p. 420.

26. *Proceedings of the National Municipal League,* Pittsburgh (November 1908), pp. 22–40.

27. Ibid., pp. 39–40.

28. Delos F. Wilcox, *The American City: A Problem in Democracy* (New York 1904). Perry Duis, *The Saloon: Public Drinking in Chicago and Boston, 1880–1920* (Urbana and Chicago, 1983), and Rosenzweig, *Eight Hours*, both offer ample refutation of Wilcox's assessment of the saloon's impact on workers.

29. Wilcox, *American City*, pp. 5–7.

30. Ibid., pp. 10–11.

31. Ibid., pp. 11.

32. Ibid., pp. 121–23.

33. Ibid., pp. 148–52.

34. Ibid., pp. 153–55.

35. Ibid., pp. 156–59.

36. Ibid., pp. 160–73. Rosenzweig, *Eight Hours,* p. 171, aptly distinguishes between the impacts on workers of Worcester's "Safe and Sane" Fourth of July Committee and local amusement parks. The few who attended the former's celebration in 1912 were "bored"; the "record breaking" crowds at the amusement parks, on the other hand, had a grand, boisterous time.

37. Wilcox, *American City*, pp. 169–71.

38. Royal L. Melendy, "The Saloon in Chicago," *American Journal of Sociology* 6 (July 1900 and May 1901): 289–306, 433–64.

39. Ibid., p. 294.

40. Raymond A. Caulkins, *Substitutes for the Saloon* (Boston, 1901), chap. 1.

41. Russell E. MacNaughten, "Local Option and After," *North American Review* 190 (July-December 1909): 628.

42. W. O. Atwater, "Temperance Reform: A Platform and a Program," *The Outlook* 72 (29 November 1902): 736. This program had the editorial support of Lyman Abbott (p. 679).

43. John Koren, "Some Aspects of the Liquor Problem," *National Municipal Review* 3 (July 1914): 516.

44. The importance of the above two organizations, particularly the Committee of Fifty, is the fact of their essentially ideological structure and purpose.

45. D. F. Simpson, "Municipal Government in Minneapolis," *Proceedings, National Municipal League, Minneapolis, 1894*, pp. 101–105. Although Duis, *The Saloon*, does not discuss the Minneapolis plan as such, Chicago and Boston both placed similar restrictions on saloons (see pp. 216–18 and 289–91). There is no evidence of direct political contacts among the cities' antiliquor elite; but then, given their circumstances, there would be no need for such contacts.

46. Judson N. Cross, "Limiting Saloon Territory: The Minneapolis Plan," *The Bibliotheca Sacra* 58 (July 1900): 405–28.

47. Cross, "Minneapolis Plan," pp. 416–17.

48. Raymond Augustus Hatton, "The Liquor Traffic and City Government," *Proceedings, National Municipal League, Pittsburgh, November 1908*, p. 440.

49. Melendy, "The Saloon," (pt. 2, January 1901), pp. 442–58.

50. Ibid., p. 461.

51. G. E. Waring, "Drink Problem in New York City," *The Outlook* 69 (26 October 1901): 504–508. In the same issue, *The Outlook* called for a similar program for New York City (see pp. 480–82).

52. "Work of the Prohibitionists," *Harper's Weekly* 46 (19 April 1902): 571.

53. "Abandoning Prohibition," *The Nation* 76 (21 May 1903): 35.

54. Charles J. Bonaparte, in an address to the League's annual meeting in 1900, told his constituency: "If you want antiliquor legislation it had better come in the shape of local option first rather than try prohibition at the beginning." *Proceedings, National Municipal League, 1900*, p. 29.

55. *Proceedings, National Municipal League, 1908*, pp. 49–72.

56. Hatton, "Liquor Traffic and City Government," p. 425. Hatton made it abundantly clear that the liquor problem was an industrial problem. Its *political* resolution should, he argued, be handled by municipal authorities. (pp. 423–25).

57. *Proceedings, National Municipal League, 1908*, pp. 54–56.

58. John Koren, "The Status of Liquor License Legislation," *National Municipal League Review* 2 (October 1913): 629.

59. Hatton, "Liquor Traffic and City Government," pp. 432–36.

60. *Proceedings, National Municipal League, 1908*, pp. 69ff. The Alcohol Committee was composed of two former state excise tax commissioners, Cornelius G. Kidder of New Jersey and Maynard M. Clement of New York. John

Koren of the Committee of Fifty; S. C. Mitchell, president of the University of South Carolina; and university professors F. Spencer Baldwin of Boston University and Hatton of Western Reserve also served.

61. Clinton Rogers Woodruff, "The American Municipal Situation," *Proceedings, National Municipal League, 1909*, pp. 125–27, reported on the general acceptance of the plan to limit licenses in proportion to the population of an area and the League's expectation that local prohibition would not damage other economic interests.

62. "Proceedings of the National Municipal League, 1913," in *National Municipal Review* 3 (January 1914): 233. In his formal address Koren described conditions as "chaotic." The "unquenchable desire," he alleged, stemmed from the tensions arising from industrial production.

63. Ibid.

64. Koren, "Liquor License Legislation," p. 634 (Koren's italics).

65. Koren, "Aspects of the Liquor Problem," p. 511.

66. Carroll D. Wright, "The Gothenburg System of Liquor Traffic," *Fifth Special Report of the Commissioner of Labor* (Washington, D. C., 1893), p. 8.

67. Hatton, "Liquor Traffic and City Government," pp. 424–26; *Harper's Weekly* 52 (25 April 1908): 6–7.

68. *Proceedings, National Municipal League, 1897*, pp. 273–74.

Chapter 8

1. Simon N. Patton, "The Economic Basis of Prohibition," *Annals of the American Academy of Political and Social Science* (reprint, n.p., 1892); Undated typescript, "Address" (ca. 1920), Henry W. Farnam Papers, Box 85, pp. 2-3.

2. Gabriel Kolko, *The Triumph of Conservatism, a Reinterpretation of American History, 1900–1916* (New York, 1963), pp. 11–17, sketches the near universality of this view. Carroll Wright in his two books, *The Industrial Evolution of the United States* (New York, 1895), and *Outline of Practical Sociology, with Special Reference to American Conditions* (New York, 1899), attempted to supply a theory of monopoly and detail the proper human response. Adams's views on both monopoly and drinking derived from his experience with the Union Pacific. His view of the latter problem can be found in the *North American Review* 115: 215; and Wright, *Practical Sociology*, pp. 355–57.

3. *Twelfth Annual Report of the Commissioner of Labor* (Washington, 1898), p. 69.

4. Ibid., p. 70.

5. Ibid., p. 77.

6. Bound Scrapbook, NNR 1231, Records of the Bureau of Labor Statistics, RG 257, NA.

7. Wright, *Practical Sociology*, pp. 350ff.

8. "Address," Farnam Papers, p. 3.

9. Samuel P. Hays, *The Response to Industrialism, 1885–1914* (Chicago, 1957), pp. 114–15; Andrew Sinclair, *Prohibition, The Era of Excess* (Boston, 1962); James H. Timberlake, *Prohibition and the Progressive Movement* (Cambridge, 1963). See Blocker, *Retreat from Reform*, for varying interpretations.

10. *Report of the Commission of the Relations and Conditions of Capital and Labor Employed in Manufactures and General Business*, vols. 1–17 (Washington, D.C., 1901), 7:22.

11. Gabriel Kolko, *Railroads and Regulation, 1877–1916* (Princeton, 1965) explores the history of the railroads' search for order. Thomas C. Cochran, *Railroad Leaders, 1845–1890, The Business Mind in Action* (Cambridge, 1953) is an invaluable source for the railroads' struggle for existence.

12. Interstate Commerce Commission (ICC), *Fifth Annual Report on the Statistics of the Railroads of the United States* (Washington, D. C., 1893), p. 12; *Railway Age and Northwest Leader* 20 (February 1895): 76; Quoted in Cochran, *Railroad Leaders*, p. 132.

13. See Thomas C. Cochran, "The Paradox of American Economic Growth," *Journal of American History* 61 (March 1975): 925–42, for an analysis of the long-range debilities of nineteenth-century capital expansion; and Cochran, *Railroad Leaders*, chap. 13.

14. ICC, *Second Annual Report, Railways of the United States* (Washington, D.C., 1889), pp. 16–17; 36–38.

15. ICC, *Thirteenth Annual Report, Railways of the United States*, pp. 41–51, 97–112.

16. Paul V. Black, "Experiment in Bureaucratic Centralization: Employee Blacklisting on the Burlington Railroad, 1877–1892," *Business History Review* 51 (Winter 1977): 444–59.

17. Ibid., 453–54.

18. Cochran, *Railroad Leaders*, p. 295.

19. Alexander Hogg, "The Railroad as an Element in Education" (John P. Morton & Co., 1901), pp. 17–18.

20. Warren Jacobs, "Early Rules and the Standard Code," *The Railway and Locomotive Historical Society Bulletin*, no. 50 (October 1939): 38–39.

21. *Railway Age and Northwestern Railroader* 20 (15 November 1895): 561–62.

22. Ibid., 24 (8 October 1897): 830.

23. Ibid., 21 (26 November 1896): 964.

24. Ibid., 20 (7 June 1895): 27.

25. Ibid., 25 (26 August 1898): 562; and 27 (24 March 1899): 208.

26. *Report of the Industrial Commission* (Washington, 1901), vol. 17, "Report on Railway Labor in the United States," p. 790.

27. Ibid., pp. 796–99. At the time of the investigation more than fifty-seven roads, which accounted for over one-third of the railroad mileage of North America, had instituted the "Brown System" of merit rating. In the first six months of its use, the Southern Pacific discharged 212 men, 77 for "intemperance," which was the largest number. But the Southern Pacific's discipline or dismissal figure was generally lower than those of companies not using the Brown System (see pp. 800–01).

28. ICC, *Eleventh Annual Report, Railways of the United States*, p. 14.

29. Ibid., pp. 24–25.

30. Ibid., p. 30.

31. ICC, *Fourteenth Annual Report, Railways of the United States*, p. 97.

32. ICC, *Second Annual Report, Railways of the United States,* p. 37; ICC, *Fourteenth Annual Report, Railways of the United States,* p. 97.

33. Black, "Employee Blacklisting," p. 453.

34. *Railway Age and Northwestern Railroader* 24 (8 October 1897), 830.

35. *Report of the Industrial Commission* 17: 715–90, and passim, contains excerpts of welfare and disciplinary programs of the largest railroad corporations.

36. Iowa Bureau of Labor Statistics, *Third Biennial Report*, 1889, pp. 213–19.

37. John S. Billings et al., *The Liquor Problem*, pp. 78, 127–34.

38. *Fifth Annual Report of the Commissioner of Labor, 1889,* "Railroad Labor" (Washington, D. C., 1899), p. 21.

39. *Second Special Report of the Commissioner of Labor*, "Labor Laws

of the Various States, Territories and the District of Columbia" (Washington, D.C., 1904), pp. 116ff. When this report appeared, twenty-five states and territories had placed drinking restrictions on various laboring occupations.

40. Billings et al., *Liquor Problem*, p. 134.

41. *Twelfth Annual Report of the Commissioner of Labor, 1897*, p. 70.

42. Ibid., p. 72.

43. Ibid., pp. 71–72.

44. *Report of the Industrial Commission* 12: 671.

45. Ibid., pp. 275–77.

46. Ibid., pp. 607–11.

47. Ibid., pp. 312–13, 626.

48. Ibid. 14:xlvi.

49. Ibid. 12:558.

50. *Twelfth Annual Report of the Commissioner of Labor*, pp. 71–72.

51. *Report of the Industrial Commission* 14: vii–viii.

52. Kolko, *Triumph of Conservatism*, pp. 26–56, details the common experience in a variety of industrial enterprises.

53. James Weinstein, *Corporate Liberalism*, details the larger purpose of the Civic Federation. Marguerite Green, *The National Civic Federation and the American Labor Movement, 1900–1925* (Washington, D. C., 1956) supplies another view. Seth Low, the Committee of Fifty's head, was president of the federation.

54. *Proceedings, Conference on Welfare Work*, 16 March 1904 (New York, 1904), p. xxv.

55. Bound Scrapbook, NNR 1231, RG 257, NA.

56. *Welfare Work*, pp. 3–26.

57. The emphasis on nutrition was not new. A Labor Bureau study entitled "Italians in Chicago," Bulletin no. 13 (November 1897), pp. 691–727, was critical of their preference for beer over milk.

58. *Welfare Work*, pp. 102–03.

59. Ibid., pp. 190–93.

60. Ibid., p. 143.

61. Ibid., pp. 47–48, 77–94. The discussion of YMCA work grew very acrimonious. Employers objected most strenuously to the religiosity of the YMCA, a posture the Committee of Fifty had urged antisaloon agencies to avoid at all costs.

62. Ibid., p. 145.

63. U. S. Congress, Senate Document No. 110, *Report on Conditions of Employment in the Iron and Steel Industry*, 62nd Cong., 1st sess., 4 vols. (Washington, D. C., 1913), 3:23.

64. Ibid., pp. 264–65.

65. Ibid., p. 274.

66. Ibid., p. 279.

67. Ibid. 2:38ff.

68. Ibid. 3:205–213.

69. Ibid., p. 91.

70. Ibid., pp. 207–08.

71. Ibid., p. 380.

72. Ibid., p. 381.

73. Ibid., p. 31.

74. Ibid. After 1904 the increase was 25 percent.

75. Ibid.

76. Ibid. 4:11.

77. Arendel Cotter, *The Authentic History of the United States Steel Corporation* (New York, 1916), p. 163. James Weinstein, *Corporate Liberalism*, chap. 2, details the nationalization of this program.

78. Fred C. Schwedtman and James A. Emery, *Accident Prevention and Relief in Germany with Recommendations for Action in the United States of America* (New York, 1911), p. 385.

79. Cotter, *Steel Corporation*, p. 106.

80. "United States Steel Corporation Accident Prevention," cutout of a "Safety Bulletin" (ca. 1912) in Seth Low Papers, Columbia University Library, Box 88.

82. Schwedtman and Emery, *Accident Prevention*, p. 388.

83. Ibid., p. 393.

84. Ibid., p. xiv.

85. Ibid., pp. 259–60; 268–69.

86. U.S. Congress, Senate Document 747, *Reports of the Immigration Commission with Conclusions and Recommendations and Views of the Minority*, 61st Cong., 3rd sess., 2 vols., 1911, 1:15.

87. Ibid., pp. 493–500.

88. Ibid., pp. 496–97.

89. Peter Roberts, *Anthracite Coal Communities, a Study of the Demography, the Social, Educational and Moral Life of the Anthracite Regions* (New York, 1904), pp. 222–23.

90. Ibid., pp. 232–43.

91. U.S. Congress, Senate Document 633, *Reports of the Immigration Commission*, 61st Cong., 2d sess., part 18, pp. 340–42.

92. Ibid., part 2, pp. 225–26, 656–57.

93. Ibid., pp. 654–55.

94. Ibid., pp. 5–6.

95. Ibid., pp. 331–32, 390–91.

96. Ibid., part 22, pp. 404–19.

97. Ibid., p. 331.

98. *Manufacturers' Record* 70 (26 October 1916), p. 41.

99. Ibid., pp. 40–44.

100. U. S. Congress, Senate Document 415, *Final Report and Testimony Submitted to Congress by the Commission on Industrial Relations*, 64th Cong., 1st sess., 11 vols., 1916, 6:5096–99.

101. Ibid., pp. 5104–05.

102. Ibid., pp. 5106–14.

103. Commission of Immigration and Housing of California, *Report on Unemployment to His Excellency Governor Hiram W. Johnson* (Sacramento, 1914), pp. 73, 60–61.

104. *Final Report of the Commission on Industrial Relations*, Senate Document 415, 64th Cong., 1st sess., 6:5148–50. The California Commission of Immi-

gration and Housing reported that 66 percent of California's floating labor population were native white Americans (see *Report to Hiram Johnson*, p. 47ff.).

105. "The Railway Track Labor Problem," *Railway Age Gazette* 55 (24 October 1913): 769–70.

106. A. Kip, "Training the Railway Employee," *Railway Age Gazette* 55 (24 October 1913): 765–66.

107. *Railway Association Magazine,* (15 January 1914): 5.

108. Ibid., p. 33.

109. *Railway Age Gazette* 56 (15 June 1914): 1414–15.

110. *Railway Age Gazette* 53 (October 1911): 746–47.

111. *Final Report of the Commission on Industrial Relations*, Senate Document 415, 64th Cong., 1st sess., 8:7598–610.

112. Ibid., p. 7600.

113. Ibid., pp. 7562–63.

114. Ibid., p. 7568.

115. See Senate Document 14, 59th Congress, "Needs of Alaska in Matters of Legislation and Government. Message from the President of the United States, 5 December, 1906." See also Dept. of Justice Files, Box 1533, no. 16982–02–24 RG 60, NA, Madison Grant to Roosevelt (and Taft). In May 1916 the Wilson administration enjoined all shipments of liquor to Alaska because of a railroad strike. The administration then pushed through prohibition for the territory, Box 1533, file nos. 16982–02–130 to 199 RG 60, NA.

116. Final Report of the Commission on Industrial Relations, Senate Document 415, 64th Cong., 1st sess., 5:4952–53.

117. Ibid., pp. 4932–35.

118. Ibid., p. 4924; *Report to Hiram Johnson*, pp. 30, 47–53.

119. Final Report of the Commission on Industrial Relations, Senate Document 415, 64th Cong., 1st sess., 5:4120–21.

120. Ibid., pp. 4249–52. Another lumberman volunteered: "There are a lot of them that just as soon as they get a stake, if it was hot . . . probably 23 percent of your crew would go down; will say 'I am going to where there is cool beer.' And you won't see some of the men in the morning, until they get all the cool beer they want" (p. 4299). See also "The Lumber Industry in California," in part 2 of the *Sixteenth Biennial Report of Labor Statistics of the State of California, 1913–1914* (Sacramento, 1914), pp. 50–150, passim.

121. Leonard Rapport, "The United States Commission on Industrial Relations: An Episode of the Progressive Era" (M. A. thesis, George Washington University, 1957) and Weinstein, *Corporate Liberalism*, chap. 7, both examine the commission's handling of the Colorado strike. Rapport's is the definitive account.

122. This was also the assumption that underlay the commission's investigations of industrial controls and philanthropic foundations (see vol. 8, pp. 7429ff.).

123. *Final Report of the Commission on Industrial Relations*, Senate Document 415, 64th Cong., 1st sess., 9:8411–12.

124. Ibid., p. 8483. In this connection one CF&I executive is quoted: "We might as well confess it, we have not given them anything but the saloon for the past 25 years" (see p. 8910).

125. Ibid., p. 8486.

126. Ibid., p. 8488.

127. Ibid., p. 8501.

128. Ibid., p. 8205.

129. Ibid., pp. 8903–49.

130. L. M. Bowers to Woodrow Wilson, 8 November 1913, Woodrow Wilson Papers, Library of Congress, Box 4, file 310.

131. *Final Report of the Commission on Industrial Relations,* Senate Document 415, 64th Cong., 1st sess., 9:8914–15.

132. Ibid., p. 8594.

133. Ibid., pp. 8501–02.

134. Ibid., p. 8772.

135. Ibid., p. 8736.

136. Ibid., pp. 8929ff.

137. Ibid., p. 8927.

138. Ibid., p. 8935.

139. Ibid., p. 8939.

140. Ibid., p. 8916.

141. Ibid., pp. 8759–60.

142. Basil M. Manly et al., *Final Report of the Commission on Industrial Relations* (Washington, D. C., 1915), pp. 113ff.

143. *North American Review* 177 (September 1903):334–39.

144. Lewis Edwin Theiss, "Industry versus Alcohol," *The Outlook* 107 (August 1914):856–61. Theiss was himself an industrialist and an active antiliquor campaigner.

145. *Proceedings of the Second Safety Congress of the National Council for Industrial Safety*, New York, 23–25 September 1913.

146. Ibid., pp. 9–10.

147. Ibid., p. 12.

148. *Proceedings of the Third Safety Congress of the National Council for Industrial Safety*, Chicago, 13–15 October 1914, pp. 203–34.

149. Ibid., pp. 208–10.

150. Ibid., pp. 211–12.

151. Ibid., p. 213.

152. Ibid., p. 221.

153. Ibid., pp. 266–67.

154. Peter H. Odegard, *Pressure Politics, The Story of the Anti-Saloon League* (New York, 1928), pp. 182–88.

155. A. R. Heath, "The Business Test of Prohibition," *The Annals of the American Academy of Political and Social Science* vols. 32–33 (November 1908): 582–90. The November session of the Academy was devoted entirely to the question of political temperance reform.

156. *Yearbook of the Carnegie Institution of Washington, 1904*, p. 9.

157. Ibid. 1914, pp. 291–92.

158. Raymond Dodge and Francis F. Benedict, *Psychological Effects of Alcohol* (Carnegie Institution of Washington Publications, no. 232: Washington, 1915), p. 252–53. My italics. Miles's task was to verify these results via another experimental approach. His work, known to safety men and industry generally, appeared in 1918 and established the Dodge and Benedict conclusions. See Walter R. Miles, *Effect of Alcohol on Psycho-Physiological Functions* (Carnegie Institution of Washington Publications, no. 266: Washington, 1918), p. 135. The Institution's research into the effects of alcohol on simple mechanical efficiency did not appear until 1924. See Walter R. Miles, *Alcohol and Human Efficiency* (Carnegie Institution of Washington Publications, no. 333: Washington, 1924).

159. Eugene Lyman Fiske, "Booze," *Proceedings of the Second Industrial Safety Congress of New York State, Syracuse, December 1917*, pp. 169–74. Other

illustrations of this propagandizing can be found in *Proceedings of the Third Annual Meeting of the International Association of Industrial Accident Boards and Commissions* (Columbus, Ohio, 1916), pp. 136ff.

160. William Menkel, "'Welfare Work' on American Railroads," *American Review of Reviews* 38 (October 1908): 446–56.

161. *Proceedings of the First Industrial Safety Congress of New York State, Syracuse, 1916* (Albany, 1917), pp. 15–18.

162. Mark Doolittle, "Temperance, A Source of National Wealth," in Edward C. Delevan, ed., *Temperance Essays* (Albany 1857), pp. 219–29.

Chapter 9

1. Peter H. Odegard, *Pressure Politics: The Story of the Anti-Saloon League* (New York, 1928). Two recent studies, Jack Blocker, *Retreat From Reform: The Prohibition Movement In the United States, 1893–1913* (Westport, 1976) and Austin Kerr, *Organized For Prohibition: A New History of the Anti-Saloon League* (New Haven and London, 1985) both accept Odegard's contention that the League was a political juggernaut and the decisive element in the arrival of the Eighteenth Amendment, while advancing arguments about its commitment to reform and internal organization. In fact, all studies of the temperance movement accept the League's own propaganda in this respect.

2. Ernest H. Cherrington Papers, series 13 (joint Ohio Historical Society–Michigan Historical Collections–Woman's Christian Temperance Union microfilm edition). See, for example, "Basis for the Formation of a National Legislative Conference Is Adopted by Representatives of Twenty Temperance Organizations at the Raleigh Hotel, Washington, D. C., March 28 & 29, 1917," attached to Howard Russell to the Executive Committee, Anti-Saloon League of America, 5 May 1917. Anti-Saloon League of America Papers, series 7 (joint Ohio Historical Society–Michigan Historical Collections–Woman's Christian Temperance Union microfilm edition).

3. Samuel Dickie to U. G. Robinson, 13 May 1912, Anti-Saloon League of America Papers, S. E. Nicholson subseries; quoted in Blocker, *Retreat from Reform*, p. 218.

4. See Blocker, *Retreat from Reform,* pp. 200–22, and Kerr, *Organized for Prohibition*, p. 127–37, for discussions of the League's difficulties with other reform agencies. The S. E. Nicholson subseries of the Anti-Saloon League Papers is replete with material bearing on such nettlesome issues.

5. "Number of Pledges in Amounts less than $200," Cherrington Papers.

6. "The Struggle for Existence," Legislative and Legal Office Correspondence, 1917–20, Anti-Saloon League Papers; Anti-Saloon League of America, *Proceedings, 1896* (Washington, D. C., 1896), p. xii; Blocker, *Retreat from Reform*, p. 156; Kerr, *Organized for Prohibition*, pp. 66–73, unveils the hand of John D. Rockefeller in these proceedings.

7. ASL, *Proceedings, 1896*, pp. 29–30, 60. Later, the Anti-Saloon League would reject such activities.

8. A. I. Root to John D. Rockefeller, 14 January 1902, series 2, box 53, Rockefeller Family Archives (hereafter cited as RFA). Root was a prominent Ohio businessman.

9. ASL, *Proceedings, 1896*, p. ii; Kerr, *Organized for Prohibition,* pp. 76–89.

10. Kerr, *Organized for Prohibition*, pp. 66–73, 79–81.

11. Starr J. Murphy to John D. Rockefeller, Jr., 29 June 1901, series 2, box 52, RFA.

12. Blocker, *Retreat from Reform*, pp. 188, 200–201; Kerr, *Organized for Prohibition*, pp. 106–10.

13. Purley Baker to George D. Rodgers, 24 December 1898, series 2, box 53, RFA.

14. Murphy to Gates, undated (ca. 5 January–5 February 1905), Ohio Anti-Saloon League File, RFA; Gates to John D. Rockefeller, 11 February 1905, series 2, box 51, RFA; John D. Rockefeller Letterpress books, Official File, vol. 87, RFA.

15. John S. Rutledge to John D. Rockefeller, and attachments, 14 September 1914, series 2, box 53, RFA.

16. ASL, *Proceedings, 1905*, pp. 10–13, 14–17.

17. Ibid.

18. Ibid. 1907, pp. 21–23.

19. Ibid., pp. 24–35.

20. Ibid., p. 54.

21. Ibid. 1908, pp. 40–50.

22. Ibid., p. 140.

23. Odegard, *Pressure Politics*; Ernest Cherrington, *History of the Anti-Saloon League* (Westerville, 1913), p. 131.

24. *Addresses delivered at the Superintendents' and Workers' Conference of the Anti-Saloon League of America* (Westerville, 1909), p. 171.

25. "What Our State Issues Should and Should Not Contain," Ibid., pp. 169–71.

26. ASL, *Proceedings, 1908*, p. 143.

27. "Substitutes for the Saloon," in *Addresses at the Superintendents' and Workers' Conference*, pp. 184–88.

28. Odegard, *Pressure Politics*, pp. 125–39, chronicles this pattern of failure. Memo, 23 February 1923, series 2, box 51, RFA.

29. Anti-Saloon League papers, Nicholson subseries, provides substantial evidence of the League's maladroitness; Blocker, *Retreat from Reform*, pp. 215–22.

30. Gates to Rockefeller, 22 October 1908, series 2, box 53, RFA.

31. Kerr, *Organized for Prohibition*, does not address this organizational problem.

32. ASL, *Proceedings, 1911*, pp. 18–27.

33. Compare Blocker, *Retreat from Reform*, pp. 218–19, for a differing interpretation.

34. ASL, *Proceedings, 1911,* pp. 43–52.

35. Ibid., p. 100.

36. "Report of the General Manager of the American Issue Publishing Company, and to the Executive Committee and Board of Directors of the Anti-Saloon League of America, June 26, 1916," Cherrington Papers, pp. 18–20.

37. "Committee of One Hundred" file, Cherrington Papers.

38. "Minutes of the Executive Committee of the Anti-Saloon League of America," 1 June 1914; Cochran to Headquarters Committee, 28 January 1915; *Baltimore Evening Sun*, 10 February 1916, Cherrington Papers.

39. Cherrington to Cochran, 28 January 1916; and Cochran to Cherrington, 3 and 10 February 1916, Cherrington Papers. The "wealthy man from Ohio" was probably Pearl Selby, a Portsmouth, Ohio, businessman who was an at-large member of the board of directors. Selby had contributed $40,000 worth of printing equipment to the League.

40. Ibid.

41. Charles S. MacFarland to Stelzle, 16 May 1916; Stelzle to Cochran, 13 June 1916; Cochran to Cherrington, 22 June 1916, all in Cherrington Papers.

42. Blocker *Retreat from Reform*, p. 201, does not connect the rural-industrial nature of the states that had weak or nonexistent organizations; Kerr, *Organized for Prohibition*, does not consider the problem either.

43. ASL, "Prohibition in the South," *Proceedings, 1915*, pp. 89–94.

44. "The Fight for Prohibition on the Pacific Coast," in Ibid., pp. 179–87. U.S. Senate, *Reports of the Immigration Commission,* 2 vols., 61st Cong., 3d sess., 1911, Senate Document 747, 2: 498–500.

45. Rev. W. E. Cadmus to Garford, 7 January 1908; Garford to Cadmus, 29 January 1908, box 20, Garford Papers, Ohio Historical Society.

46. Speech of A. L. Garford, 21 September 1912, box 128, Garford Papers. George W. Perkins to John W. Weeks, 28 November 1917, box 28, Perkins Papers, Columbia University.

47. "NCW" to Garford, 6 February 1914, box 37, Garford Papers. "NCW" was the publisher of the *Toledo Blade*.

48. Ibid.

49. Milo G. Kesler to Garford, 13 July 1914, box 40, Garford Papers. Kesler, field secretary for the Ohio Anti-Saloon League, described himself as "personally . . . a 'BullMooser'."

50. "Shall Special Interests Control Our Government," box 128, Garford Papers.

51. The Anti-Saloon League could not agree with the Ohio Progressives' formulation of national prohibition and did not give the party a partisan endorsement for fear of losing the churches' support. Root's father. A. I. Root, was one of the first Ohio manufacturers to back the League financially. Garford had written to Root asking him to bring the League into line. Wheeler found the situation "embarrassing" because the League was "working hard for Progressive candidates" behind the scenes in many parts of the state. Eventually, the League did work for statewide prohibition in Ohio. See Wayne B. Wheeler to Ernest Root, 13 July 1914, box 40, Garford Papers.

52. Garford to J. P. Brophy, 14 January 1914, box 37, Garford Papers. H. E. Nunn to Brophy, 11 April 1914, box 38, Garford Papers.

53. Garford to T. S. Conner, 23 November 1915, box 47, Garford Papers.

54. Garford to Brophy, 16 December 1915, box 48, Garford Papers.

55. Garford to Timkin, 16 July 1917, box 59, Garford Papers, and Garford to Henry D. Gibson, 2 April 1917, box 58, Garford Papers.

56. Perkins to McCormick, 8 February 1917, box 28, Perkins Papers. After

passage of the Eighteenth Amendment, Perkins gave $10,000 to the New York Anti-Saloon League and agreed to organize financial contributions for the ratification fight in the state. He failed to do so, however, because he went overseas to supervise the YMCA's work with enlisted men. See William H. Anderson to Rockefeller, 8 July 1918, box 52, series 2, RFA. Also, "Memo to Anderson, 24 November 1920, from New York Anti-Saloon League Assistant Treasurer," box 51, series 2, RFA.

57. Cyrus McCormick to Perkins, 2 May 1916, box 27, Perkins Papers; McCormick to Perkins, 23 January 1914, box 25, Perkins Papers. For details of the YMCA's industrial antiliquor welfare, see "Report upon the Possible Service By the Young Men's Christian Association in the Mining Communities of the Colorado Fuel and Iron Co.," box 18, series 2, RFA. The object of this service was summarized as follows: "If these mine employees of 25 different nationalities are to be welded into one people, efficient, sober, and content, it must be done by something more than recreative games" (p. 44). To implement the program for CF&I, Rockefeller hired International Harvester's C. J. Hicks, who had supervised this program, originally developed for the railroads, on behalf of the McCormicks. See C. J. Hicks file, box 17, series 2, RFA.

58. "Minutes of the Progressive Social Service Commission, Monday, 22 September 1913," box 112, Samuel McCune Lindsay Papers, Columbia University.

59. Perkins to Roosevelt, 24 April 1914, box 25, Perkins Papers.

60. Press release, 31 October 1914, box 128, Garford Papers, and speech dated 2 February 1914, Garford Papers.

61. "Industrialism," box 129, Ibid.

62. Ibid.

63. Ibid.

64. U. S. Senate, *Reports of the Immigration Commission*, 61st Cong., 2d sess., Senate Document 633, part 22: *The Floating Immigrant Labor Supply*, pp. 331, 404, 425–29, 459–60.

65. Bowers to John D. Rockefeller [hereafter JDR], 21 February 1912, box 21, series 2, RFA.

66. Bowers to C. O. Heydt, 13 May 1913, RFA.

67. Handwritten memo, ca. 3 April 1914, box 11, RFA.

68. Bowers to F. T. Gates, 15 April 1912, box 21, RFA.; Bowers to JDR, 16 May 1912, RFA.; handwritten memo, ca. 3 April 1914, box 11, RFA.

69. "The Church and Industrial Welfare, a Report on the Labor Troubles

in Colorado and Michigan, prepared by the Rev. Henry A. Atkinson, Secretary of the Social Service Commission of the Congregational Churches and Social Services of the Federal Council of Churches of Christ in America," n.d., Atkinson file, box 20, RFA.

70. Ibid., pp. 18–19.

71. Bowers to JDR, 21 February 1912, box 21, RFA.

72. "Report of the Federal Grand Jury, Pueblo, Colo., December 2, 1913," in "The Church and Industrial Welfare," Atkinson file, box 20, RFA.

73. Russell to JDR, 9 June 1914; Murphy to Bowers, 11 June 1914; Bowers to Murphy, 15 June 1914; Murphy to JDR, Jr., 16 June 1914; Murphy to Russell, 18 June 1914; Russell to Murphy, 2 September 1914, all in box 51, RFA.

74. John S. Rutledge to JDR, 4 September 1914, box 53, RFA.

75. Russell to JDR, Jr., 5 July 1916, and Richardson to Murphy, 11 July 1916, box 51, RFA. Rockefeller gave $5,000 on the strength of his son's conviction that "I believe it to be of the utmost importance to the State of Colorado, as well as to father's financial interest." See JDR, Jr., to Murphy, 28 July 1916, and Murphy to JDR, 2 August 1916, in RFA.

76. ASL, "The Failure of Regulation in Massachusetts," *Proceedings, 1915*, pp. 261–64.

77. "Colorado's Conclusion," pp. 175–79, Ibid.

78. L. Ames Brown, "Prohibition and Politics–II," *North American Review* 202, 6 (December 1915): 858–72; Kerr, *Organized for Prohibition*, pp. 1–2.

79. A. J. Barton to R. P. Hobson, 28 September 1915, box 5, Hobson Papers, Library of Congress.

80. Wilber F. Crafts to Hobson, 14 September 1915; and G. W. Eichelberger to Hobson, 11 October 1915, Hobson Papers; "Strategic Analysis and General Plans for National Operations in the Prohibition War," 18 September 1915, box 3, Hobson Papers.

81. William D. Anderson to W. S. Richardson, 23 August 1917, box 52, series 2, RFA.

82. Hobson to William J. Bryan, 22 June 1908, box 1, Hobson Papers; "Draft of announcement of candidacy for U. S. Senate," 12 June 1912, Ibid.

83. Hobson to Theodore Roosevelt, 9 November 1904, box 45, Hobson Papers; "Draft . . . candidacy for U. S. Senate," Hobson Papers.

84. Hobson to Edward M. House, n.d., House Papers, Yale University.

85. Hobson to H. D. S. Mallory, 1904, box 48, Hobson Papers; Hobson to Roosevelt, 9 November 1904, box 45, Hobson Papers.

86. "For New York American," 2 March 1915, box 45, Hobson Papers.

87. Ibid.

88. "The Truth About Alcohol," box 46, pp. 10–14, Hobson Papers. I say "supposed productive capacity" because neither Hobson nor any of his followers ever demonstrated the existence of unrealized laboring capacity attibutable to drinking. Such expressions should be seen as expressions of hope, the hope itself based on an ideology that took for granted, indeed required, perpetually mounting production to secure profit margins necessary to achieve the national dream of individual fortunes for every holder of property in the nation.

89. "The Red Menace," typescript, n.d. (ca. 1921), box 46, Hobson Papers; Hobson to K. R. Kingsbury, 29 December 1921, box 47, Hobson Papers. Hobson became so extreme in his views that he eventually alienated both big business and the League. See J. J. Wilt to Hobson, 30 December 1921, box 57, Hobson Papers. Wilt was general superintendent of Standard Oil of California's Pipe Line Division.

90. Cherrington to Hobson, 14 and 17 November 1916, box 57, Hobson Papers; Hobson to Cherrington, 5 July 1916, box 4, Hobson Papers.

91. George H. Hull to Hobson, 10 July 1916, box 4, Hobson Papers.

92. Ford to Hobson, 7 October 1914, box 1, Hobson Papers.

93. Nyce to Hobson, 26 January 1915, box 3, Hobson Papers.

94. Minutes of the Executive Committee of the Anti-Saloon League of America, 4 June 1914, Cherrington Papers. "Council of One Hundred" file, Minutes of the Executive Committee, 20 November 1918; and Witham to Purley Baker, 11 October 1915, all in Cherrington Papers.

95. "Report of Howard H. Russell, Assistant Superintendent of the Anti-Saloon League of America, For the period 15 December 1915 to September 1916, Inclusive," Cherrington Papers.

96. Ibid.; Cherrington to Cannon, 26 November 1915, Cherrington Papers; untitled memo, June 1916, "Council of One Hundred" file, Cherrington Papers; Minutes of the Executive Committee, 20 November 1918, Cherrington Papers.

97. Statements of the Special Emergency Fund for 26 June 1917 to 1 October 1917 and 1 October 1917 to 1 December 1917, Cherrington Papers; W. S. Richardson to Starr Murphy, 3 July 1915, series 2, box 52, RFA; Kerr, *Organized for Prohibition*, p. 154.

98. Cherrington to Cannon, 26 November 1915, Cherrington Papers.

99. Ibid.; "Strategic Analysis," box 3, Hobson Papers.

100. E. J. Davis to Purley Baker, 17 August 1915, and Baker to Davis, 19 August 1915, Hobson Papers; William H. Anderson to Charles Whitman, 22 December 1915, Anderson Papers, University of Chicago.

101. Reports of the Legislative Committee for 30 March 1916, and January 1917, Cherrington Papers.

102. Cannon to Cherrington, 27 December 1916; Cannon to Baker, 27 December 1916; W. S. Witham to Baker, 23 December 1916; Howard H. Russell to the Executive Committee of the Anti-Saloon League of America, 5 April 1917, all in Cherrington Papers.

103. Fisher to William G. Eliot, Jr., 2 December 1915, box 6, Fisher Papers, Yale University.

104. Fisher to Hobson, 23 December 1915, box 3, Hobson Papers.

105. Fisher to Hobson, 27 March 1916, Hobson Papers.

106. Foss to Judson, 29 January 1917, President's File, "National Prohibition," University of Chicago. Fisher forwarded the memorial directly to Woodrow Wilson in January 1917. See Fisher to Wilson, series 4, box 151, Wilson Papers, Library of Congress.

107. President's File, "National Prohibition" folder, University of Chicago, has the published list of those who endorsed Fisher's petition.

108. Cherrington to Hobson, 14 November 1916, box 57, Hobson Papers.

109. JDR to Murphy, 28 November 1916, and W. S. Mitchell to Murphy, 29 November 1916, box 53, series 2, RFA.

110. Frank G. Vanderlip to Gustave Pabst, 26 January 1917, part B, series 2, Vanderlip Papers, Columbia University.

111. Anderson to JDR, 18 December 1917, box 52, series 2, RFA.

Chapter 10

1. U. S. Congress, Senate, *Final Report and Testimony Submitted to Congress by the Commission on Industrial Relations*, 64th Congress, 1st Sess., Senate Document 415, 11 vols.: 8: 7622–23.

2. *Proceedings of the National Conference of Social Work* (Atlantic City, 1–8 June 1919), p. 513.

3. Ibid.

4. Cheerington to Cochran, 18 February 1916; and Stelze to Cheerington, 4 May 1916, Cheerington Papers. See also John M. Barker, *The Saloon Problem and Social Reform* (Boston, 1905), pp. 197ff.

5. Lincoln Steffens, *The Autobiography of Lincoln Stephens* 2 vols. (New York, 1931), 2: 859–60.

6. News Clipping: "Acceptance Speech at Shadow Lawn," Wilson Papers, Library of Congress.

7. Higginson to Wilson, 29 June, 1917; and Wilson to Higginson, 3 July, 1917, series 4, box 152, Wilson Papers. Woodrow Wilson to the President's Cabinet, Care [Joseph] Tumulty, 17 January 1919; William B. Wilson to Woodrow Wilson, Care Tumulty, 18 January 1919, Records of the Department of Labor, RG 174, NA. "Memorandum for the Attorney General," 21 January 1919; Tumulty to Wilson, 21 January 1919, Department of Justice Memorandum, 24 January 1919, file nos. 187130–36, Records of the Department of Justice, RG 60, NA.

8. Scholars are now addressing such questions. See Harry G. Levine, "The Alcohol Problem in America: From Temperance to Alcoholism," *British Journal of Addiction* 79 (1984): 109–19.

Epilogue

1. David E. Kyvig, *Repealing National Prohibition* (Chicago, 1979), is the standard work.

2. David E. Kyvig, "Objection Sustained: Prohibition Repeal and the New Deal," in *Alcohol, Reform and Society: The Liquor Issue in Social Context*, ed. Jack S. Blocker (Westport, Conn., 1979), pp. 211–33. Here Kyvig establishes a link between the AAPA and the anti-New Deal Liberty League.

3. See above, chap. 1, p. 12, for Edwards's report. Its gist was that workers' off-the-job deportment was much improved by a temperance regime. That is, they attended church regularly, were not given to "sprees," nor to political "agitation."

4. See above, chap. 10, pp. 186–87.

5. Kyvig, "Objection Sustained," employs the terms "modest," "comfortable," and "self-made" (pp. 212ff). One is provoked to speculate why such terms are used to describe men of such obvious power and influence.

6. Biographical data is taken from *Dictionary of American Biography*,

ed. Allen Johnson and Duman Malone, 20 vols. (New York 1928–37; supplements 1-2, 1944–58).

7. AAPA, *Annual Report for 1931*, pp. 21-30, in AAPA Papers, Library of Congress. Harkness, himself, well illustrates how a network of wealth and power developed in the United States between 1875 and 1925 – a mere fifty years. His father, a man of "modest" origins, became a partner of John D. Rockefeller, Sr. Young Harkness eventually married a daughter of New York corporation lawyer Thomas E. Stillman, who was trustee of the estate of Mark Hopkins, the Amherst College moral theologian. Hopkins owned 25 percent of the Southern Pacific Railroad and had succeeded William Earl Dodge as president of the National Temperance Society. Subsequent to his marriage, Harkness found himself appointed to Southern Pacific's board of directors.

8. AAPA, *Annual Report, 1933*, "Historical," pp. 4–6, in AAPA Papers.

9. "Who, How, Why of the Association Against the Prohibition Movement" (Washington, D.C., 1931), p. 4, AAPA Papers.

10. *Dictionary of American Biography*, s.v. "Wadsworth, James W." Wadsworth himself married a daughter of New York banker William R. Travers, whose name today adorns the oldest thoroughbred stakes race in the United States, "The Travers," run at Saratoga Springs, New York.

11. Wadsworth to Clyde H. DeWitte, 4 June 1926, James Wadsworth Papers, Library of Congress.

12. Ibid.

13. "Speech, Saratoga Springs, 1 September" [1925?], Wadsworth Papers.

14. Ibid..

15. "Radio Talk, Station WJZ," 15 December 1929. Reprinted by AAPA as "A Business Man's View of Prohibition," AAPA Papers, Library of Congress.

16. "Speech to be delivered by Senator James W. Wadsworth, Jr., at Labor Day celebration at Fort Hamilton Reservation, Brooklyn, on the afternoon of Monday September 6, 1926," Wadsworth Papers.

17. "Radio Talk," pp. 4–5.

18. Ibid., p. 5.

19. Ibid.

20. James W. Wadsworth, "Prohibition Passes in Review," *The Kansas Repealist* (May 1933): 10–11.

21. Kerr, *Organized for Prohibition*, pp. 222–31, provides an account of this thrust.

22. Kerr, *Organized for Prohibition*, pp. 247–48, discusses Anderson's problems with the Rockefellers. Both the Anderson and Rockefeller papers furnish pertinent details. For the Rockefellers' support of national prohibition see chap. 9, above, pp. 182–83.

23. Kerr, *Organized for Prohibition*, p. 265.

24. The commission's first budget provided $50,000 for prohibition. The investigation of the "Causes of Crime" received the next highest allocation, $15,700. See Records of the NCLOE, "Minutes," 4 December 1929, RG10, NA.

25. Kerr, *Organized for Prohibition*, p. 268, for Webb-Keynon; 59th Cong., 1st Sess., Senate Document No. 14, "Needs of Alaska in Matters of Legislation and Government" for antisaloon activities. The fact that the League, which, in happier times, had taken on House speaker Joseph Cannon, did not protest Wickersham's appointment suggests further its eclipse in the antiliquor circles that counted.

26. Wickersham to Richard A. Ballinger (Sec. of Interior), 1 May 1908 and 10 and 19 October 1910; to George R. Walker, 21 October 1910; Walker to Wickersham, 14 December 1910; Wickersham to Hudson Stuck, 28 October 1911; Ballinger to John Wilson Wood, 16 July 1910; Commissioner of Education to Ballinger, 10 October 1910, Records of Department of Justice, RG60, NA.

27. NCLOE, "Minutes," 29 May 1929, RG10, NA.

28. NCLOE, "Minutes," 30 May 1929, RG10, NA.

29. NCLOE, "Minutes," 22 July 1929, RG10, NA.

30. NCLOE, "Minutes," 6 June 1929; 22 July to 3 December 1929, RG10, NA. No record of Mellon's meeting with the commission, which lasted from 10:45 am to 1:00 pm, exists. All that is known is that Mellon informed the commission that as early as 1922 the transfer of the Bureau of Prohibition to the Justice Department had been contemplated, but he could produce no record of that policy issue. See NCLOE, "Department of Treasury file" in "Communications with Public Officials," RG10, NA.

31. NCLOE "Minutes," 22 July to 3 December, 1929, "Testimony of Labor Leaders"; "Miscellaneous Records," RG10, NA.

32. NCLOE, "Testimony of Labor Leaders"; Report of James J. Forrester," 16 July 1930, RG10, NA.

33. National Commission on Law Observance and Enforcement, *Report on the Enforcement of the Prohibition Laws of the United States.* House Report

722, 71st Cong., 1st Sess., Wash. 1931, pp. 80–82. See also Wickersham to Editor of *Colliers*, 11 March 1931, NCLOE, "General Correspondence," RG10, NA.

34. Quoted from Kerr, *Organized for Prohibition*, p. 269.

35. Draft "Memorandum" ca. January 1933, Edward M. House, House Papers, drawer 32, file 126, Yale University.

36. Ibid.

37. See NCLOE, "Testimony of Labor Leaders," RG10, NA.

38. Harry G. Levine, "The Birth of American Alcohol Control: Prohibition, The Power Elite, and the Power of Lawlessness," *Contemporary Drug Problems* (Spring 1985), pp. 63–115.

Sources

Manuscript Sources

Henry Farnam Papers, Yale University
Irving Fisher Papers, Yale University
Edward M. House Papers, Yale University
Seth Low Papers, Columbia University
Samuel McC. Lindsey Papers, Columbia University
Frank G. Vanderlip Papers, Columbia University
George W. Perkins Papers, Columbia University
William E. Dodge Papers, New York Public Library
Richard W. Gilder Papers, New York Public Library
William H. Anderson Papers, University of Chicago
Presidents' File Papers, University of Chicago
Julius Rosenwald Papers, University of Chicago
James W. Wadsworth Papers, Library of Congress
Papers of the Association Against the Prohibition Amendment, Library of Congress
Richmond P. Hobson Papers, Library of Congress
Woodrow Wilson Papers, Library of Congress
John D. Rockefeller Papers, Rockefeller Family Archives

John D. Rockefeller, Jr., Papers, Rockefeller Family Archives
Arthur L. Garford Papers, Ohio Historical Society
Ernest H. Cherrington Papers, Ohio Historical Society
Papers of the Anti-Saloon League of America, Ohio Historical Society
Papers of the Scientific Temperance Federation, Michigan Historical Collections, Ann Arbor
Papers of the National Temperance Society and Publication House, Presbyterian Historical Society.
Rumbarger Family Papers, Forest History Society, Durham, North Carolina

Unpublished Government Records

Records of the Bureau of Labor Statistics, National Archives, Record Group 257
Records of the Department of Justice, NA, RG 60
Records of the Department of Labor, NA, RG 174
Records of the U. S. House of Representatives, NA, RG 233
Records of the U. S. Senate, NA, RG 46
Records of the National Commission on Law Observance and Enforcement, NA, RG 10

Index